D1121541

More Praise for *Inside the Box*

"*Inside the Box* addresses one of the most over-hyped but under-valued issues in business today: corporate values. There are so many examples of companies pursuing essentially the same strategy and positioning with vastly different business performance. I am convinced that it's the quality of the leadership that is the source of the difference in performance, and without strong values that leadership is elusive. Companies with strong enduring values are companies that endure."

> ~ *Martha Clark, Global Human Resources Director, AXA Rosenberg*

"Inside the Box, Inside Corporate Headquarters, Inside the Locker Room…the game plan for success is spelled out clearly by David Cohen. The values formula is wonderfully articulated and so applicable in all of our worlds."

> ~ *David Poulin, Athletics Development, the University of Notre Dame; 13-year NHL career, 3-time NHL All-Star, playing for the Philadelphia Flyers, Boston Bruins, and Washington Capitals; 10-year Notre Dame Head Hockey Coach*

"Reading David's new book underscored the appreciation I have for the importance of values in my organization and in my life."

> ~ *Paul Bottero, President, Computer Horizons Canada*

Inside the Box

Inside the Box

LEADING WITH CORPORATE VALUES TO DRIVE SUSTAINED BUSINESS SUCCESS

DAVID S. COHEN

JOSSEY-BASS
A Wiley Imprint
www.josseybass.com

Library and Archives Canada Cataloguing in Publication Data

Cohen, David S., 1947-
    Inside the box : leading with corporate values to drive sustained business success / David S. Cohen.

Includes bibliographical references and index.
ISBN-13: 978-0-470-83832-7
ISBN-10: 0-470-83832-9

    1. Industrial management. 2. Corporate culture. 3. Values.
4. Leadership. I. Title.

HD30.19.C64 2006   658.4   C2006-903782-5

Production Credits:
Cover design: Adrian So
Interior text design: Natalia Burobina
Printer: Tri-Graphic Printing, Ltd.

John Wiley & Sons Canada, Ltd.
6045 Freemont Blvd., Mississauga, Ontario L5R 4J3

Printed in Canada

1 2 3 4 5 TRI 10 09 08 07 06

This book is dedicated to my grandfather Ed Roth, my parents, Irving and Florence, and my wife, Naomi, who have and continue to live values-based lives

and

to Ezra Jacob and, God willing, his brothers, sisters and cousins, to be named at a later date, that they may ensure the continuity of the values from generation to generation.

TABLE OF CONTENTS

Acknowledgements

This book did not begin with my career transition to corporate consulting twenty-one years ago. This is a lifelong work that began generations before me. The ideas that shape this book originated during long rides from Irvington, New Jersey, to Bradley Beach, New Jersey, with my grandfather. My grandfather shaped them as he told stories along the journey of growing up. As the reader will soon understand, the title of this book is not a flip turn of a phrase. My early education on what is a values driven company came during my time "inside the box" companies of my father and grandfather.

Over the last two decades I have spent working with corporations large and small around the world, I have come to realize that there are no correct values to drive business. The values that help one corporation succeed can be very different from those of another. In both cases, however, it is the corporation's people that embody those values and behave according to them. Accordingly, I have some people to thank for this book. I begin by acknowledging those who knowingly or not provided me with insight into values. I think it's safe to say that I have learned more from them than they have learned from me.

In my career, I have received valuable feedback from my clients and from many participants at conferences who have challenged my ideas and forced me to look at things from diverse perspectives. If this book causes readers to revise their own thoughts, I will have given something back to the ongoing dialogue about the centrality of people and the importance of values in the sustained success of organizations.

This book became a reality thanks to the support and encouragement of many people. When the proposal for the book was presented to my editor, Karen Milner, I was both surprised and pleased by her enthusiastic response. Her enthusiasm for the ideas of the book forced me to continue the creative process and to write even when I thought I would not finish the work. Once the manuscript was completed, Elizabeth McCurdy and Pamela Vokey's support during the editing process helped maintain and hone our focus. Once again, copy editor Nancy Carroll provided a critical and essential perspective on the editing and helped improve what was unclear.

From the beginning, I was assisted by some very supportive and encouraging friends. But the one who made it all happen and brought it all together was Keith Hollihan. During the past three plus years Keith offered encouragement when I was not focused and was frustrated when I was not writing. Keith did not just help with the writing of this book but played an important role in shaping the original ideas, challenging my thoughts and making suggestions. I believe that in the end, Keith has more co-authored this than helped with the editing and writing. For that I am grateful to him and I appreciate his friendship even more.

I must also thank Gil Cohen, who besides being my son also works with me as a consultant. He has never stopped asking questions and challenging my ideas for their pureness and consistency. He drew his commitment to our shared values from his hero, my dad. Frequently, Gil would remind me of our perspective on the world and our understanding of where we come from. There are sections of this book that are better because of his comments and passion. I also thank Gil's wife, Michaelanne, who has brought a renewed sense of calm and focus to Gil's life.

The central theme of this book is the importance of passing values from generation to generation. The encouragement and support of both my other son, Ari, and my daughter-in-law, Sarah, helped me get to the end of this journey. They put the journey into crystal clarity when they began the next generation of our family by producing Ezra Jacob to whom, along with my parents and grandfather, this book is dedicated and without whom it would not have been written.

Finally I thank Naomi, my wife of thirty-five years, who has put up with many frustrations, including sacrificing our quality time together for the sake of this book. Naomi has always been supportive and optimistic, despite my ever-changing and frequent travel schedule, and my lack of focus or my hyper focus on things. I cannot thank her enough for putting up with me, my ADHD and my attempts to do too many things at one time.

Daring to Think Inside the Box

For a few years, in the late 1950s, my father owned a box company in West Orange, New Jersey. The company produced folding boxes for toys, model airplanes and games. To me, it was a place of wonder. Any parent who has ever bought a present for a child knows that the box itself can be a bigger hit than the toy. Maybe it's because the box, although empty to the critical eye, holds all the potential in the world.

Sometimes I did jobs on the factory floor, running one of the punch machines. I noticed how hard the employees all worked. They were motivated, disciplined and productive. They kept the work area clean. My father had been a union organizer in the 1940s and 50s, a socially conscious leader. Later, when he became a boss, he treated people fairly and with respect. He wasn't the type to strike fear into those around him, but he did keep everyone focused on the job. Even from a young boy's eyes, I could tell he enjoyed what he was doing. Watching my dad at work was one of my first exposures to leadership in action.

Values were very important to my father and our family. I came to understand that values formed the basis of my father's leadership style in all circumstances, whether as a union organizer, a small business owner or a parent. As I grew older and became an educator and principal, I saw that values were important in schools, too. When schools are organized around a clear set of values, children know the difference between right and wrong and have the freedom to grow. Teachers can rely on those values when providing guidance and discipline and encouraging learning. Later, after I left the field of education and began a new but related career as a business consultant and executive coach, I saw that organizations were energized and inspired by values, too. Indeed, it was apparent that the best organizations succeeded not because of their products, market strategy or people but because all three factors were fueled by the same source — the organization's values. This revelation rekindled a lifelong quest to understand what values mean, what they do for individuals and groups, and how they can be brought into alignment with what we do and what we strive to become.

Over the course of twenty years, I visited many organizations, large and small, in the private and public sectors in North America and around the world and took a good look inside. In a few very successful organizations, values were clearly articulated. Everyone, at all levels, understood the values in the broader context of the organization's vision and culture; they also understood how to apply those values to their jobs. Values provided a direct connection between the CEO, the factory worker and everyone in between. Values formed the basis of the organization's brand as understood by employees, customers, suppliers and even shareholders.

In a larger number of less successful organizations I encountered, values were not so clearly articulated or widely understood. Sometimes the leaders of those organizations needed help expressing their values in concrete ways that could be communicated to everyone. Other times, the organizations needed help aligning values to vision, strategy, work processes and people systems. When the work was done right, values provided an organizing principle, a directional compass, which helped the organizations succeed and became a source of energy for an organization's vision, strategy and day-to-day efforts.

And then there were those many organizations in which values were unclear and inconsistent. Usually, this meant that there were conflicts between the values that the leaders expressed and the values that they actually supported. Just as often, there was a hidden curriculum of values within the organization, which overrode the values that the leaders espoused. Such organizations were usually in distress. Even the ones that were thriving for a time fell apart at the first major crisis. If the senior leadership turned over or the market shifted or a new competitor appeared, those organizations were quick to panic, lose their way and break down. No matter how primed for success they seemed, their tremendous energy and vision was unsustainable in the long run.

Over time, it became obvious to me that vision, strategy, market share, reputation or profits were all very important, but having a clear and consistent set of values was far more critical in predicting whether an organization would continue to succeed and grow as its people, markets, competitive landscape and technology changed. In other words, I learned what every child knows. What's inside the box — an organization's values — is just as important and more exciting and satisfying than what comes out of the box — an organization's vision, brand, business strategy and products.

But why do some organizations harness the power of values so well when so many others fail? Many people have written about the importance of values to leadership. Others have written about the importance of values to organizational culture and performance. But few have explained the mechanics of values —

how they form the foundation of an organization's culture and
shape and influence strategy, brand, products and people. Many
businesses talk about the importance of culture or leadership
but fail to draw the links between what culture and leadership
is based on and how to most effectively communicate, reinforce
and build from that. In other words, they do not explain how
values are expressed in vision and strategy, and how they guide
leaders and managers in providing an environment of discipline,
reinforcement and effective learning.

This book aims to do just that. You do not need to be the
CEO of your organization to read it and implement these ideas.
However, CEOs and senior leaders will benefit immeasurably from
the clarity of the practices described. Leaders who are passionate
about making their work environment more productive and
supportive and who want to make a meaningful contribution to
the world through the organization to which they have committed
themselves will find this book inspiring and useful. In addition to
the senior team, this book will be a helpful guide for managers
who need an organizationally consistent language, framework
and set of tools for getting the best out of their people. This book
is also invaluable for the leaders of spin-offs, divisions, groups or
teams who want to strike a special tone separate from the larger
organization and for the human resources professionals who
need detailed action plans to make a business case for why the
leaders, not human resources, must be setting the standard and
paving the path to success. Finally this book is for anyone who
wants to take a leadership role in guarding, celebrating, fostering
and living their organization's values as if they were their own.

This last role is absolutely vital. Every organization needs its
rebels, fanatics and whistle-blowers to be successful, but they
must be rebels, fanatics and whistle-blowers *with* a cause, namely,

their organization's own values. Organizations need people who embody values through their actions and are simultaneously guardians and messengers of them, people who will keep the organization in line, regardless of who is failing to live up to those values. No matter how much management might wish that its people would fall expediently into place behind every initiative, strategy or action plan, the truth is human beings are not motivated by decree, reward or demand, but by the stirrings of their own hearts.

People must make their contributions to an organization willingly and independently to bring passion, commitment, creativity and energy to a job. But they will do so only so long as they believe that what they are doing is authentic and meaningful, and is part of a code of commitment shared by the organization as a whole. If an organization does not live up to its values in everything it does and thus fails to keep true to those values in striving towards its vision, it loses the energy, passion and loyalty of its people. Cynicism, increased stress, reduced quality, corner cutting and apathy are the inevitable results.

Without values, everything may be permissible, but few people will stay committed and loyal to such an organization for long. They may collect their paychecks every other Friday; but they won't be thinking about how they can solve a problem or achieve an objective on the drive home or even, in all likelihood, while they are sitting at their desks. As one front-line employee of a telecommunications firm said to his union representative about his company's values, "If our company will begin living this way from the top and throughout, this will stop being a job and become a career again."

Thinking Inside the Box

A few years ago, I visited a client on site. The client was a company that happened to make boxes. I didn't think about that connection to my past until I entered the plant. Suddenly, the smell of the factory brought all those memories of my childhood rushing back.

I thought about my father, and I began to see how his leadership style affected the people around him. As a consultant and coach, I was now in the business of helping people grow their organizations through hiring and leadership development. I realized, from an adult perspective, that my father's disciplined approach to the way things should be done was not restrictive; it provided a structure that the people who worked for him found comforting and liberating. As his adolescent son I had always thought that he boxed us in with his values, but now, as an adult, I saw that box in a very different light. Adults look at boxes as limiting, but children see them as filled with potential. Parents who have bought presents and witnessed their child spending more time playing with the box than the toy understand this profoundly. I began to reflect on the way people in organizations talk about the need to "think outside the box" and why that always annoyed me. "The box is not your problem," I'd always wanted to say. "Figure out what you've got in the box and you'll be all right." I had no idea what I really meant by that until recently. Finally, I understood: organizations are boxes. People, ideas, emotions, dreams and values live inside them. Thinking "outside the box" always seemed like an excuse to ignore what made an organization special by trading all that away for whatever was fashionable or trendy. I knew, however, that what's deep inside the box — organizational values — was the real treasure.

In the end, this book's approach and message can be summed up by this metaphor: instead of thinking outside the box, I am calling on people to think inside the box. This means a shift in thinking which is necessary if your organization is to be value-focused. It is a recognition that what an organization stands for on the *inside* is equally as important as the vision it tries to make real to the world *outside*.

What an organization is thinking inside the box has long been overshadowed and overwhelmed by external concerns: what the shareholder is thinking, for example, or what competitors seem to be doing, or what customers are demanding, or what the market makes financially profitable in the short term. The problem, however, is that without an internal grounding for those concerns many organizations lose focus and lack consistency of principle when it comes to the way they do business. They fail to harness the full extent of the energy at their disposal through their own values. They have no center of gravity or reliable compass to support their direction. They make decisions for bottom-line, expedient or opportunistic reasons. Sometimes they achieve short-term goals, but they always pay a long-term price. In my twenty years as a consultant, executive coach and advocate of a value focus for organizations, I have seen it happen time and time again.

Thinking outside the box has become such a common cliché in organizations in recent years that some firms impose fines for using the term. But the expression continues to hold sway. You hear it, especially, anytime there is a call for ideas that break through the confines of what has always been done. Organizations continue to need the shake-up that such a phrase represents. Twenty years ago, most large organizations had bureaucratic cultures that inhibited fresh ideas and promoted an inwardly focused myopia. IBM, for example, was famous for not being overly concerned about what was going on outside its own high walls. Why should Big Blue care about what its customers wanted or what its competitors were doing or what innovations were being hatched in the garages of teenaged inventors? After all, what made sense for Big Blue was naturally going to be right for the market or the customers; just as a few decades before, what was "good for GM was good for America."

But now that a succession of break-out-of-the-box organizational theories and fads have firmed their grip on a generation of managers' minds, there is a need for a renewed counterbalance to that thinking. Organizations that think predominantly outside the box are prone to quick fixes and inappropriate solutions, or to simply following the latest trend set by a popular business journal or author. Lacking the center of gravity that values provide, they focus on results without consideration for how those results are achieved. They benchmark, mimic and play catch-up with their competitors; they bring in outside charismatic leadership as saviors regardless of value fit; and they merge with or acquire other organizations without considering the ramifications of culture or values alignment. They may be nimble, flexible and profitable in the short term, depending on circumstances, but they do not last or make their mark on the world.

Organizations that know how to think inside the box have a limitless resource of positive energy and single-minded focus at their disposal. Their values are a treasure chest, complete with map and tools. Thinking inside the box is a deliberate check against what the organization's own values dictate the right answer, strategy, standard or direction to be. Should a manager promote or celebrate the actions of an employee? Think inside the box to measure that person's performance against the organization's values. Should the board hire a particular CEO? Think inside the box to determine if that candidate's values are a match for or would be a shift from the organization's values. The latter would create a negative impact as it would be countercultural. Should a customer service representative agree to or reject a customer's demands? Think inside the box to independently and efficiently decide the right answer.

In this book, we will help you do some inside-the-box thinking about your organization, your people, your leadership and your terms of success. In the chapters that follow we look at famous value bellwether organizations like Johnson & Johnson, GE and even the New York Yankees for the way that they achieve greatness consistently over time. We also look at equally well-known organizations that have struggled recently and publicly with issues, challenges and failures linked to value conflicts. Finally, we closely examine a number of lesser-known organizations like Federal Home Loan Bank of Pittsburgh and sanofi-pasteur that are currently striving to integrate their values with their leadership discipline and daily work processes.

Our journey will cover the following terrain. In the first chapter we look closely at the importance of values and value-based systems. I will show you what they mean, why they are real and what they do for an organization. In chapter two, we look at how much the CEO or top leader influences the organization's values, and how an organization can define and roll out those values to be embraced and understood by everyone, at all levels, in all roles. In chapter three, we look at how values create organizational culture, the means by which values are expressed through unofficial rules, guidelines and corporate legends. In chapter four, we link values to work by defining the behaviors that employees need to use in order to be successful. I also detail how employees can be hired, identified, supported, developed or dismissed according to their values performance. Managers and supervisors become the living embodiment of the organization's values, and as such they are responsible for defining them with their direct reports and honoring those who live according to them in tough or unusual circumstances.

In chapter five, we look at how to develop leaders and develop a real succession planning strategy by using values as a standard and guide. We also discuss the impact on your employees when you promote a person who others do not perceive as a standard-bearer of your values. In chapter six, we look at values and change. A frequent criticism of inside-the-box thinking is that organizations need to be responsive to the outside world. I couldn't agree more. Staying true to principles is the way lasting organizations navigate change without losing their bearings and sense of direction. Actually changing values and culture is a phenomenally difficult task that few organizations have managed successfully, despite many attempts. Finally, in chapter seven, we look at the measurable outputs of values. Organizations that operate under consistent and long-standing values systems have been called "enduring companies" and "institutions." This book, in large part, is about how organizations achieve such success.

Although values come from top leadership and are cascaded down through the ranks, the authenticity, impact and worthiness of those values can only be measured through the people doing the work of the organization. Asking your own employees is one way to make that determination. They are the ones who know you best, who are sensitive to whether you are consistently living up to the organization's values and who are unfailingly aware of whether your organization is on the right track. Most leaders who fail to make values real, deny or protect themselves from the insights of their employees as a matter of course. This book will provide the framework and questions to prompt productive self-examination. In education, we say that the best way to know the capability of a teacher is to ask the students. Students always know, very quickly, if their teacher is prepared, committed and effective. So, too, a salesclerk at Home Depot can tell when the new CEO comes from an organization with an entirely different value set. But we'll tell that story in detail in chapter five.

Remember, what's happening inside the box is far more important to your people than what's going on outside the box. Leaders should be prepared to refocus and unashamedly reaffirm their values. Sometimes that requires looking at the world from a different perspective.

CHAPTER ONE

What's Inside the Box?
How Values Work

❑ When people feel alignment between their personal values, their organization's values and their manager's values, they call it a "good fit."

❑ When values are clear, they guide all business and personnel decisions — especially when those decisions are tough and emotional.

❑ When an organization's declared values and its real values don't match, people become stressed, confused and cynical.

❑ When an organization's values serve as the foundation for its vision, business strategy and talent development, it outperforms its competition and becomes a lasting institution.

What are your organization's values? Can you list them without looking at the back of your business card? Do those values define what's unique about your company and communicate that difference to employees, customers and even shareholders? Do they impact your own work on a daily basis? Do they drive your organization's long-term mental picture or does the vision drive the values? Most importantly, do you feel (deep inside) as though your personal values and your organization's values are a good fit?

Values come from the top. They are set by the founder, and get cascaded and reinforced — or distorted and blocked — by each manager through each direct report. What does it mean when a store clerk, telephone sales rep or lab technician fails to demonstrate an organization's values in the way each does his or her job? Chances are, somewhere along the chain of command, a breakdown occurred in the way those values were communicated, demonstrated or reinforced. Sometimes that breakdown originates at the very top.

Few of us are CEOs, but we all have the potential to feel a powerful, emotional investment in what our organization stands for, what it's striving to accomplish and how it behaves in the world. We long for that connection, whether we admit it or not. Those people who believe that organizations and values are really like oil and water have probably experienced so much disconnect between word and deed over the years that they have earned their deep cynicism. At heart, they do not feel safe and free within the environment of their organization, and their organization probably does not appreciate and draw out the best from them in return.

LOOK INSIDE THE BOX

Leaders Earn the Cynicism of Their Employees

People don't leave organizations, they leave managers. They leave managers because the manager does not live up to the promise the company made the employee about how the person could expect to be treated once they join the firm.

Signs of potential grounds for cynicism include managers who:

- Break promises
- Circle the wagons but don't live the values and defend themselves against criticism during times of crisis
- Don't apply the values to those who are "getting the results"
- Follow the management fad of the moment
- Talk about respect but don't give people the support, training and/or tools they need
- Promote people who don't live the values

But what do "values" really mean? As a modern business term, the word has become commonplace, a concept that can seem utterly divorced from the blood, guts and heart of how an organization operates. In truth, there's no product, idea or strategy as powerful as an organization's values. A leader's most important job is to clarify, live by and pass on those values to others. In fact, that could serve as a pretty good definition of leadership itself.

Do CEOs realize this? In my experience, 95 percent believe that values matter. They buy into the conventional wisdom that high-performance, built-to-last organizations are based on something called core values. But there is plenty of evidence to suggest that many of those same CEOs and senior leaders are less confident when it comes to the mechanics of values. This means that, like most people, they do not think about how values need to be defined, articulated and reinforced in order to spread. Nor do they understand how critical it is that leaders and managers within the organization rely upon values as the basis for all decisions. This is especially the case when those decisions occur at *defining moments*. As a result, such leaders fail to capitalize on the power of values to foster a winning culture, build a coherent people system and communicate a meaningful brand to employees and customers.

LOOK INSIDE THE BOX

You can identify a **defining moment** or **corporate legend** by the way it feels — a gut-wrenching emotional choice that seems to physically impact an organization's morale and energy because those involved in the incident stuck to the values at such times. People will understand and support whatever decision you make; if you ignore the values because it's easier, more expedient or more lucrative in the short term to do so, you will be able to look back one day and recognize that decision as the moment when the organization lost its way.

One Set of Values Does Not Fit All

Often I am asked about the notion that one set of values does not fit all. I recently attended a presentation on organization and culture. The presenter made a case that by using a particular approach you can measure a culture. The presenter claimed to have created a tool that measured culture against her own definition of a good culture. She defined the desired organizational culture as a democratic, flat and humanistic organization. She took a perspective that she believed to be appropriate for all companies. I see this imposition of one set of values on other cultures as corporate cultural imperialism.

If you subscribed to the one-culture-fits-all and one-leadership-model-fits-all mentality that she and her partner advocate, you would have to believe that conformity to this model works for all companies in all places. It does not. If you work in a family-run business that has always been paternalistic, what is wrong with continuing with the values that are behind that success? I have worked with large family-owned and -operated firms in Europe and Southeast Asia. Imposing her culture model reminds me of a book written in 1958 called *The Ugly American*, by William J. Lederer and Eugene Burdick. In that book, the authors assert that events similar to those described in the book have happened again and again in the developing world. Indeed, most of the book seems very authentic. The phrase "ugly American" is invoked to embody America's incompetent, heavy-handed foreign policy. The book describes a sequence of very competent, as well as incompetent people, who are trying to win the Cold War for America in Asia. Would not having one culture for all firms be akin to corporate cultural imperialism?

Without too much imagination we can apply the lessons from *The Ugly American* to all the people with good intentions and good ideas for North America who try to impose a set of behaviors and corporate concepts in environments and economic, political and social structures that cannot accept them. But this discussion is for another day, since it is complicated by the ever-increasing globalization of the

Continued

corporate world. As barriers to trade and the exchange of ideas begin to break down, perhaps the world of economics will do what nation states have tried and failed to do for generations — achieve one world economic village.

Many North American corporations such as Google, Yahoo and Cisco are wrestling with the compelling question of cross-cultural values as they expand their business globally.

A Flash Test on Values

I had an opportunity to assess the uncertainty about the meaning of values first-hand at a conference organized for high-ranking executives from several different sectors within the finance industry. I was speaking to a group of senior leaders from sixty different companies, made up mostly of CEOs and CFOs from across North America. I had a great deal of respect for these people. They were seasoned executives running organizations that were experiencing significant change. The rules governing their industry (finance, banking and insurance) had been re-written, the traditional nature of competition transformed. Customers were demanding a different kind of service and even a different relationship. How should their organizations respond? Most of the discussion that day had revolved around strategy related to that changing landscape. Indeed, it had been a long day of talking heads, and a noticeable number of participants had snuck out for a late afternoon round of golf. Those left behind must have felt even more desperate for strategic ideas than the others. But it was my turn at the podium and I was there to talk about something I believed to be more critical than strategy — namely, the values from which strategy arises. I decided to do a little investigation into what was really *inside the box* by conducting a flash survey.

"How many of you lead organizations in which values have been clearly articulated?" I asked.

More than three-quarters of the hands in the room went up, including the hands of the CEOs in the room. It was an encouraging number, but I suspected that not every response would be so rosy.

"How many of you can tell me what those values are?" I continued, pushing them a little out of their comfort zone.

There was a bit of mumbling, some sheepish smiles. I allowed them to think about the question and talk among themselves. In a few cases, two or three people from the same organization were present, so they were able to confer and come up with a complete list. Even then, it took them a while to bring that list of six or seven values forward.

This would be alarming, of course, to anyone who believes that values really do matter. But more alarming still was the fact that all of those values, from all of those different companies, sounded basically the same. I wrote them on the white board as they were called out to me. I stood back to give everyone a clear view and we admired the list for a moment. Then I started crossing off those values that were identical or nearly identical to others on the list. Despite having sixty different organizations represented in the room, we ended up with a baker's dozen of cookie-cutter phrases describing those organizations' values. Do any of these phrases sound familiar? "Is there anyone here," I asked next, "whose organization does not subscribe to at least three or four of these values?"

No one put up his or her hand.

"Then let's try an experiment," I suggested. "What do you think would happen if, at the end of this discussion, you didn't go back to your own companies but switched with the person on the other side of the room instead and went back to his or her company? Would you still be just as effective as a leader?"

There were a few uncomfortable laughs. One woman spoke up:

"We couldn't do that. It wouldn't be successful."

"But if your organizations have the same values, then you should be able to interchange positions without missing a beat. You may need to learn a few new names and get used to a different business card, but the behaviors that led you to be so successful in your current environment should be identical to the behaviors that will lead to success in the new company."

Perhaps because these leaders knew each other's organizations fairly well, my comment touched a raw nerve. Many protested that it wouldn't work.

"Why wouldn't it be successful? Your companies are obviously extremely similar," I said. "In fact, I'd even go further than that and suggest that your companies could merge, and you might never notice the difference."

Their companies were in the same industry, competing for the same customers. If their values were identical, then they should have welcomed a merger. Perhaps a few jobs would be lost, but the fit between those companies would make a merger feel more like a family reunion than a hostile takeover.

That's when the debate really came to life. Everyone in the room was suddenly in agreement on one thing: their organizations' cultures were distinctly different. Some were customer-focused, others were great at marketing. Some had long and venerable traditions; others were new spin-offs of older companies and had a vigorous entrepreneurial spirit. A few people had worked in more than one of the organizations and spoke up about how different their experience of those companies had been. Just walking into the offices of company X, I was told, you could feel the difference from company Y. Each organization made decisions differently, talked differently, rewarded people differently, hired differently and selected leaders differently. You felt at home in one organization or the other, but rarely in both. People were very passionate about the extent of those differences.

"Ah," I said, "so why don't your values reflect that?"

And that's when a light went on. In fact, it burned so brightly that during the evening reception many of those who had chosen the golf links over the lecture approached me to confess that they should have stayed because they had heard that the conversation was meaningful and thought-provoking. Perhaps that was my first understanding that leaders do not forego values because they dismiss them but because they struggle to make sense of them like everyone else.

Values Create Behaviors

Companies have unique cultures because their values are distinct. You can feel the difference when you walk in the door, whether you are a brand-new recruit, a lifelong employee, a customer, a vendor or a security guard. Values are a reflection of that difference. They are the essence of what makes each organization and each person unique.

Why? Because values define what we think is right or correct; they influence how we see the world and how we act. When my group of insurance executives began to get specific about what distinguished their different companies, they didn't use words like "respect," "integrity" or "customer-focus." Instead, they described what a sales representative would do to help a customer, or how a manager would handle an employee who needed disciplining, or why a CEO was or was not a successful leader. When I listened to them describing customer service at their various organizations, I could see and feel the difference.

When I pointed out how concretely those descriptions captured the essence of their organization's unique qualities, they began to understand. Nothing about this idea is revolutionary — in fact, it's so simple that no one consciously thinks about it. Instead, we're so used to thinking outside the box when looking for compelling ideas, strategies and new ways to win that we forget how rich and resourceful our organizations are *inside the box*. What's inside really does matter. In fact, it makes all the difference in the world.

LOOK INSIDE THE BOX

Values List

Take a moment to write down your organization's values here. If, like those senior financial leaders, you don't remember them, check the back of your business card. (After GE's Jack Welch stated them on GE's cards, many companies followed suit — much in the same way they copy each other's values.)

Your organization's values:

1._____

2._____

3._____

4._____

5._____

6._____

My CEOs and senior leaders recovered quickly. They explained to me that their value statements — integrity, respect, honesty, and so on — were not distinct because they were only words. People knew what they really meant. Their organizations are distinct because of their unique cultures, and culture is an intangible that can't be described in a mere handful of words.

Let's try, I thought, and pressed on. I pointed to our list of values on the white board. "Integrity. Teamwork. Respect. What do you mean when you say that 'respect for others' is a value?"

There was a brief hesitation and then a deluge. "Respect for others" was very important. It was critical for the organization to treat people with respect, to acknowledge them when they contributed to the business, to provide them with the tools to succeed. Other executives declared that respect did not just refer to employees but also to customers and the public at large. Respect was a value that described the people-focused nature of the business. If the organization showed customers respect, then the business itself would succeed.

Not everyone agreed. Their viewpoints were rich and varied, textured and nuanced. But what emerged was a robust and powerful debate that got to the core of how those companies differed when it came to the value they all called "respect." They didn't resolve their vagueness about the issue completely, but they did do a lot of serious thinking about what the value meant to them, and they were able to articulate that meaning with greater clarity, little by little. Respect as a value was a passionately held belief that really mattered. It affected how everyone did their jobs. It touched on feelings about the larger meaning of the organization's vision. It reflected what the organization wanted to accomplish in the marketplace. It was the basis for the kind of employees that the organization looked to for leadership and hoped to recruit for future generations.

The difficulty, however, was that none of the senior executives in the room really knew what respect meant until they began to discuss it and think about it. If those leaders needed to struggle to come to that understanding, just think how varied the interpretation must be among the twenty to thirty thousand employees of each of their organizations. Imagine how twenty to thirty thousand different understandings of respect affects customer service, employee relations, coaching, development, compensation, performance management, execution, decision making and ethics. Sure, respect was important. But the real question is how does a company demonstrate that importance on a customer-by-customer, manager-by-manager, employee-by-employee basis?

LOOK INSIDE THE BOX

Most Common Values

Customer satisfaction 77%

Ethics/integrity 76%

Accountability 61%

Respect for others 59%

Open communication 51%

Profitability 49%

Teamwork 47%

Innovation/change 47%

Continuous learning 43%

Positive work environment 42%

Diversity 41%

Community service 38%

Trust 37%

Social responsibility 33%

Security/safety 33%

Empowerment 32%

Employee job satisfaction 31%

Have fun 24%

Survey on "Corporate Values in 2002" by the American Management Association.

The Tower of Babble

If there's no clarity at the top about what values really mean, then there's certainly no consistency at the management level. This means that there's no way to measure, coach, assess, promote or fire people in line with those values. Any organization that does not articulate its values concretely functions like a modern Tower of Babel. No one can be quite sure that they are speaking the same language at different levels or different locations within the organization. Decisions don't always make sense or feel right. Confusion reigns. No matter how compelling and inspirational the organization's vision may be, its aspirations fall far short in reality.

LOOK INSIDE THE BOX

Achieving results in the *right way* is about top performance that is consistent with organizational values.

Consider the value of respect again. We can put forward a million-dollar process about what we mean by respect. We can be very articulate and careful in our corporate communications when we use that word, but then blow it all in the way we hire, fire, promote and manage. For example, it's a truism that most managers hire for technical capabilities but fire for personality

— i.e., poor alignment to the organization's behavioral norms. What this means is that we bring people on board because they have the skills and technical abilities to do the work we need them to do, but we end up firing them because they do not use those skills and abilities to do their jobs in a way that fits with the organization's way of doing things. How does this happen? It occurs when our values, as defined by the behaviors that demonstrate those values, are not clearly articulated and included in the job profile. Should we expect that just because someone has the requisite technical talent to do a job that he or she also will demonstrate respect in the workplace? Of course not. No one believes that a soft attribute like respect goes hand-in-hand with a technical ability. Instead, we look for respect in other ways — by evaluating the individual's personality in the interview process and hiring him or her based on our gut feeling. Nevertheless, how do we really know whether that person has the value we call respect and will demonstrate it in the way that people in our company believe is right? The truth is, we have no way of knowing. And the largest root cause of that uncertainty is our own lack of understanding about how respect gets demonstrated by people who truly fit our company's culture.

It's bad enough when an organization hires someone who does not fit the values, but the impact is even more toxic when the organization rewards someone who does not demonstrate its values. This happens all the time in companies for a simple reason: people who don't demonstrate cultural values can still achieve bottom-line results; they just don't achieve those results in the "right" way. And yet, hold the presses for a moment. Aren't results all that really matter? Organizations are struggling just to survive in the marketplace today; does any leader really care *how* a star employee meets strategic objectives? A leader should care. After all, that star employee's colleagues and customers care very much. They are the ones who are most directly affected by the actions employed in achieving those results.

If respect, for example, is the value in question, and a star salesperson gets a key account but does not demonstrate the behaviors associated with respect in doing so, other customers and employees are the first ones affected. Immediately, their value antennae are quivering. What will the leaders in the organization do about something that has rocked the culture, ruffled feathers and negatively swayed morale?

The moment those leaders praise, reward or promote that employee, all credibility in respect as a value is lost. It is now understood that respect is just a word, not a real value. It is a cheap form of currency used by the leadership to puff up a speech, decorate a website or motivate the group in a mission in which no one truly believes. When the chips are down, and success is at stake, the leaders have made it clear that profit comes before principle. To the people of the organization, any sense of common mission or larger meaning has been tarnished and cheapened. They now understand that it is acceptable to get ahead by doing whatever they feel like, as long as it produces results.

Nothing is more corrosive to an organization's culture. And yet it is a challenge to prove to leaders that consistency between stated values and actual behaviors — at every level of the organization and at each critical moment — truly does make a difference in the firm's long-term profitability and success. No doubt, that's because in our society we have a tendency to reward leaders for their short-term wins. But who said leadership was about taking the easy path?

Staying true to values is an uphill battle. There are many temptations to break faith with values and make expedient decisions. Leaders should realize, however, that when it comes to values, employees and customers are always watching. Leaders can destroy their personal credibility and damage their organization's culture by not acting in accordance with their values or preserving them at all costs. As leadership experts have long understood, it's all about what you do, not what you say. For the organization's people, it's about how you get there, not where you arrive. Those companies that stick to their values, in good times and bad, always win out in the long run. But before we look at that evidence, let's examine more fully what values do and why they really matter.

Why Values Hit Home

Values are emotionally charged. They really matter to people. They impact what people choose to do with their lives and where they feel at home. Although values are most often inadequately understood, barely articulated and hardly noticed on a conscious level, they actually explain how people think and what they believe in. If we are united by a common set of values in our companies, countries, volunteer groups, book clubs or religious organizations, we are also divided by our value differences — nation from nation, religion from religion, bowling team from bowling team, voting block from voting block. The power of values to bind and separate us cannot be overstated.

LOOK INSIDE THE BOX

Values are strongly held beliefs that are emotionally charged and highly resistant to change.

So what are values? Consider the following definition as you read this book: values are strongly held beliefs that are emotionally charged and highly resistant to change.

Now, let's take the definition apart. As stated above, values are not facts — they are beliefs. Nevertheless, values are so strongly held that their proponents view them as facts. Those who hold certain values believe they should be self-evident and obvious to all, without any deep analysis or overall explanation. That other people can view those "facts" so differently, and believe in contrary "facts" just as passionately, is part of the wonder and challenge of the human condition.

Values are highly resistant to change. A run-of-the-mill belief can change over time or in the face of sufficient argument. If you believe that the world is flat, for example, I can probably provide you with sufficient proof to change your opinion, as long as you're a reasonable person. A value, however, will almost never change, no matter how persuasive a counter-argument may be. Think about some of the most contentious debates of our times about evolution, abortion, capital punishment or gun control. If you are an ardent believer in science, then you will never be able to join the intelligent design or creationist side of the debate and claim that the facts of evolution are up to religious interpretation. It's simply wrong to you. The opposite, of course, is also the case. If you believe that the universe was formed in seven days as the Bible states, or that it evolved according to the designs of an intelligent creator, then you can't shrug your shoulders and agree with evolution proponents by saying, "Maybe it happened that way; maybe it didn't." Neither side will understand the validity of the other side's argument. No matter how rational, factual or emotional a counter-argument may be, it will never dissuade someone from a deeply held belief when that belief is a value.

Consider some of the more contentious, emotional and passionate arguments you have faced in the work world. Upon reflection, I bet you will discover that those arguments were less about facts than deeply held values. Most of us can remain fairly rational and objective in a formal work setting when an argument concerns something that doesn't affect our sense of right and wrong. But when the argument touches on values, an emotional button is pushed.

For example, if your business desperately needs to increase its profits in the next quarter, then you are probably open to a number of different ways to accomplish that improvement. But if you have a value belief that holds that learning is critical for the long-term success of your organization, then you will not be okay with a proposal to slash the training and development budget in order to bump up profitability. The counter-argument may be very logical and compelling: training is a luxury that we can always reinvest in when times are good again; training is a long-term tool, but we have an immediate crisis; training is something that employees view as a perk, but we all need to batten down the hatches until this storm is over. Nevertheless, you believe that training is not a nice-to-have; it is a strategic necessity. In your view, training is a covenant between employees and leadership that says, "We believe in you; we want you to believe in us. We invest in your growth because we want you to invest your effort, creativity and commitment in us." In fact, you believe that if the training budget gets cut, your employees will see that decision as a huge violation of a larger promise that will hollow out your credibility. Training, in other words, is a line in the sand. If your organization crosses that line, it may as well wave the white flag — the larger battle would be pointless.

Individual versus Organizational Values

Why wouldn't everyone in your organization see the argument the same way as you? There are a number of possible explanations, none of which bode well. The first and most healthy possibility from an organizational standpoint is that you are alone on this issue because it is a value for you but not to the organization as a whole. In other words, you hold investment into the development of people to be a critical value but your organization does not. Nor has it ever said that it does. In your fight with others on the leadership team, you have no recourse to point, Perry Mason–style, at the organizational values listed on the boardroom wall and say, "See, learning and development are not just words to us; they're values! If we cut training now, we're breaking faith with those who believe in us!" Instead, you can only think, deep inside, that cutting training and development is wrong, and wouldn't it be nice to work for a company that actually felt the same way.

If you are working for a company where your values do not match the organization's explicit and clearly stated values, then you may be a bad fit for that organization. At critical moments, and perhaps frequently, you will run into value conflicts with others in your organization, and with your overall sense of where the organization should be going and what it stands for. This can be extremely stressful on a personal level. People who do not fit with their organization's values are not at home in its culture. They are likely to feel alienated from others, and they will probably find themselves increasingly shunted aside from key decisions and decision makers. A strong culture has a way of making those who don't fit feel rejected and out of place.

In fact, an organization that is really clear about its values probably would never have hired you in the first place. But let's say you slipped through the cracks somehow. Chances are you will be found out. Take, for example, performance appraisals that are based on an explicit understanding of the organization's values. You may decide to go your own way when the "right" decision, according to what the organization believes in, is something entirely different. Your direct supervisor should not give you a stellar grade in your performance review; nor should you be promoted or rewarded, no matter how hard you worked, how good your intentions were or even how great your results turned out to be. After all, you did not achieve those results in the right way. To reward you for them would be to send the wrong message to others about what the organization stands for.

This may seem unfair to you, since you are working so hard, but ultimately, aren't you better off finding a home where you really belong? Perhaps you think that a job is just a paycheck, and you shouldn't have to sell your soul to the organization in order to make enough to eat. Maybe so, but an organization that is based on values has the right and the obligation to hire, retain and promote the right people in order to reinforce its culture and achieve its vision. In fact, if the organization keeps you on, it is probably doing a disservice to the others who believe in its values and are striving everyday to make them real. In most cases, it is easier to get rid of one individual than to change the organization's values to accommodate that person. The exception, of course, is when the individual in question is the newly hired CEO — a circumstance we will examine in chapter two.

Not everyone is going to be a perfect fit in every organization. Individuals are complex beings, and organizations are complex matrices of dynamics and priorities. But as much as possible, we should strive to see that individual values and organizational values overlap. Where they don't overlap, we should be so clear about organizational values that people know they have to make a decision contrary to what they actually believe in, because that's the way the organization would do it. The danger to an organization is when they espouse a set of values and then the organization's leadership acts contrary to the stated values thus "inviting" right-minded people who joined the firm, believing in the truth of the values as stated, to become morally appalled and clear their consciousness by blowing the whistle on the leaders. Organizational alignment is when the values are lived consistently day to day, moment to moment by everyone without exception.

One other question often raised and referred to above is the correctness of one set of values over the other. Let's take a moment to further explore that issue. I have been asked, on occasion, what about when institutions take on fake or immoral values. My sense of right and wrong is only right from my perspective. I cannot impose my beliefs and values on others. However, I do have the right and obligation to point out my differences if the other side's values might impose a threat to me. For example, I have said that in Nazi Germany the leadership and even, unfortunately, the people had a heightened sense of integrity. Why? Because, they acted with great consistency on their values at all times. I have to take a strong objection to their values, but from their perspective they acted with consistency. I would also say that within organizations we do not find those extremes. Within organizations the behaviors that define the values define their ethics. When they find like-minded individuals, the organization is healthier and stronger.

Rebels with a Cause

Does this mean there is no room for dissent in an organization? Of course not. Even in healthy organizations, dissent over leadership decisions is not uncommon. Sometimes it is an indication that employees believe organizational values are being violated by those in power. In fact, I have witnessed times where rank-and-file employees care so deeply about an organization's values that they fight decisions that threaten the culture. If customer service is a value, for example, and a new dictate from the executive floor forces salespeople to cut corners, the members of the sales team will not take that order sitting down. They may grumble, complain and fail to follow through. They may take a vocal stand and try to make a change. Or, they may seem to acquiesce but actually undermine the order by continuing to serve customers the old way. Regardless, morale will be lowered. Retention of employees may become an issue. A toxic mood of cynicism may begin to pervade the organization. If the leadership doesn't recognize this dissent and seek to rectify its mistake somehow, it may have a big problem on its hands. Should these dissenters be punished for their resistance? In an ideal world, absolutely not. They may be rebels, but they are rebels with a cause. They believe in their company's values, maybe even more than the leadership does.

There is always going to be tension in organizations over values. In healthy organizations, those tensions indicate the normal process of working through the ramifications of decisions and actions. Does the decision feel right? What will happen as a result? Who will be affected and how? We don't always know right away when a decision or an action is in conflict with a value. Something feels wrong, people begin to argue, lines get drawn. In some organizations, this tension divides the organization into factions or along political lines. But if the values of the organization are clear, consistent and well understood by everyone, eventually people will sort out the issues and get to the heart of the matter. Values are like a compass. They help organizations right themselves and recognize the way forward no matter how chaotic things may temporarily be.

Stated versus Real Values: The Organization's Underground Culture

Quite often, organizations have two sets of values. One set comprises cherished and prominently displayed values that the organization thinks it believes in. The other set comprises the values that the organization actually believes in and, in fact, operates by. Those are the values of the underground culture.

You might hope that such a split personality is rare in the world of organizations, but think about how common it is among people. How many politicians, religious leaders, senior executives, union leaders, social welfare proponents, moral crusaders, role-model athletes and ordinary men and women get caught doing or saying something that feels completely antithetical to what they profess and we think they believe in? There are so many recent examples to choose from, one hardly knows where to begin. Here's a favorite. Michael Sears, a former CFO of Boeing, was considered a likely successor to the CEO. Sears was such a rising star in the executive world that he had a contract for a leadership book called *Soaring through Turbulence.* One critical chapter in the book was about the importance of workplace ethics. Unfortunately, the book never made it to the stores. Mr. Sears' publishing contract was canceled when he was indicted for negotiating a deal with the U.S. government while secretly offering his negotiating partner a job at his company. Ultimately, this scandal touched others in the organization and led to the resignation of Philip Condit, the CEO that Sears had been touted to replace. Although Mr. Sears wrote about the importance of ethics, his conduct during the government negotiation doesn't sound or feel ethical. Certainly, it was illegal. If you read the values that Boeing holds to be true, Mr. Sears' conduct sounds antithetical to his organization's principles, too.

Boeing's list of eight corporate values includes integrity, which is described in the following manner: "We will always take the high road by practicing the highest ethical standards, and by honoring our commitments. We will take personal responsibility for our actions and treat everyone fairly and with trust and respect."

LOOK INSIDE THE BOX

Boeing's Values

In all our relationships we will demonstrate our steadfast commitment to:

Leadership

We will be a world-class leader in every aspect of our business and in developing our team leadership skills at every level; in our management performance; in the way we design, build and support our products; and in our financial results.

Integrity

We will always take the high road by practicing the highest ethical standards, and by honoring our commitments. We will take personal responsibility for our actions, and treat everyone fairly and with trust and respect.

Quality

We will strive for continuous quality improvement in all that we do, so that we will rank among the world's premier industrial firms in customer, employee and community satisfaction.

Customer Satisfaction

Satisfied customers are essential to our success. We will achieve total customer satisfaction by understanding what the customer wants and delivering it flawlessly.

People Working Together

We recognize our strength and our competitive advantage is — and always will be — people. We will continually learn, and share ideas and knowledge. We will encourage cooperative efforts at every level and across all activities in our company.

A Diverse and Involved Team

We value the skills, strengths, and perspectives of our diverse team. We will foster a participatory workplace that enables people to get involved in making decisions about their work that advance our common business objectives.

Good Corporate Citizenship

We will provide a safe workplace and protect the environment. We will promote the health and well-being of Boeing people and their families. We will work with our communities by volunteering and financially supporting education and other worthy causes.

Enhancing Shareholder Value

Our business must produce a profit, and we must generate superior returns on the assets entrusted to us by our shareholders. We will ensure our success by satisfying our customers and increasing shareholder value.

So how was it that Mr. Sears engaged in conduct that violated the values of the company in which he held a leadership position? We can only speculate. Perhaps Mr. Sears was a bad apple, or maybe he got caught the one time he engaged in unethical behavior. Since he was a prominent leader at Boeing, however, it seems more likely that Mr. Sears was engaging in conduct that the organization, at that time, didn't really believe was unethical. In the culture of the organization, securing a contract might have been more important than the means by which that result was accomplished. Other values, such as enhancing shareholder value, may have taken precedence over integrity.

This discrepancy between stated values and actual values is very common, and indicates a basic tendency to which organizations are highly susceptible. We are inclined, for whatever reason, to treat values like works of art. We view them as nice to hang on the wall and beautiful to look at, but we don't act as though they truly mean much to us in the real world. Business-minded people may be especially prone to this problem. Values are idealistic — they think — but the real world is ruthless. Leaders must be pragmatic and realistic by nature. Sometimes you need to play outside the lines in order to make something happen. At the end of the day, winning is essential, or else your values won't even matter, business people sometimes reason.

In fact, the opposite is true. The best organizations understand their values, articulate them clearly and hold them higher than any short-term concerns or short-cut methods. This does not put such organizations at a competitive disadvantage. It is the source of their competitive advantage — an idea we will be exploring in depth in the chapters to follow.

Sometimes a leader or a rank-and-file employee knows that he or she is violating a value but knows that the organization will sanction his or her actions. This is a clear-cut sign that the organization's stated values and its real values are different and distinct. Real values cannot be violated under any circumstance. It should also be noted that all values are created and applied equally in a healthy organization. No one value trumps the others.

How much more powerful would an organization be if it articulated its real values accurately? In such an organization, there would be no hidden agenda or second-guessing. Employees who joined wouldn't have to go through a six-week or six-month acculturation period during which they must figure out what the real rules are. When leaders made a decision, people would be able to judge immediately whether that decision fit with the organization's beliefs, and embrace or disallow that new direction accordingly. Such an organization would be aligned and committed, steps ahead of the competition.

Why are we so averse to thinking of values in down-to-earth terms? No one should be ashamed if his or her values don't sound lofty, poetic, inspirational or idealistic enough. Concrete values that affect how decisions get made and how actions get evaluated will have far greater meaning and impact for those who live under those beliefs. Every manager and every senior leader should welcome the opportunity to create clarity about values.

To determine whether your organization lives by its stated values or by an implicit set of values that don't get talked about, try listing your values again. Do you really believe in them? Can you think of examples when those values were demonstrated? Can you describe what happened when any of those values were violated?

LOOK INSIDE THE BOX

Values Test

Stated Value 1:

Real Value 1:

_____

Stated Value 2:

Real Value 2:

_____

Stated Value 3:

Real Value 3:

_____

Stated Value 4:

Real Value 4:

_____

Stated Value 5:

Real Value 5:

_____

Stated Value 6:

Real Value 6:

If you know rich stories that answer those two questions, and if other people in your organization know the same stories or have similar ones, chances are that your values are real. If some or all of the values you list do not really matter to your organization, then you will be able to think of different examples that illustrate that discrepancy.

The distance between an organization's stated values and its real values measures the gap a leader must straddle to achieve organizational credibility. In truth, no leader can continue to straddle that gap for long. It's not a very dignified position in which to find oneself.

Aspirational or Core Values

Sometimes value conflicts arise not because there is an unconscious gap between stated and real (or underground) values but because the organization does not treat its values like a code for daily living. Instead, the organization views its values as an ideal to strive for or a promised land just out of reach but always in sight. While this attitude seems to indicate understandings of how hard idealized values are to stick to, it also provides a built-in excuse or rationale for failing to live up to them. This drives home the point that we don't actually know if something is a value until it is tested in the real world when something significant is on the line.

As a result, it is reasonable to argue that there is no such thing as aspirational values. Values are either important enough to live by, especially in difficult times, or they are unrealistic and meaningless. An organization cannot aspire to become something better or more pure than it is, no matter how noble or worthy those goals may be. Values are about how an organization's people consistently conduct themselves every day. They are not a nice-to-have, but a have-to-have.

While it's tempting to be idealistic and lofty when discussing values, doing so creates difficulties. Consider how much trouble the United States of America gets in when it espouses democratic principles for nations around the world but does not live up to those ideals by enforcing such principles in every situation. Of course, the world is not a perfect place, and real political strategy often takes understandable precedence over idealistic hopes, but this gap between what it espouses and what it strives for leaves the United States open to critics' charges of hypocrisy. If American leaders held firm to the idea that the United States is a beacon or example of democracy that others can choose to emulate, it might be given a bit more leeway in how it conducts its foreign affairs. It is easy for political leaders to be swept away during flights of rhetoric, using values not as an operating principle but as a description of an ideal future. Most human beings have an incurable desire to feel good about themselves. The hypocrisy comes when people speak one way and act another, while maintaining a self-satisfied belief in their ethical superiority. Companies sometimes act this way, certainly nations do, and so do people.

Business leaders are also prone to idealistic messages about values when they rally the troops. It's very easy to speak in lofty, idealistic terms about values. We feel great emotion when we think our organizations are better or purer than we are. But the ability to communicate in such lofty terms is a sign that we are discussing values vaguely and they are thus open to interpretation in any way that each listener sees fit. In other words, the Tower of Babel is back. If values are articulated concretely in ways that people can connect to how they do their jobs, they will have real impact on performance. They will also ultimately be more inspiring as people see the link between living those values and the organization's success in achieving its goals. When an organization can draw on its own history with a powerful corporate legend and explain through that oral history the actions taken to bring those values to life, then the value is not aspirational but a reality. Everyone in the organization knows exactly what to do and how to act, in good times and bad, with or without a rule book.

The use of the term "core values" reflects a similar problem as that of aspirational values. The term "core" implies something that is deeper and more essential than anything else. It's as though an organization can have one set of values that are like regular work clothes and another core set of values which are its Sunday best. I have seen leaders in organizations talk about core values particularly when the chips are down and times are tough. "We need to get back to our core values," they say, in an acknowledgement that they have strayed from what makes their organization special. If they had stayed true to those values all along, they would not view them as core, but as guiding principles. Nevertheless, it's difficult, if not impossible, to be true to values when they are idealistic or (worse) borrowed from a firm that has been held as a benchmark for others to emulate. Most of us are not saints. Organizations operate firmly in the real world. Values are about achieving results in a way that is consistent with what an organization stands for, not about being morally superior to the competition or bettering ourselves as human beings.

Universal Values, Morals and Relativism

Aspirational values are ultimately about doing what's right in an ideal sense, but not all of us can live up to that standard. Many people schooled in religious values go through life conscious of a gap between how we are supposed to live as opposed to how we do live. Few of us are able to live up to the full spectrum of religious commandments, nor do we expect to. If there is a gap, and we feel comfortable living that way, then I suggest that our actual values are different from those that we learn through our religious institutions or schools. We can strive all our lives to follow that better way, but we can only be judged by what we do, not what we say. Just ask any student of any religious belief system. While it is important to have a set of values to guide our lives, living accordingly is a journey along an arduous path, a lifelong activity. In the end, living your values, not talking about them, defines who you are. There are incredible examples of people who stood up for their values in extreme situations, but they are rare. Consider Sandy Koufax, the Jewish baseball pitcher who refused to pitch a World Series game because it was Yom Kippur. Nor was this act a solitary display of values adherence by Koufax. Years later, when team owner Rupert Murdoch stated that there should be no gay men on the squad, Koufax resigned from his position in the organization because Murdoch's values conflicted with his own. Both acts took courage.

Nevertheless, values, for our purposes here, should not be confused with ideals or codes of conduct. Values supercede the latter and are more realistic than ideals. As noted above, an organization, like a society, can be immoral and still have corporate values. Corporate values are:

1. Related to issues of right and wrong and to how individuals within an organization are to act individually and how the company should behave collectively.

2. Based on what the founding leadership of the company states to be right and wrong, rather than on what the law or other professional standards say are right and wrong.

3. Regarded in terms of what is known to be right or just as opposed to what is officially or outwardly declared to be right or just.

4. The touchstones that provide guidance on how to behave decently and honorably *within* the company.

5. Good or right when judged by the common or collective understanding of the average employee.

6. Provided for individuals to have the ability to distinguish right from wrong and to make decisions based on that knowledge.

7. Based on an inner conviction, in the absence of physical proof.

To put these points into perspective, let's look at simple nation states, as they are in fact large corporate entities. Whether a nation state, a religious group or a business, all have a foundation rooted in a set of values. No one can determine if someone else's values are right or wrong you can only say, based on your own values set, that the other nation states, religious groups or companies' values are not yours. For example, let us consider Islamic belief. Many nations guided by Islamic principles believe that women should wear bhurkas in public and be completely hidden from view because it is immoral for them to be seen by men. In western cultures, on the other hand, forcing women to adopt this way of dressing would be considered immoral and oppression of women. Which culture is right? The answer depends on your values; each side is right, depending on your side of the argument.

Some people view values as universal. Some people view them as relative. The universalists think that the same values apply to everyone. The relativists believe that different people embrace different values and we need to respect those differences. Both sides find themselves holding positions with inherent contradictions. How do two groups of universalists, for example, co-exist when they each have absolute values? As we know all too well today, fundamentalist religious beliefs can be a source of great conflict between cultures. We need only think it is a "jihad" or the "war on terror." But those who hold relativist views often get in trouble, too. Respecting unique values can become an excuse mechanism. In the late 1990s, for example, totalitarian leaders in South East Asia were able to tell western critics that democracy wasn't an Asian value, so there was no need for reforms. Western critics replied that democracy was a human value, equally applicable anywhere. According to the relativists, we need to leave the dictator's statements unchallenged. But this is a tough pill to swallow for dissenters living under oppressive totalitarian regimes.

Fortunately, we don't have to deal with political or human rights issues in this book — we just need to talk about organizations. But a word of caution. When an organization has a clearly stated set of values, those values are for everyone in every place the organization operates. This does present a problem when the local culture or laws differ and don't allow for the company to successfully conduct business in that country in a way that is consistent with their values. For example, many manufacturing organizations in China and Asia treat the employees that produce goods for them in a way that is not aligned with their values. Corporations don't exist in a vacuum and unless their values enable them to ignore human rights issues they need to step up and act at all times in all places with consistency. Not doing so opens the box for employee cynicism if not consumer cynicism. It is reasonable to argue that there is no universal definition of the same value between companies because each company comes to its values through a different collective experience that validates its values only for itself. When it comes to values within organizations there are three ideas:

- First, values are universal for the entire company — the values that an organization holds true are absolute inside the walls of the organization. Different divisions or regions of the organization don't have different values, not even if they have very different leaders. The values are universal across the organization, regardless of circumstances.

- Second, when it comes to different organizations, values are relative to that organization's experience. The values of one organization are not the same as the values of another. What is right in one organization is not right in another. Values do not transcend organizations. They can't be benchmarked, borrowed or replicated. We can't take the successful values of one organization and apply them to another and expect anything good to happen as a result. The values have to come from inside the organization. In truth, they are already there; they just need to be discovered.

- Third, corporate values are not about right or wrong, good or evil — they are about consistency to a standard of action that defines the right behavior. Whether someone is good or bad in the context of an organization depends on whether they act consistently with the organization's behaviors that define the values. If an organization's values are in conflict with societal values, a person is still considered "good" within that organization as long as they stay true to those values. In the same way, those who hold different values might consider that person a monster outside of the organization. At Enron, for example, it was okay to create fake offshore accounts in service of higher share value. Outside the organization, most of us were appalled.

In addition to the intersection between values inside the organization and values outside the organization, we need to think about the intersection between individual values and organizational values. This intersection can be a source of tension and alienation or it can be a source of confirmation and belonging. If you believe that people development is a value and you work in an organization where it is a value, then you will feel comforted and confirmed when your organization makes decisions that support that value. If you believe that respect for the customer is a value, but your organization treats customers without respect, then you will feel conflicted and alienated about working there. In other words, it all depends on what you believe in and where the group you belong to stands in relation to that belief.

It's possible for us to fake or adopt an adherence to values we don't really believe in. If an organization is articulate about its values and consistent in upholding them, then it can be relatively easy for a member of the organization to follow those values, as long as they don't conflict with their own. It may not be the most powerful, satisfying or fulfilling way to be in the world, but it's possible. So the question becomes, how do we know when something is really a value to us or not? It's like the ten-thousand-mile test that young people often experience when they first move away from home. Now that you're in college, or half way around the world on some inexpensive beach in a south-east Asian country, what are your moral limits? If you are true to your values, then you will behave the same way regardless of whether anyone you know will ever find out what you are doing. If your values are only standards that apply when you might get caught, then they are not living principles. You will do one thing under one circumstance and another in a different circumstance.

Value-Driven Organizations

Business theorists have long recognized that values are important and organizations with a strong culture are more successful. But, despite all the hoopla, the link between values and organizational performance is still poorly understood. While we give lip service to the idea that successful organizations are value-driven institutions, and talk about successful leaders as value stewards, we do not sufficiently explain the mechanisms by which values are made meaningful in organizations. It helps to get a broad stroke explanation of where we've come from, to understand where we need to go.

In the early 1900s, Chester Barnard was the president of New Jersey Bell Telephone Company. As an executive and a thinker, he was profoundly interested in the web of social and personal relationships within organizations. When he retired, he wrote *The Functions of the Executive,* published in 1938, a classic work about cooperation and communication. To Barnard, an organization has coherence when individuals come together to contribute their efforts in service of a common purpose. This notion of purpose was a key breakthrough. Every organization has a purpose, but a purpose does not create cooperation unless it is accepted willingly by the organization's members. A leader's job is to harness action in pursuit of a purpose.

Philip Selznick furthered this idea of purpose by declaring that organizations have specific competence which gives them unique character. By character he was touching on the idea of culture. "Organizations become institutions as they are infused with values…" he wrote. Leadership, Selznick believed, was about defining a basic vision and building an organization capable of fulfilling that vision.

Many theorists picked up on this wave of insight, but the issues didn't really become urgent for business practitioners. In the 1970s, Henry Mintzberg began describing the different configurations of organizations in terms of structure. One configuration, the "Missionary Organization," seemed important because Japanese companies like Toyota had adopted it so successfully. Japanese organizations managed people not by standards and procedures but by norms and beliefs — that is, values. Their approach was making a difference in terms of healthier, more productive and more innovative work environments.

Mintzberg looked at this phenomenon and wondered why more organizations weren't like Toyota. In Mintzberg's view, every organization has a culture but only value-driven organizations have an ideology. An ideology is a "rich system of values and beliefs about an organization, shared by its members, that distinguishes it from other organizations. ... It ties the individual to the organization, generating an 'esprit de corps,' a 'sense of mission,' in effect, an integration of individual and organizational goals that can produce synergy."

I would go further and suggest that all companies have a value set that is handed down by management to succeeding generations of employees. Organizations that are particularly effective at passing on their values usually have a strong founder who identifies a vision, then gathers others around him to accomplish that desired future state, yet to be achieved. As Mintzberg writes, "The individuals who come together don't do so at random, but coalesce because they share the same values associated with the fledgling organization." Leaders reinforce those values through authentic belief in them, clear articulation of them, and by backing up their words with consistent deeds. Over time, the belief system establishes a pattern of behaviors that result in a codification into values. The stories that best exemplify the values become part of the corporate mythology. Crisis points that highlight how living the values leads to desired results establishes an oral tradition that one generation of employees shares with the next, hence, reinforcing for the next generation that there is a correct way of acting to succeed. The confluence of repeated similar actions, the stories they generate and the pride that results create the habits of behavior that define the shared ideology or values. The collective experience enables and sustains this. The foundation for this is the founder of the organization who leaves the "right way of acting" as his or her legacy. As Selznick had articulated years before, the organization gains a distinct identity and becomes an institution.

In the early 1980s, Terrence Deal and Allan Kennedy spelled out and coalesced what we knew about the importance of values and culture to successful organizations. In their book, *Corporate Cultures: The Rites and Rituals of Corporate Life*, they used anthropology, the study of culture, to come up with terms and language for explaining what organizational theorists had been struggling to articulate. Strong cultures, they said, were the new "old rule" of business success because so many of the great companies like Procter & Gamble, IBM and Johnson & Johnson, had understood that truth from the first day and lived by it all along. Organizations with strong cultures are based on values. They have heroes, individuals within them who "personify those values" by serving as value stalwarts, role models and standard-bearers. Heroes have a strong sense of mission.

To demonstrate, Deal and Kennedy tell a favorite story of Adolph Ochs, founder of the *New York Times*.

> A traveler meets three stonecutters and asks each of them what they are doing. The first says, I am cutting stone. The second says, I am shaping a cornerstone. The third says, I am building a cathedral.

Culture heroes believe that they are not just doing their jobs; they are building cathedrals. One of the jobs of managers within the organization is to celebrate such heroes and reinforce heroic behavior through rites and rituals that support the culture.

Deal and Kennedy nailed it. But it wasn't until 1994, when Jim Collins and Jerry Porras wrote *Built to Last: Successful Habits of Visionary Companies*, that the idea of a value-driven organization really took hold in managers' minds. Collins and Porras built a very convincing case for the link between values and superior performance by analyzing the stock performance of a number of institution-like or visionary companies over many years and comparing that to a set of well-known rival companies that operated during the same time period and in the same industry. They found clear evidence that the valuation of the institutions far exceeded both the market average and the noteworthy comparison companies. For example, Johnson & Johnson markedly outperformed Bristol-Meyers Squibb in stock price, brand recognition and new product development. Same went for Boeing versus McDonnell Douglas, Sony over Kenwood, Wal-Mart over Ames, Walt Disney over Columbia.

The results are impressive, visually and otherwise: Collins and Porras then looked at what those visionary companies had in common. They found that the high-performing companies were all driven by a relatively unchanging set of values. The comparison companies, on the other hand, tended to flit and change with the wind when it came to values, undergoing many transformations over the years. The comparison companies were focused on short-term profits, shifts in the market or business process improvements. The visionary companies also changed with the times, improved themselves and achieved profitability; they simply did so within the rationale and guidance of their values. They were more consistently aligned to their values when it came to goal setting, strategy, tactics and organizational design. In other words, the visionary companies did their thinking inside the box.

Selznick used the word "institutions." Collins and Porras called these companies "visionary" because they are inspirational and seek to change the world; in other words, they know what the cathedral they wish to build will look like when completed, even though they are still in the midst of constructing it. What else do we know about them? Visionary companies are widely admired by their peers and draw a cult-like devotion from their employees. Visionary companies have long illustrious track records that include more ups than downs. They embrace change, innovation and improvement and go through multiple product life cycles. Even when they face setbacks and crises, they do not compromise their ideology, and therefore they survive and ultimately thrive. Even more impressive, visionary companies outlast their original product ideas, and even the powerful personalities, motivations and entrepreneurial spirits of their founders. Indeed, their enduring greatness is not the result of one great person or a single great idea but an underlying process, as Collins and Porras put it, of "stimulating progress while preserving the core."

This analysis cemented what many other theorists and leaders had also discovered about the importance of values. It did little, however, to explain how those great companies established, articulated, preserved and operated under those values, much less how future organizations could strive to do the same. Collins even acknowledged this fact in his follow-up study, *Good to Great: Why Some Companies Make the Leap … and Others Don't*. The visionary companies he and Porras described had always been great. But how could other companies get there? Collins' answers in *Good to Great* were about leadership, selecting the right people, steadfastness, discipline and continual improvement. These are all important points, but they still don't explain how his visionary organizations turn dry principles into a code for living to such great effect.

Values and Visions

Even the term "visionary" created some confusion, inspiring a mania for vision and mission statements instead of values articulation. If you've ever been involved in the development of a vision or mission statement, you know how difficult this process can feel and how unrewarding its impact can seem.

A few years back, I sat next to a woman on a flight from Chicago to San Diego. I was working away on my PowerPoint presentation for a conference workshop, and she was reading a business book. We began to talk. She mentioned that her organization was currently going through a very painful vision statement exercise. Despite all their efforts and the guidance of the consultants at a prominent school of management, they just couldn't get it right. It was rending the senior management team apart, diverting resources and distracting the organization.

I asked her if they had defined their values yet. She said no. I told her that the correctness of the vision could only be determined by checking against the values. You couldn't develop the vision first and fit it to the values later. Value discussions are emotionally charged as it is; if you don't recognize that you are actually arguing over value-based issues when you are debating an organization's future vision, you have very little hope of reaching a productive consensus. In fact, it's likely that your vision will not match up with your values and will therefore be meaningless or even destructive to the organization as a whole. She paused and reflected on her organization's values and its culture; the concept resonated. She told me to hold that thought while she got her boss from the row behind ours. After she introduced me to him, he sat in her chair, and we discussed the relationship between values and vision until the plane landed in San Diego. When he got back to the office, they halted the work they were doing on defining their vision and went back to the drawing board with their consultants, this time focusing on their values first.

I suspect that vision or mission statements have been so popular in recent years because they lend themselves to executives' natural orientation towards action and results. Vision is about accomplishment and setting future goals. CEOs find the idea of developing such a legacy compelling. But values are how you get there and what makes your organization the kind that can do it in the first place. The dream comes true only if you maintain an unwavering belief in the future state. Dreaming it without passion and without being on constant watch creates a vision without energy. "If you will it, it is no legend," Theodor Herzl wrote in "Altneuland" in 1902. It is not the will alone that gets you there; it is the passion and belief in what you are creating that moves you forward. Yet, many CEOs don't wish to articulate their values. As one major bank CEO once said to me "my people should 'just know it' by the way we work around here. I shouldn't have to lay it out for them." If only it were that simple. In that bank misunderstanding about values was a serious problem, creating customer service issues that were costing the organization market share. Managers and supervisors just didn't know how to communicate values articulately, or how to reinforce them consistently.

Visions Can Change; Values Don't

A company or an organization can finally accomplish a great visionary goal, pat itself on the back and develop a new and equally audacious visionary goal, and still retain the same principles. The values guide the direction and growth of the organization, provide an ethical barometer, help identify employees who belong and employees who don't, act as a filter for strategy and people decisions, and offer satisfaction and meaning when objectives are reached. Without values, an organization's vision has no direction or energy source.

Want some examples of visionary organizations that rely on values first and foremost? How about the United States of America? The founding fathers defined the principles of the emerging nation and left the details to the major government bodies, the state and local governments, and the leaders of successive generations. They declared the United States to be a democracy that celebrated equality of opportunity and provided freedom of worship, speech and lifestyle. But this declaration did not make it so. Many in the population (including women and African-American slaves) were, at the time, still disenfranchised. Not everyone was equal.

While freedom and equal rights became the anchor to the American way of life, this did not happen overnight. First there was an amendment to bring equal status to women and later to African-Americans. Then there was a civil war over the issue. In fact, it wasn't until 1963 when Martin Luther King led a march on Washington (at which I was present) that real change began to occur. The social impact of Jackie Robinson's inclusion into Major League Baseball in 1947 resonates as one of the civil rights movement's significant triumphs. This achievement was in part made possible because of Walter O'Malleys vision in 1946 to integrate professional baseball. Through the heroic efforts of Jackie Robinson and many of his teammates, the line between black and white began to fade. By 1963, some twenty years after Robinson was sent to the Montreal Royals in the minor league and opened the gates, Dr. King had the momentum for his famous march. The integration of baseball happened during World War II, when many of the players enlisted into the armed services. As a result the number of quality players dwindled. To fill the stands and ensure cash flow Bill Veeck, Jr., in 1943 in Philadelphia considered integrating baseball by bringing in players from the Negro Leagues. Having the dream without the courage to act on it made Veeck's idea a footnote in history. (Thomas Oliphant, *Praying for Gil Hodges*) The reality of integration waited until O'Malley acted on his beliefs and began the long civil right's journey that culminated in King's speech in 1963. Over the years, many such visions and missions have gripped the country — from Manifest Destiny to winning the space race — but the values of the United States have never changed. Millions of immigrants have been drawn to the country because of those values, which have stood the test of time and become stronger with each crisis.

Or consider the New York Yankees. Somehow they manage to win World Series after World Series. Love 'em or hate 'em (and I'm a holdover Brooklyn Dodgers' fan whose family loved Them Bums for generations and felt abandoned when they moved to Los Angeles), the Yankees are the most successful franchise in the history of any professional sport, despite the recent Red Sox championship! In the last one hundred years, they've won twenty-six World Series — one out of every four World Series, or 40 percent of all pennant championships. Four of those World Series teams played in the 1990s during the height of free agency, in which there was an average annual turnover of 40 percent of their roster. How do they manage to attract, retain, develop and utilize the top performers who lead the team to the pinnacle of success, approximately once every four years? As one sports writer said after another brilliant late-season trade brought yet another underutilized impact player to the team: "The Yankees know how to find Yankees." What he meant was the team knows how to identify, recruit or obtain players who fit and excel under the particular circumstances of being a Yankee. They maintain the tradition of what it means to be a Yankee through eras, owners, coaches and stars. In 2002 in a piece called "Why the Yankees Are So Great," Jimmy Cannon wrote that fifty years ago, Hank Greenberg, general manager of the Cleveland Indians, asked "What happens to them when they become Yankees?" Greenberg replied,

> ... The ballplayers on other clubs are ballplayers. They are Yankees. ... They are serene elite, graceful and humble ... because their pride is not disfigured by vanity.
>
> ... There have been drunks and malingerers and complainers but they seldom last. ... They respect the tradition of Ruth and DiMaggio. ... They are not humorless but they reject buffoonery. They are not seized by despair ... in times of crisis. ... They can't be bullied. They are a team with little animosity.
>
> ... The managers are the same way although their methods and their personalities vary. You are a Yankee, they feel, and you are the best.

The vision, undeniably, has always been the same: to win the World Series. But it's a vision shared by thirty other teams. Yankee values are the engine of their vision and that is what makes them successful. When you think of the Yankees of the late 1990s and early 2000s it's clear that this tradition, culture and atmosphere remains unbroken. Joe Torre, the current manager, sounds more like a values coach than a tactical master when he describes what it takes to make his team win. The Yankee players in our star-powered era still don't display names on their uniforms, a sign that they put their personal ego below the team. Nor do they have hair on their faces, a sign of respect for Yankee discipline. Whether elite stars or role-players that are outstanding, old or young, Yankees come from all backgrounds and types, but they must all fit in or be traded away. Players who are diverse in personality, background and outlook on life all worship the tradition of Babe Ruth, wear the same uniform and fight for the same goal.

The Yankees, like other value-based organizations, exhibit clear traits. The Yankees:

- Outlast and outperform their competition.
- Execute better because they are able to make faster and more consistent decisions.
- Recognize, celebrate and reinforce the work practices that contribute to achieving their visionary objectives.
- Know who is a star, who fits in, who doesn't and why, and can make rational people decisions.
- Have a clear understanding of the "right" thing to do in any situation, under their terms.
- Project their brand in a compelling way to employees, customers/fans, competitors and shareholders.

If that sounds like the Holy Grail of leadership, it should. Great leaders have always recognized the significance and utility of values as ideas and inspirational tools. They know that if you get the values right, everything else falls into place.

Getting There

That's the end state, the objective, the promised land. No organization is a values paradise. Perfection is not possible because staying true to values on a daily basis is hard work. In fact, the organizations most known for their values work the hardest at acting consistent with those values.

Without an understanding of how values work, leaders fail to take advantage of their organization's most precious resource— the unique culture and vision that employees, customers and partners have bought into and believe in. Those organizations that do understand how values work are easy to spot. They outperform competitors. Their employees and customers are more satisfied. Their success and viability is sustainable over a long period of time and through a great deal of change. The formula that they operate by is a simple one, though difficult to replicate. In the chapters that follow, we will learn exactly how value-driven organizations make this formula real.

LOOK INSIDE THE BOX

The Values Formula

VALUES **Strongly Held Beliefs** that an organization has about itself and what it thinks it needs to do in order to be successful in the world.

VISION **Dream or Mission** that grows out of the values, a long-range goal that the organization consistently strives to achieve.

~~~

LEADERSHIP   **Consistent Demonstration** of those values at all levels, thereby reinforcing the culture and holding everyone accountable without exception.

~~~

EXECUTION   **Ways People Work** within that cultural discipline to achieve the organization's objectives, despite pressures to act in a way that is inconsistent with the organization's values.

MEASURES OF GREATNESS

❏ **Organizational Integrity** — a healthy work environment in which people understand the organization's values, act consistently with them and can independently judge whether something is right or wrong.

❏ **Business Results** — a healthy bottom line where the way people behave moves the organization steadily towards its vision.

Employee Brand — a healthy sense of loyalty and commitment in which people function willingly as volunteer cheerleaders of the organization's culture in front of potential employees and customers. Employees are engaged.

CHAPTER TWO

Reinforcing the Box: Making Values Meaningful Throughout the Organization

❑ Values are set by the founders and leaders of the organization; they don't arise from a grassroots committee of employees.

❑ Engage employees in an ongoing series of conversations about the values in order to facilitate understanding and common language.

❑ For employees to live the values, they have to see them modeled by their direct boss and have them reinforced in day-to-day tasks.

❑ Celebrate your past and tap into your corporate legends when moving into unchartered waters. Don't think you need to reinvent the wheel — or the organization — when tough times arise.

Where do values come from? Who decides what's a value and what's not? How do values take root in an organization? In this chapter, we'll answer those questions by looking at the way organizations have re-energized themselves not by thinking exclusively about the future, but by drawing on the lessons of the past.

The Wizard, the Jam Session and the Gridiron

The Wizard of Menlo Park was Thomas Edison. Edison left a legacy of patents, and created the groundwork for the company now called General Electric (GE). As part of his legacy he left an organization deeply rooted in his way of looking at the world. International Business Machines (IBM) is an organization where pride in learning and being a leader has been part of the very foundation. While the company might make an effort to "update" its values, in fact, they only discovered that they affirmed the values. The University of Notre Dame is synonymous with college football heroics, hence the gridiron connection. But before athletics became the focus of celebrity, academics were embedded as the university's foundation.

GE

When it comes to vision and values, few companies rival GE in terms of being admired and emulated. Because of the long-term success of the company, it's not surprising that many companies have come to adopt GE's ways, including its adherence to values. It's probably only my imagination, but it seems like executives at every company now carry around a values and vision card like GE's. In fact, many companies don't even bother to come up with their own unique set of values, but cherry-pick words and phrases that GE uses and tag them onto their own culture. GE-celebrated concepts like Six Sigma (originally from Motorola) have spread like wildfire, and top GE executives have been plucked to run other companies in the hopes of tapping into some of GE's storied leadership development.

For the record, GE's values card looks something like this. On the front side, it lists words that describe its values: Curious, Passionate, Resourceful, Accountable, Teamwork, Committed, Open and Energizing. Its slogan is "Imagination at work." On the flip side, it lists its actions: "Imagine — We put imagination to work for our customers, people and communities; Solve — We help solve some of the world's toughest problems; Build — We are a performance culture that builds markets, people and shareholder value; and Lead — We are a meritocracy that leads through learning, inclusiveness and change." Below those actions, the card has another slogan in caps: "ALWAYS WITH UNYIELDING INTEGRITY."

GE is a resilient, innovative, energetic and successful company because of its values. I'm happy to showcase them as a winning model because values are critical to every organization's success. The problem is that values can't be copied or carried over from one company to another. Every vibrant company's values are unique, forged by the personalities and passions of the organization's founders, reinforced or further shaped by critical top leaders over time, and polished and held dear by generations of employees, who see them as a strict code for the right way to do the job. Adopting the values of GE or any other admired company won't work in your organization because the organization itself will struggle mightily to reject those values. Even if you ultimately succeed in grafting new values onto the patient in some Frankenstein-like operation, prospects of survival, let alone vigorous health, are slim.

For example, GE's values and leadership style today was not created out of whole cloth by super-CEO Jack Welch. Instead, Jack Welch was selected and molded in the shape of GE's values. He did an outstanding job living that culture as steward of the values and leader of the organization. The GE approach to doing business follows a direct lineage through its other CEOs to its founder, Thomas Edison, one of the world's greatest inventors. Edison was responsible for many prominent inventions, none more transformative than the electric light bulb and the idea of powering a city's electricity through a grid attached to a generator. Imagine the world without electric light and consider his impact today. GE was formed when Edison's company, Edison General Electric, merged with a rival. In 1896, General Electric was listed on the new Dow-Jones Industrial Average along with eleven other companies. It's the only one that remains on the Dow Jones today.

When you look at the personality of Thomas Edison, you get a strong sense of the way that personality has infused GE, 110 years later. As an inventor, Edison showed incredible breadth of interest in a wide variety of devices. He did work on the early telephone, the phonograph, the light bulb and electric power, and took out an incredible number of patents. GE, built to capitalize on his industrial endeavors, was probably the world's first corporate conglomerate, operating businesses in eleven industrial areas ranging from aerospace to nuclear power, television to finance. Despite his wide variety of interests, Edison was no dilettante, rushing from one fascination to another. Instead, he focused on a particular problem for years, solving the many challenges that showed up along the way. These challenges were never just technical but often involved marketing and discovering how a product would gain widespread adoption, which would draw public attention and finance to his work to make it a success. He took an immensely long-term view of his work, foreseeing the way his inventions would create new markets. He was also relentlessly practical. Once he said, "I find out what the world needs; then I proceed to invent it." He also admonished himself: "Never waste time inventing things that people will not want to buy."

That sounds a lot like the GE of today. Jack Welch's declaration that GE would be number one or number two in any market, or get out, reminds one of Edison's desire to build only what people want to buy. According to GE's website, "What we do and how we work is distinctly GE. It's a way of thinking and working that has grounded our performance for decades. It's a way of talking about our work and ourselves that takes the best from our past and expresses it in the spirit and language of GE today." It goes on to say that every business needs a reason to exist. "For GE, the big question has a simple answer. We exist to solve problems — for our customers, our communities and societies, and for ourselves." Like Edison, the company enjoys thinking big and thrives on being curious and driven, but it also brings a "commitment to sweat the small stuff that brings ideas to life." In terms of vision and direction, "It's not so much a vision for our future" ... that motivates the company but ... "where we're headed is in many ways a reflection of where we've already been."

Enduring companies understand this connection to the past. They know that the reason for their past success is rooted in their cultural DNA. That source code comes from the earliest leaders and founders of the organization. It gets shepherded by the subsequent leaders who — if they are to be successful — must be selected to fit the spirit of those values. It is made meaningful by the way employees work, think and talk. It is communicated in the stories and legends that the organization tells about itself — a distillation of myths that capture the essence of truth.

IBM

When it comes to achieving something in the future, an enduring company knows that any great accomplishment requires standing on the foundation of the past. IBM is another storied American technology company that has achieved great success over the last hundred or so years, albeit with a few more bumps in the road than GE. Its blue-suited sales force and brilliant researchers characterized the success of American business for several decades. Nevertheless, it has reinvented or refocused itself through several crisis periods while always maintaining a strong connection to its culture and sense of meaning. Most recently, in 2003, the company decided to revisit its values.

According to CEO Sam Palmisano in a note to employees found on the corporate website, "When IBMers have been crystal clear and united about our strategies and purpose, it's amazing what we've been able to create and accomplish. When we've been uncertain, conflicted or hesitant, we've squandered opportunities and even made blunders that would have sunk smaller companies. It may not surprise you, then, that last year [2003–2004] we examined IBM's core values for the first time since the company's founding. In this time of great change, we needed to affirm IBM's reason for being, what sets the company apart and what should drive our actions as individual IBMers."

In order to examine those "core" values, IBM launched a seventy-two-hour on-line "jam session" with all 319,000 employees around the world. A passionate and sometimes painful debate ensued, expressing pride in the company and frustration with the ways that the bureaucracy sometimes impedes accomplishment. In the end, the process came up with three values: dedication to every client's success; innovation that matters, for our company and for the world; and trust and personal responsibility in all relationships. In fact, rather than formulating a new set of values, the jam session seemed to clarify and confirm the existing IBM values. Indeed, Palmisano concluded that the effort was a success, stating, "We are getting back in touch with what IBM has always been about — and always will be about — in a very concrete way." Surely, this reflection and affirmation helped IBM make some tough decisions going forward, like the decision to sell off its PC business to Chinese computer manufacturer Lenovo.

Notre Dame Football Program

The University of Notre Dame's prestigious football program is another institution that went through a serious dilemma and found guidance, not by looking forward but by looking backward. My work was with Notre Dame's slightly less celebrated hockey team, and it was fascinating to see the way Notre Dame's hockey team's values were part of the overall university's values. During this time the university's prized football program was going through what could have been a significant values crisis.

To put this all in perspective it is important that one recognize that, above everything else, Notre Dame is a school that has long prided itself on academic excellence. Even its top athletes have to meet high academic standards. But as almost any college football fan knows, Notre Dame is also handicapped by that same value. Other college programs have no qualms about letting athletes be athletes and students be students with little or no overlap. If most school's top-ranked athletes see the inside of a classroom, I bet it's only because they were put under pressure to attend classes by the athletic director or they wandered in by mistake. Notre Dame's academic requirements seem quaint if not naïve in contrast. In this day of big bowl games and big television coverage, having a top football program generates tens of millions of dollars for a school. And in recent years, Notre Dame's status as an elite team was slipping badly, threatening its status as a top program and top money generator. After all, why would you want to see every Notre Dame game on national television if they weren't winning?

Some missteps in coaching selection contributed to the crisis. At the end of the Lou Holtz era, Notre Dame needed a new leader to carry the torch. New coach Bob Davie didn't pull that off. Whispers of trouble began at the end of his tenure, as Notre Dame's elite status slipped. When an ostensibly highly competent football coach named George O'Leary was hired to lead the program after Davie's retirement, disaster struck. O'Leary resigned five days later when it emerged that he had lied on his resume. This scandal of integrity seemed to stain the football program too.

But then Notre Dame hired Tyrone Willingham, and all seemed to be right in the world. Willingham was the first black coach in the history of the Notre Dame program. No academic slouch, he had coached at Stanford University and had been able to somehow build teams that won with high-performing students. Many believed that Willingham's ability to connect with the modern athlete and draw him into Notre Dame would overcome Notre Dame's values handicap.

Could he pull it off? If you think this concern was limited to just the higher-ups of Notre Dame, you'd be surprised. Students on campus and coaches from the other Notre Dame programs all held their own strong opinions. What's more, national sports talk radio was also abuzz with the topic. Many passionate fans around the country called in to argue both sides of the issue. Some insisted that the program needed to forego its value of academics before athletics in order to grow with the times, while others insisted that Notre Dame needed to stick with its values because they were what made the university and its football program unique. As someone who worked with organizations dealing with such issues, I recognized this as a full-blown values crisis and was very interested in seeing how it would shake out.

When I made a presentation about values at a conference for Notre Dame staff, I drew on the history of the university to frame the ongoing debate. The founders had established the university with a standard of excellence for academics and only introduced sports and athletics many years later, long after that academic excellence had become sanctified as a value. Even in the heyday of Lou Holtz, Rev. Theodore M. Hesburgh, the former university president, would often question the coaches on how many class days the students would need to miss while on the road. He insisted that it never exceed six full days. When the hockey team had to play in Alaska, for example, they needed to schedule the game so that their travel could take place over the Thanksgiving holiday in order to avoid missing too many school days. At local conference games, they put themselves at a competitive disadvantage because they traveled later than other school's teams — classes always came first.

In other words, the value that held academic excellence above athletics was set early and was very formative in the culture of the organization. It had withstood a great deal of pressure over several eras. In a win-at-all-costs college sports world (not unlike, I would note, our win-at-all-costs short-term corporate mentality), it was half-jokingly said that even a 10–1 season was considered a losing record. How would the school deal with pressure to change a value when it was truly under siege for having failed to appear in noteworthy post-season bowl games, let alone national championship games?

At first, the choice of Tyrone Willingham looked good for
upholding the university's value of academics and turning
the team around. In Willingham's first season, he exceeded
expectations in terms of the team's record, and hopes began to
soar. In the second season, he faltered and the program came
back down to earth. In the third, he had another losing record
and was fired with two full years left to go in his contract — a
stunning decision and a bewildering fall from grace.

Of course, many in the media and around the country
decried the racism implicit in Willingham's being fired. After
all, Willingham was black, and no other coach in the history of
the program had been fired after just three years. But despite
the question of race, the pressure to fire Willingham had been
strong, from students and alumni alike. They simply would not
stand for a losing season. It was interesting to see the extent to
which Notre Dame's students and alumni didn't really care about
the charges of racism. The bigger crisis was the importance of
winning. The Willingham page was quickly turned and Notre
Dame put its hopes on getting a truly great coach. Eventually,
Charlie Weis, the offensive coordinator with the three-time
Super Bowl champion New England Patriot team, was lured to
the Notre Dame head coaching job. Many saw him as a distinct
second or even third choice. But although Weis had never played
for Notre Dame or coached there before, he had attended Notre
Dame as a student, and he cared deeply for the traditions and
values of the institution, while also believing that it could be a
winning program. Weis was very smart about dealing with those
values conflicts up front. Publicly and in team meetings, Weis
assured everyone that the values of winning would not come
before academic excellence. He made it known that winning a
national championship is the goal, but that the achievement is
all the more sweet when the importance of the classroom is not

lost in the process. He even told a star national recruit who was still in high school that he would have to improve his grades if he hoped to make it at Notre Dame, a concern no other college coach in the nation would even think of raising.

Weis connected the great teams of the past to what Notre Dame could become again. To hammer his point home, Weis invited Rudy Ruettiger, on whose life the football movie *Rudy* was based, to make a surprise speech to the athletes before the season began. In the movie, Rudy Ruettiger was an undersized dyslexic student from a large poor family who struggled to get into Notre Dame, struggled to stay in while he was there and barely made the football team. Yet his perseverance and devotion won his classmates and teammates over so much that he got carried off the field as a hero when he made a game-saving tackle. When the real-life Rudy Ruettiger spoke to the players of Notre Dame's 2005 football program, it was the first time he had been invited back to the campus since his own playing days in the 1970s. Weis understood the power of that living legend. Rudy Ruettiger was a living embodiment of the values of hard work and winning against the odds which Notre Dame prides itself on; Rudy's story made it personal.

Despite low expectations, the 2005 Notre Dame team went on to have a strong winning season and make its first significant post-season bowl game appearance in years. Fans were elated. And so were the TV networks.

The North Star

When a company is in distress or under immense competitive pressure, the temptation is to give the values and culture of the organization a makeover. But enduring companies know that not everything old is bad. Expressing long-standing values in contemporary terms, like GE does on a regular basis, or IBM did with its jam session, can help energize an organization by clarifying and confirming its reason for existence. When an organization is in trouble, chances are the values are not the source of the problem. Often, the values have slipped over the years, as a gap grows between the words the leaders use and the way they act and operate. Indeed, IBM's former CEO Lou Gerstner acknowledged this phenomenon in his book, *Who Says Elephants Can't Dance?* As Gerstner put it:

> Most companies say their cultures are about the same things: outstanding customer service, excellence, teamwork, shareholder value, responsible corporate behavior and integrity. But, of course, these kinds of values don't necessarily translate into the same kind of behavior in all companies — how people actually go about their work, how they interact with one another, what motivates them. That's because, as with national cultures, most of the really important rules aren't written down anywhere.

On the other hand, many companies ignore misalignment of their values and charge ahead to deal with their problems, looking to the future instead of the past. This mentality leads them to focus on their corporate vision or mission rather than on their values. Indeed, visions are sexier than values. They're about action and direction rather than touchy-feely reflection, and CEOs like that kind of mandate. It's important, however, to consider how everything fits together, and the hierarchy of concerns: values first, then vision, strategic plans, business unit or divisions objectives and team and personal objectives which result in the overall operations.

A vision statement provides you with a clear mental picture of a desired future state, a North Star that shows the direction to be taken. It's challenging and exciting and represents something significant yet to do. While the strategic plan enables you to move forward, without the vision statement, ambiguous as it might seem, how do you know you are going in the right direction? As that great American philosopher Yogi Berra once noted: "If you don't know where you are going, you will wind up somewhere else."

You will never be greater than the vision that guides you. No Olympic athlete ever got to the Olympics by mistake; a compelling vision of his or her stellar performance inevitably guides all the sweat and tears for many years. The vision statement should require the organization's members to stretch their expectations, aspirations and performance. Without that powerful, attractive, valuable vision, why bother?

From my perspective, a vision statement is a goal that a company or organization wishes to achieve in the distant future. When President John F. Kennedy said that America would send a manned spacecraft to the moon within ten years and return him safely to earth, that was a short-term vision — a daunting, inspiring glimpse into a future state capable of catalyzing great energy and resources. President Kennedy didn't say how he would get a manned space flight there and back again (the strategy), and he didn't say how much it would cost, or what operational resources would be employed. But he got us excited, put a target in front of our paths and said, "Let's make this happen."

But how did Kennedy tap into that energy? His vision resonated so strongly because it was based on the values of his nation. The United States has always had a pioneering spirit and a sense of manifest destiny based on the great resources of a free people. In a global competition with its rival, the U.S.S.R., Kennedy's lofty charge touched a very real emotion in the American people.

As I said, Kennedy was vague about the details. Vision statements are deliberately left vague to allow great flexibility in developing a strategy to achieve that desired end. How you get there is about the strategy you employ. Your strategy organizes your resources — time, money, people, etc. — in pursuit of the vision. It all resonates and works because it is based on your values. A vision statement is not an aspiration to become number one or number two in your industry. Why not? Because that statement does not clarify what being number one means, how you will measure it, or why it's important. Similarly, a vision statement does not merely describe the scope, such as, for example, "Our vision is to become the largest international widget company in the world." That kind of statement says nothing about why your company is unique.

Vision and strategy both have to be based on a company's values, or they will not feel right to employees. Values are "what you're all about," vision is "where you want to be in the future," and strategy is "how you're going to get there." Values and vision are not situational or up for renewal every time something new comes along or someone new becomes the CEO. Strategy can and should change as detours pop up during the journey or conditions and opportunities change. As people in the organization change, values and vision usually remain the same. However, given different skill sets and personalities, you can implement better or different strategies. Even when the CEO changes, values must remain the same. Vision can change with a change in CEO, but that's a wrenching shift that often requires deep changes to operational, financial, market and people strategy.

LOOK INSIDE THE BOX

A Sampling of Vision Statements

Federal Home Loan Bank of Pittsburgh

We will be a catalyst for building thriving communities, working creatively with our partners until a warm home and steady work are within the grasp of every person in our region.

Coca Cola (original vision)

To have a Coke within arm's reach of every person in the world.

Coca Cola (new vision)

To Refresh the World ... in body, mind, and spirit.

PepsiCo Sustainability Vision

PepsiCo's responsibility is to continually improve all aspects of the world in which we operate — environmental, social, economic — creating a better tomorrow than today.

Lockheed Martin

Powered by Innovation, Guided by Integrity, We Help Our Customers Achieve Their Most Challenging Goals.

Starbucks

To become an enduring, great company with the most recognized and respected brand in the world, known for inspiring and nurturing the human spirit.

When I think about values and vision, I'm always reminded of my high school and the way our baseball coach, Mr. Macaluso, would focus each year on winning the state championship. That was the vision, and it never changed. From year to year, the players and lineups changed, and the strategic plan changed accordingly, but the vision was the same. What I didn't recognize at the time was that our values were also constant. Our values were the emotional driver of our team. They were the reason we all felt connected and special to be playing under the school's colors. Our values created an unusual bond that has kept many of the players connected for some forty-plus years. If I could sum up those values in one statement, it would probably go something like this: "Treat one another with respect." We supported one another despite differences in skill levels. Only Mr. Mac could call a player "meatball" and not mean any harm. Outsiders who heard the expression may have thought he was being disrespectful. In today's politically correct school environments, he might have been disciplined or dismissed, but we knew the difference. If you violated our value, you were off the team. It was the only "fireable" offense we had, despite the pressure to win the state championship.

LOOK INSIDE THE BOX

The Power of a Vision

In an amazing longitudinal study on goal setting, Yale University surveyed the graduating class of 1953 on commencement day to determine if they had written goals for what they wanted their lives to become. Only 3 percent had such a vision. In 1973, the surviving members of the class of 1953 were surveyed again. The 3 percent who had a vision for what they wished their lives would become had accumulated greater wealth than the other 97 percent combined.

As I mentioned in the first chapter, every company out there seems to use respect as a value these days, but it can mean very different things in different cultures. In the same way, benchmarking or copying mission or vision statements from other companies also makes no sense. I have seen consultants copycat visions in companies to much fanfare, only to leave employees completely bewildered because the changes run interference with work processes that are based on long-standing values.

Of course, strategies can be copied too. Witness the airline industry where many different companies, struggling under the pressures of high fuel costs, burdensome employee contracts and service overreach, decide to emulate the more successful Southwest Airlines and go no frills with shorter flights and significantly reduce customer amenities. But Southwest is able to execute its strategy successfully because it is based on its values and all shared in the vision. The employees of Southwest believe in what they do on the job. Strategy needs to be based on what is unique about your company and what you do differently than the competition to achieve your own distinct vision or mission. If you have no vision or mission, how can you possibly evaluate the success of your strategy?

A vision is not a strategy or a business plan; it's the place where strategy needs to take you. It is a destination, a beacon, a North Star, nothing more. The correctness of a strategy can only be assessed based on how it works to achieve a vision, and both vision and strategy need to be assessed for correctness based on your values. If you don't base everything on values, then the most brilliant strategy can put you out of business. Your employees will not put their heart and soul into it. And making the strategy real will inevitably cause your organization to violate some of its own values.

Especially in a large organization, this common thread between values, vision and strategy is vitally important. Each department can have its own strategy to achieve the vision or mission of the organization. All departments need to have the same set of values as the rest of the organization, or the vision and mission will be meaningless to them. If the organization starts to look for ways to improve itself, merge, change marketing plans or do business more efficiently, that change needs to be assessed based on the values. Otherwise, depending on how out of line the new approach is, you will find that you reach a point where the effort of change is in inverse proportion to the benefits.

Three Rules for Defining Values

Many leaders, especially old-school ones, believe that values are something that exist in the company and are understood implicitly by employees, but are weakened or cheapened by articulating them publicly. While I understand the misgivings of those crusty warriors, I also believe that convulsive changes in organizations and markets, the impact of globalization, and the state of fluid workforces dispersed geographically and connected mostly by email creates a new imperative for the stability of explicit values. So, how do you clarify, articulate or create a set of values that will have lasting and meaningful impact on the organization?

Rule #1: Organizational Values Are Set by the Founders

The first rule is that values are set by the founders or leaders of the organization — with no exceptions. In this day of flattened management hierarchies, we expect input into critical decisions to come from all parts of an organization. But when it comes to values, organizations are not democracies — they are benevolent dictatorships, firmly ruled with a velvet-gloved fist.

I worked with a start-up company that specialized in storage space for large amounts of data previously not capable of being captured digitally. They struggled in clarifying and articulating their values because the company itself was growing at warp speed. The culture of the organization was highly democratic and entrepreneurial with a high threshold for risk, so the leaders decided to include a wide range of key employees in the values discussion. Problems soon surfaced, however, because it turned out that employees and top leaders were at odds about the values, in particular the behaviors that defined living the values within the context of work. For instance, the founders of the organization wanted to be pioneers in their industry. They took a great deal of pride in being the first to discover how to take enormous video and film quantities and store and catalog them digitally. To the employees, however, a pioneer was someone who got shot full of arrows and left for dead, while settlers were those people who reaped the rewards of new exploration. The founders wanted that sense of risk and adventure in their value set. It was partly why they'd gone into business together in the first place. The employees preferred a more safe and conservative approach to doing business.

The founders and employees attempted to compromise and come to an agreement, but these two visions of what the company stood for were fundamentally at odds. Eventually, the founders gave up on the democratic exercise, but a certain amount of damage had been done in attempting it in the first place. In fact, the values of the founders should have trumped or preempted all discussion about values; they never should have allowed the employees to fundamentally form and define the company's values. They should have hired only people who believed in those values. As a result they should not have hired those who do not share their values in the first place. The foundation for fit to the company and fit to the job is having the correct skills, knowledge and behaviors that are consistent with the company values. A vision that expressed those values should have been articulated and a strategy that went about achieving that mission should have been created. Instead, lacking coherence between those critical pressure points, the company floundered because of the difference between employees. The sales team was unsuccessful in selling the product because it had a different understanding of what it meant to live the values. Eventually, the trouble got worse as differences in belief systems between the head office and the major regional center hampered progress, and the company went from fast growth to limping along before finally selling itself off.

There are many colorful examples of historical companies whose values were forged by their founders. Take Standard Oil, which eventually became Exxon Mobil. Whereas a competitor like BP seems to pander to the public, trumpeting its innovations and focusing on conservation and alternative fuels, Exxon Mobil is a behemoth that makes few lists of most admired firms and seems to go about its business quietly and rather secretly. It has an engineering culture that focuses on maximizing revenue and minimizing mistakes. It makes bold, strategic deals but downplays the attention and accolades that spice up flashy moves. Despite its low-key approach, Exxon Mobil keeps growing and growing. In 2005, it generated the largest annual revenue in history.

If you read a biography of John D. Rockefeller and the early days of Standard Oil, you will be amazed at how closely the personality of today's Exxon Mobil adheres to the personality of Rockefeller, one hundred years earlier. A somber, religious man, he was a shipping clerk and bookkeeper as a youth who made his trading partners rich by being highly disciplined and clear-headed about the principles of accounting. While he was quiet and unflashy, Rockefeller was not afraid of taking incredible gambles when he had calculated the odds and knew that the benefits outweighed the risks. Many of his antagonists and partners were astonished to find themselves outmaneuvered by some bold play that Rockefeller had planned with great, and very quiet, strategic care. The fact that he always seemed to win rubbed people the wrong way. He was maligned by many critics, who saw the growth of Rockefeller's empire as contrary to the American dream of free enterprise. (Eventually, the U.S. government would step in and break up Standard Oil on antitrust grounds, creating offshoot companies like Esso, Mobil and Standard Oil of California in the process.) Rockefeller was also lumped in with the robber barons of the Gilded Age, a time when the gap between rich and poor had never been greater. But unlike men such as Cornelius Vanderbilt, the shipping magnate, and Andrew Carnegie, the steel magnate, Rockefeller shied away from ostentatious displays of wealth. He kept his own money and attention on Standard Oil, never losing his focus on growing his business.

Before anyone knew it, Rockefeller had cornered the oil market in the United States and was seeking to make Standard Oil the dominant oil company in the world. As a manager,

Rockefeller was the original model of "Management by Walking Around," watching accountants doing the books and giving them tips that set the tone for the careful work he demanded. As an amateur engineer, he oversaw his refineries very closely, pushing for efficiency, quality and safety because they were good for business. As a strategist, he was in on every deal, negotiating relentlessly until he had obtained what he wanted. And as a visionary, he believed that the growth of the world economy ensured the growth of his company, advising friends, colleagues, employees and partners to put their money in Standard Oil and keep it there. The company itself was only going to continue to increase in profitability and market share.

If that sounds like Exxon Mobil, it should. Today, Exxon Mobil's vision remains essentially the same: to be "the world's premier petroleum and petrochemical company." It has a long-term view, a strict letter-of-the-law attitude about doing business, and a focus on safety, quality and flawless execution that outperforms its peers. Rockefeller's personality and values put a stamp on Standard Oil that still exists in its distant descendant today. His actions and behaviors demonstrated his firm convictions and provided a model of right conduct for his top managers and employees. Right and wrong — or at least what Rockefeller would consider right and wrong — became evaluated through Rockefeller's eyes. People saw success the way he saw success. Within a generation, the culture based on those values had been set. Nobody ever dreamed of arguing with Rockefeller about those values during his tenure as leader, despite any pressure from critics, competitors and government overseers. Nor did Rockefeller ever turn to his employees and underlings for their advice in shaping or forming those values. It was his company and his vision, and he allowed his employees to execute the details accordingly, though he also reinforced his values with frequent coaching. Imagine how difficult it would be for a leader to shake up Exxon Mobil and change those values today. It wouldn't happen overnight, and it wouldn't happen easily. It's also difficult to imagine that many employees of the company would ever willingly accept the new belief system.

Rule #2: A Company Should Have No More Than Six Values

A hallmark of a successful company's value set is its simplicity. A company's values should be few in number, no more than six (preferably five or less) in total, since they need to hone in on those meaningful touch-points which truly make that company unique. Any more than six values and you are watering down what is important, or allowing employees to make selections of favorite values while neglecting other values. It's important to note that all values are equally sacred. No one value supersedes or trumps any other, especially in a crisis. Organizations cannot say for certain whether a value is a value until that value is tested. Only when a painful decision is made according to the value does the moment of truth come. Those are the moments that make for corporate legends, stories that provide the proof that the values are real.

In coming up with those values, it is best to first seek to understand what the executive leadership team believes is the legacy it wishes to leave for the next generation of employees. It's a challenging question. When leaders think they are the guardians of the future and not the person reaping the benefits of the present, they take on an entirely different perspective on employees, business decisions, shareholder relationships, etc.

Step I: The values they bring to work: The first step is to interview the top executives and get them to tell stories of how they live what they perceive are the values and how they see others doing the same. This helps them understand a common definition of what a value is and to see how values and corresponding actions have already benefited them in their lives and in business. As a result of this first part of the conversation, they begin to realize what are their personal values and how they hope others perceive them living these values in their lives.

Step 2: The values of the company (positive or negative) based on decisions the executive has made that impact others. The next activity is to get them to look at the company values from the perspective of how customers, suppliers, contractors, and especially their employees are treated. By doing this you get to see how values impact their current decisions. They also begin to see why others have taken actions that they thought consistent with the unspoken values. A word of warning — often, this is like getting the emperor to realize he or she has no clothes. You discover through this discussion the ideas they have about the business, the correctness of their business strategy and whether they feel passionate about their belief system. A key learning point is that the stories have to come from within the current firm to be authentic. When the leaders don't discuss stories from their current firm, but rather draw from previous employment, they wind up imposing a foreign element on the organization. We have all heard the new executive who would refer to his or her former employment situation as the "right way of doing things." It is annoying and shuts down listening.

Next comes an off-site meeting with the executive team — without their BlackBerries or Troes. What happens off site is covered in Rule #3.

Rule #3: Values Must Be Articulated as Concrete Behaviors

Step 3: Getting the executive team together off site. Values are the DNA of an organization. Values are the foundation for the organization's culture, strategy and work styles. Values certainly influence and shape those things. In my view, a strong leader is someone who understands and recognizes how to use the values of the organization in further shaping and guiding how the organization does business. In other words, an effective leader strengthens the bond with values because it brings what the organization does more closely in line with what the organization is.

Values are not always explicitly understood by everyone in the organization, although they should be. When values are explicit and clear, they provide a road map for success by giving people an internal (and external) sounding board to check the correctness of every decision and act. Employees who fit the organization are those who demonstrate the organization's values through the way they talk and behave.

Step 4: Decoding what the executive team has articulated as the values and corresponding behaviors. One warning to those exploring the articulation of the values of the company leaders: make certain that the leader is passionate about the exercise! Working with the executive team, once you have heard the stories that support the values you must decode them into behaviors and then look for the behavioral patterns that define the values. During this time you will discover that there are many more behaviors than you need. As long as you have five or six clear and well articulated behavioral statements, you have enough to generate consistency in interpretation. (Example of values and corresponding behavioral statements are found in the following chapters.)

Step 5: Sharing your articulation of their behavioral statements: You next take all the decoded information back to the executive team for its members to review a second time. It is interesting how a time span of one or two weeks can provide a perspective on what the values mean and how they feel for the individual. At this meeting the group reviews the content, plays with the wording, realizes that what it thought was a value is in reality only a belief or a behavior needed to do business and eventually comes to a consensus (no voting) on the values and corresponding behavioral definitions. You know you have it right when the energy in the room is electric and there is a common sense of pride in what you have discovered.

Step 6: Employee engagement for validation: The next step is to run the ideas past a select cross-section of employees. The cross-section should cover all geographic locations and all salary levels as well as non-salaried (especially your unionized) employees. It is important to note that the way in which the values conversation is introduced is essential for success. At no time do you want the employees to feel they can overturn a value and substitute their own. That is a ground rule up front to avoid gripe sessions. During these focus groups, it is very common to hear that employees are surprised that the leadership "got it right." This is a sign that the leadership and the employees are on the same wavelength and that the leaders are currently as consistent in living the values day to day.

Step 7: Executive team sign-off: The next step is to bring the values back to the executive team with a summary of the report from the employee focus groups. This meeting is where the leaders have an opportunity to modify the wording of the behaviors to meet the language of the rank-and-file employees.

It is also here that they find out whether the values resonate with stories or corporate legends from both the employees and the executives. Through this process you can fine-tune the number of statements that define the behaviors that describe the value as a living, current and authentic definition of the culture.

Step 8: Rolling out the values: Once the values have been articulated and endorsed by the leaders, you move onto the next step: how to spread the word in such a way that the employees know it is meaningful and something they need to know. The process of discussing values through on-the-job behaviors is powerful. Nobody really understands what "respect" means, or rather, everyone understands respect in his or her own terms. But if I define respect as meaning X as opposed to Y, Z or any other letter in the alphabet, and I further articulate X in concrete rather than abstract terms, then we can develop a shared understanding of respect that will begin to shape how we act, and eventually how we think. When more than three people are acting, talking and thinking in a certain way because they all mutually believe it to be correct, you've got culture. And a strong culture is the hallmark of every successful organization. The story of the City of Pickering serves as an example that puts all the steps above into perspective.

City of Pickering, Ontario, Canada

Working with the City of Pickering, Ontario, Canada, on its values I saw the importance of this alignment firsthand. A township for 150 years, Pickering was the first new city of the millennium within Ontario. Appropriately, it focused on its values in advance of developing a new people management system that would be capable of handling its new size and responsibility. We began with the values in the traditional manner, individual interviews followed by a two-day, off-site executive meeting and then a number of follow-up meetings with the executive to clarify and fine-tune the working. We then brought the draft — a compilation of the executive team's ideas as to the values and vision of the company — to a cross-section of employees. At one of those meetings, an employee muttered about how poorly the values were followed by the managers. "Around here," she said, "they earn our cynicism." As a phrase that captures the pain and disappointment of employees working for leaders who don't walk the talk, "earned cynicism" deserves to be enshrined in every board room in corporate America.

Thomas Quinn, the chief operating officer of the city, was in charge of the process. He is a genuine leader who cared passionately about leaving the organization in strong and stable condition. Quinn was concerned that people on his team were just saying the right things for his benefit and not really doing the right things when it counted. So we took some time off between articulating the values and rolling them out.

The values they came up with were clearly defined in behavioral terms.

LOOK INSIDE THE BOX

Values of City of Pickering, Ontario, Canada

Respect: Treating one another equally with courtesy and empathy, as you would like to be treated.

1. Provides all people with an informed response, within the time commitment made.
2. Asks clarifying questions of individuals to achieve a full understanding of their needs and perspectives.

3. Collaborates with other areas/departments of the City to help ensure that ideas and issues are properly directed or considered.
4. Listens with an open mind to the ideas, suggestions and opinions of others.
5. Recognizes the value of each person towards the success of the organization.
6. Supports decisions one is involved in, regardless of one's initial position on the matter.

Honesty: Acting with integrity, ethics and sincerity

1. Tells any employee of the City who behaves contrary to our values why their behavior is inappropriate.
2. Provides timely feedback based on factual events and specific behaviors.
3. Takes ownership and responsibility for one's own actions; admits mistakes and acknowledges successes.
4. Shares relevant information with co-workers in a timely manner, even if not asked, so everyone can make an informed decision.
5. Acts within the framework of the laws and professional obligations and the City's values, policies and codes of conduct.

Enthusiasm: Speaking and acting with energy and passion while following through on commitments to conclusion

1. Works with a positive attitude and energy.
2. Speaks passionately and with conviction to build support for programs, ideas and concepts.
3. Seeks opportunities within issues, as opposed to impediments.

Continued

4. Does what it takes to get the job done within the values of the City.
5. Celebrates with pride the good work, services and actions of employees that are above and beyond what is expected of them.

Progressive and Innovative: Applying creative thought, using sound judgment and reasoned decision-making

1. Looks continuously for areas of improvement through improving current methods or finding new ones.
2. Provides positive recognition of innovative behaviors in others.
3. Works on skills and self-improvement to meet own job-related needs as well as the needs of the City.
4. Looks outside one's own department and also the Corporation for ideas (e.g., technology or services) in order to improve.
5. Takes calculated risks, owning accountability for outcomes.
6. Builds on past experiences in developing approaches and undertaking the current activities.

Community Responsibility: Being socially, environmentally and economically responsible

1. Places present and future needs of the larger community over the immediate needs of any one individual or group.
2. Recognizes that through diversity we become a stronger community.
3. Contributes to the safety, security and quality of life of the community.

4. Responds to the needs of the community as they change over time.
5. Addresses behaviors and actions that reflect poorly on the City or the community, regardless of whom is involved.

It all sounded wonderful until an incident happened that shone an unfavorable light on the reality of those values. A firefighter employed by the city died of a kind of cancer that was only recently defined as an occupational hazard. As such, his widow was entitled to compensation. At the same time, however, the city had switched insurance plans to save employees money, and the widow was sent a letter stating that her claim had been denied because of the changeover. It was a bureaucratic mistake, but one that should have been avoided based on the behaviors that described the values of the city. The city's lawyer shouldn't have been the one to send that letter. Although the lawyer and everyone involved followed policy in the way they handled the claim, to Tom Quinn the actions clearly violated the values of respect, honesty and community responsibility. As Quinn put it, "The correctness of any policy has to be measured against the values, and if they don't jive, then the policy is wrong. And we weren't flexible enough to handle that." To make it up, a plan was developed in which Quinn and the Fire Chief, Bill Douglas, visited every fire hall in the city to apologize. Human resources was against the actions because they undermined policy. Quinn, and the Fire Chief went ahead, took heat from HR and heavy criticism from the fire halls, but everyone respected the fact that he was willing to face the music. Next, Quinn met with the widow personally and gave her his word that she would not be affected financially by the change.

Demonstrating the values so explicitly during a time of crisis, Tom Quinn helped to make them real. He realized that the values weren't real yet for the whole organization, however. The mindset of some employees had to change, and that meant some people might have to go. But he took a giant step in making that shift happen when he decided to live the values rather than take the easy way out.

Rolling 'Em Out

The disconnect between all the work that goes into articulating values, the hoopla of celebrating the arrival of those values, and the way people in the company actually end up behaving on the job begins almost immediately after launch. No wonder values work is often considered a waste of time and money and, worse, a distraction. The great disappointment makes the frustration even worse. Coming up with values at the top executive levels is an exhilarating process, one that confirms and enlightens, even as it engages executives with their passions for the business like few other activities. Confirming values and linking them to job behaviors throughout the ranks is just as exciting. Employees feel that the company is becoming transparent and enlisting their on-the-job expertise, sometimes for the first time. They have a chance to say what's really meaningful about their work and why some approaches lead to success and others don't, and it all makes wonderful sense because it is based on the true values of the company.

Not surprisingly, a satisfied executive team is eager to trumpet and herald the new values when they have been fully articulated, spending big dollars in promotional activities to do so. The fireworks display is like the Fourth of July; it gets the whole company rocking and rolling. Then reality hits in the workplace. Nothing has really changed. Behaviors stay the same. Values violations occur frequently, without consequences. Everyone is disappointed. If the CEO is attuned to the situation, the values stop being discussed in speeches, but they still get remembered ironically. Employees are embittered. Cynicism sets in. "Do as I say, not as I do," becomes the de facto ruling code. The entire values exercise ends up being seen as worse than a waste of time; it may have actually helped to sabotage the culture and critically harm the organization.

Don't blame the values. Blame the execution. As with anything else in business, good ideas and best intentions are meaningless without a sound strategy and committed follow-through. The simplest explanation for why values fail comes down to the fundamental relationship between supervisor and direct report. It doesn't matter what values the CEO proclaims in a speech, a direct report is most affected by the values exhibited by his or her supervisor. In order to please the boss, the employee starts to emulate and reflect the boss's behaviors. When the boss is not living or reflecting the values of the company, the breakdown is total. In a company with many thousands of supervisors and direct reports at many levels dispersed around the world, how can this kind of disconnect be prevented? It seems an impossibly complex issue, more complex and challenging than any business problem.

To spread a vital understanding of values throughout the organization, I recommend the cascade, or trickle-down, approach. Although values are set by those at the top of the organization, employees only find values meaningful when they are modeled or demonstrated by their immediate boss — what he or she says and does. When values are being rolled out, each member of the senior leadership team needs to engage their direct reports in a discussion of what the values mean in concrete terms and how that will affect the way they do their jobs.

In turn, those who have had that discussion with their superiors have the same discussion with their own direct reports, and so on, throughout the organization. In all of those discussions, a meaningful two-way dialogue takes place in which managers and reports are teaching and learning simultaneously, up and down the line. Noel Tichy, professor of organizational behavior and human resource management at the University of Michigan, describes this as creating a "virtuous teaching cycle."

But breakdowns can still occur. In real life, values are not always fully embraced by every manager at every level. Some managers are cynical; others feel a genuine lack of commitment to the values and are just going through the motions. Some managers see the values a little differently than the organization would like and put their own spin on things. This lack of clarity between the values at the top and the values as they are communicated by the manager can create a tremendous disconnect. It's a little like the game of telephone that children play. A message is whispered in one child's ear, he or she whispers it in the next person's ear, and so on, until the message is passed around the room. The joke is, when the message finally gets revealed, it has so thoroughly changed from the original as to be unrecognizable.

In order to counteract this effect, the cascade strategy requires that every discussion about values with a direct report involve not only the immediate manager but a second manager, preferably from a different region or division of the company. This check-and-balance approach reinforces the fact that values are truly organization-wide and not specific to one business or region over another. It keeps managers honest and on message, and gives reports a more in-depth sense of why values matter across the organization.

The process of holding active and animated discussions about values throughout the organization has profound and measurable rewards. Namely, it:

- Brings shared values to life.
- Increases commitment to the culture.
- Defines what is right and what is wrong in the context of achieving business results.
- Demonstrates how a strong culture is essential for business success.
- Increases employee ownership and accountability for learning and performance.
- Guides managers in coaching, evaluating performance, celebrating the right behaviors and dismissing those who perform contrary to the values regardless of their talent.

Remember, values come from the top, but they must be embraced throughout the organization. The process of sharing values through cascaded discussions does not mean that those values get changed along the way; they get clarified. Each employee at each level of the organization is able to identify the reality of the values based on his or her own experiences. From those experiences come corporate stories that reinforce moments when the values have been demonstrated. Corporate storytelling is the most powerful means of reinforcing values in an organization because such stories amount to a celebration of the values in heroic situations. In addition, good values discussions enable the leadership to judge how real values are for the employees and what efforts will be needed to make them clear. As a result the meaning of living the actions that defined the values get celebrated through discussions.

Not all is a rose garden. Early in my consulting career I was working with a firm that was going through a transformation from a government-regulated monopoly to a free market in the natural gas business. As the discussion evolved, it became clear three of the top twenty executives were acting in a way that was counter to the articulated behaviors for the future. From the values articulation they created a leadership profile for the future to anticipate the changing business environment. The new leadership behavior of "Intelligent Risk Taking" was created. This required executives to allow themselves to be challenged by their direct reports and in turn be open to new ideas. This concept of being challenged by others was foreign to those who grew successfully in what was a traditional utility run as if it was a para-military operation.

While the values of the company had not changed, the behaviors that defined them had evolved. Subsequently the leadership behaviors needed alignment. The consequence was that two of the three senior employees realized this and approached the CEO to resign. They came to a mutual understanding and they left knowing it was the best thing for both sides. As an outcome of this early experience, I begin the values journey with a warning to the CEO: once the values are clearly articulated, the consequence might be that one or two of the members of the team realize why they are not a good fit. We will see this again in a story later in the book.

Living the Values

The Federal Home Loan Bank of Pittsburgh (FHLBP) showed me how powerful a re-engagement with values could be in energizing and focusing an organization's spirit and workforce. Let me tell you their story.

The FHLBP was created during the Depression in 1932 when Congress established the national system to fill a dire need for a stable source of funds to prevent home foreclosures. The Great Depression had undermined the existing banking system, and with it, the American dream of private ownership. Each of the twelve Federal Home Loan Bank districts was independent to serve the needs of its own local areas; each developed its own culture.

The current generation of the FHLBP leadership joined the organization with a passion akin to the founding philosophy of the system. Many specifically desired to find a meaningful way within the mandate to use their skills in finance to give back to the community. Leaving the financial institutions they came from required a cut in salary, so you know that those beliefs in social responsibility were serious.

The CEO of FHLBP, James Roy, was one such man. He had joined the organization from Melon Bank, where he learned through a variety of experiences, lessons about the ways he did not want to treat people. He wanted to put his own Christian philosophy to work in business. The FHLBP needed a new focus, however. It had a regulatory mentality for business without a sense of customer service. The system of Home Loan banks needed to change with the times. But how could that shift be managed? "I had a vision," Roy says. "My eleven peers around the country were very concerned that the Federal Home Loan Bank system was going to disappear. My vision was to serve the large commercial banks and thrifts, but I knew that it would take a dramatic change in our character for them to see us as an organization they wanted to deal with. We had to look like a bank instead of a regulator."

This meant developing a caring service-oriented focus, and Roy believed such a major overhaul needed to start with a new look at the values, vision and behaviors of the organization. In 1989 and 1990, the senior management team engaged in a discussion of the values. What were they? What was their place in the organization? What function did they serve? What should they have been? The debates were lengthy and emotional, but then something amazing happened. "I can still remember one of the guys in the room saying, 'Why don't we simplify this?'"

Roy recalls. "'Our values should be, Value the individual, work as a team and customer first.' We all looked at him with our jaws dropped and thought, holy smokes, he nailed it. We knew that if we got our relationships right on the inside of the firm, it would carry over to the way we related to our customers on the outside. And we also knew why we wanted to do this — not so the bank would be more profitable but because it was the right thing to do."

In the end, the discussion articulated the vision and values as captured in the following box.

LOOK INSIDE THE BOX

Values of Federal Home Loan Bank of Pittsburgh

Our Vision...
We will be a catalyst for building thriving communities, working creatively with our partners until a safe warm home and steady work are within the grasp of every person in our region.

Our Culture...
Fostering a values-driven culture that focuses on our values:

Value the Individual
- The belief that each of us is a unique person of exceptional value.
- Each of us deserves the kind of respect, dignity and appreciation reserved for the very best. We deal with each other in the light of this principle.

Work as a Team

- We're all in this together: co-workers, customers, partners, all.
- We all have a stake in the Bank and its future. We strive to build trusting relationships on a foundation of fairness, integrity and understanding. We seek to be dependable, mutually supportive and consistent in our relationships.

Put the Customer First

- All that we do is for and about the customer.
- Our objective is "surprising service" — service inspired by the understanding that we are partners with our external customers. It's the kind of service that earns trust and respect, the two key qualities on which great partnerships are built.

"Before we took them to the rest of the organization," Roy says, "we spent considerable time thinking about what these values meant, what the implications were and how they had to be actualized. It's one thing to talk about them; it's something else to get them to a point where people own them." At first, not everyone was fully gung ho, as is the case in every endeavor, but vigorous discussion and articulation led to full acceptance. Then they rolled them out.

They decided that the initiative would be called a "Catalyst for Communities." As CEO, Roy worked with each of the department heads and small groups of department employees to begin to talk about the values. This took place over several sessions where people could question what the values meant and challenge them in situations where the firm's programs and policies didn't line up. The work of actualizing the values through programs was still to come; they needed to get the people behind the values first.

In a program called "Bringing Your Values to Life™," each manager took responsibility for "localizing" the meaning of the values and the vision in a series of conversations over the next six-month period. The conversations lasted from fifteen minutes to an hour. Following the discussion with their managers, the direct reports would conduct the same discussions with their own direct reports all the way to the front line. The process worked. As Roy says, "You can't legislate values any more than you can morality, but you can create an atmosphere out of those values that becomes so compelling that over time people say, 'I get it, I understand it and I buy into it.'"

Those few who couldn't accept the values, or didn't believe in them, got a lot of attention and discussion, but eventually were shown the door without apology. To check whether it worked, Roy commissioned focus groups with staff to see if they could express the values in terms of how they saw the culture of the organization without prompting. The feedback was tremendous. "Man, did they get it!" Roy enthused. "They fed it back to us, talking about what the culture of the home loan bank was like, and their description could fit categorically under each of the three values. It was just amazing."

Next came the process of putting the values in place with specific developmental approaches, including hiring, orientation, performance management and leadership development. This ensured that the conversations about the values were frequent, ongoing and meaningful in terms of people's day-to-day work and careers. It also ensured that executives and HR were getting regular feedback about how the values were being interpreted and whether they were sticking, and whether the culture was perceived to be living the values.

"The [business] results speak for themselves," Roy states. "When I started here in 1987, the Bank was just a little over 5 billion dollars in assets, with 200 thrift members, organizations that owned stock in our bank. Today, we are a 72-billion-dollar organization and have recruited over 400 commercial banks that are all part of us now. It's been a dramatic success story. Looking back, the values have been at the heart of it."

Indeed, the success goes deeper than the numbers. During some of the initial discussions with employees about values, the employees debated issues and concerns about the values, and the positive feedback trickled up the system. One of the employees came up with a suggestion for how to live and celebrate the values and vision: "We will be a catalyst for building thriving communities, working creatively with our partners until a safe warm home and steady work are within the grasp of every person in our region." To bring that vision to life, the employees decided to take one week per year and give it back to the community by putting "sweat equity" into the building of a home. To kick off the yearly program Catalyst for Communities, each employee arrives at work on a Monday to find a package on his or her chair containing a booklet capturing the vision, a baseball cap with the logo of the project and a disposable camera to capture visually the meaning of the vision in their own communities. The houses built through sweat equity are proudly displayed on the corporate website. The FHLBP was also deeply involved in providing housing assistance for the victims of Hurricane Katrina. Making those efforts did not distract from the business of the bank — those efforts expressed what the bank was all about and brought the bank's people and communities together in a sharing of those values.

Celebrating Values

In making values meaningful across the organization, our research shows that one thing is critical. Successful institutions celebrate their values and pass them on from one generation of employees to the next through the sharing of stories between people. This oral tradition, not unlike the sharing of myths and tales around a campfire in tribal societies, focuses on events and memories that reflect and elaborate on the values of the organization. In doing so the stories capture the heart and soul of the group.

For those who work at IBM, one corporate legend would be the IBM PC Jr. The PC Jr. was in response to the upstart Apple 128K and Commodore Computers, which against all expert belief at IBM should not have been successful. After all, the thinking at IBM was: who would want to have a computer in their home? So at first they stayed out of the home computer arena. When they did enter the field, it was the first time IBM introduced a product that failed. To save face for the design team, the project leader flew to Armack, New York, to tender his resignation. But instead of accepting the resignation the response was something to the effect that "it just cost IBM millions to educate you, why should [we let you go work for the competition]"? That story circulated through IBM like a highly charged circuit, energizing employees who were not feeling very proud of Big Blue and reinforced the fact that learning was and still is a value.

Employees don't tell corporate stories in the past tense or the future tense — they always retell them in the present tense for emphasis. Despite the fact that they happened in the past, the stories live on as if they are still happening and relevant today.

I have seen this time and again in organizations. At first, confused about the timeline of a story, I would ask. More often than not, the events could have taken place years ago or yesterday — it makes no difference to the storyteller or those listening when the story concerns some heroic act that revolves around values.

Some companies do a credible job creating values yet do not successfully transfer the "word." They create corporate websites that laud the values or design fancy business cards, or launch expensive public relations campaigns, yet fail to hit the mark with employees. The reason is due to the differences between oral and written history. When stories move from the tradition of oral history to the facts of written history, the passion and impact is diminished or even lost. Telling a story means believing it. Repeated frequently, a values myth gains the foundation of truth. Hearing a true story that really matters to the organization, individuals are able to interpret its meaningfulness in the context of their own lives, and thus embody the essence of the value and pass it on to others. That's another reason why values discussions between superiors and reports are so critical. It's natural that we use stories to illuminate the values of the organization. There's no better way to connect the abstractness of values with meaning. As individuals, organizations and nations, we are the stories we tell.

CHAPTER THREE

The Discipline of Working Inside the Box

- Success equals desired business outcomes attained in accordance with values.

- A strong culture is built on clear values that drive long-term success.

- A strong culture is linked to an environment that enables employees to recognize what is expected of them.

- What is right and good will remain right and good over many years in a strong culture.

- Identification with values and culture becomes the basis of employee engagement.

- If you allow people to violate the values and "live" another day, your integrity will suffer and you will lose credibility.

Why do people work for your organization — is it for love or money or something else?

Whenever I speak to CEOs and top executives about corporate values, I always ask them why they think their frontline people work for their organizations. Without much thought, most of them are quick to answer that rank-and-file employees work for a paycheck. They need the job. They see the company as a place to work or spend the day, a way to pay the mortgage, put food on the table or support the family. Is this a cynical point of view, a jaded or a realistic perspective?

In Toronto, Ontario, I once met with a group of janitors (custodial engineers) and maintenance workers employed by sanofi-pasteur — known as aventis-pasteur at that time, a world leader in developing vaccines. I was there to discuss the Facilities Group's internal customer service issues. The facilities maintenance team was in frequent conflict with the engineering group due to the fact that, in the eyes of their internal customers, they were uncooperative with one another and often put down the other group's work and efforts. This was driven by the schism between the directors who were leading each group. The vice president of the Facilities Management divisions wanted to develop a better working relationship to improve overall teamwork and, as a consequence, improve customer service. The maintenance workers were a diverse group, mostly immigrants with limited formal education, a mix of accents and ethnicities. Their length of service at the firm ranged from three to twenty-five years. What I learned from them about how they view their jobs and their organization was inspiring.

As a company, sanofi-pasteur traces its lineage to Louis Pasteur, who was the father of microbiology. If you remember your high school biology, you might recall that it was Pasteur who in 1857 finally demonstrated that infections are caused by micro-organisms. Before Pasteur, medical and agricultural scientists believed that infectious diseases arose through spontaneous generation. As with any fresh scientific leap, a door had been opened to countless applications. Pasteur's ideas led directly to other discoveries such as the pasteurization of milk and improvements in the care of livestock. Continuing his research over many years, he explored the possibility of vaccinating animals to prevent infectious diseases by inoculating them with attenuated microbes. After experimenting with diseases that beset livestock, Pasteur was able, by 1887, to develop a rabies vaccine for humans — an advancement that saves lives to this day.

Pasteur formed an institute to further his research. In 1889, one of Pasteur's students, Marcel Merieux, founded his own laboratory to concentrate on industrial virology. Merieux's institute worked first in veterinary medicine before expanding its applications to human medicine. Foot-and-mouth disease, tetanus, diphtheria, tuberculosis, syphilis and typhoid fever were all treatable with the vaccination process discovered by Pasteur.

The Institut Merieux Biologique was acquired by Rhone-Poulenc in 1968. A few years later this wholly owned subsidiary formed an alliance with the descendant of Pasteur's own laboratory, the Institut Pasteur Production. It was a combination of one organization's research acumen with the other's multinational industrial capacity. In 1989, Pasteur Merieux Serums et Vaccins acquired Connaught Laboratories, based in Toronto, Canada. Connaught Laboratories had been founded just before World War I by Dr. John Fitzgerald, who had himself been inspired by the way Institut Pasteur prepared serums. Connaught Laboratories in Toronto and its own subsidiary in Swiftwater, Pennsylvania, had made great strides over the century in treating diseases such as polio. In fact, Connaught was the first company in the 1930s to voluntarily answer the U.S. government's need for a supply of polio vaccine by donating it to the cause to protect U.S. citizens.

In 1999, Pasteur Merieux Connaught was renamed aventis pasteur. (In 2005, it was named sanofi-pasteur.) Into this storied tradition I came to discuss customer service issues with the Toronto facilities maintenance team just after Pasteur Merieux Connaught was renamed aventis pasteur. In order to determine whether the rank-and-file employees perceive an organization's values as embraced by their leaders, I always recommend going out to various sections of the organization and checking directly. In that spirit, given the opportunity to talk to these employees, I asked them a simple question: "When your neighbor or relatives ask you what company you work for and how you feel about that company, what do you say?"

The first answer I got was: "I tell them I work for Connaught, a company that is making the world safer for children through vaccination." Before I could even ask a follow-up question, another janitor intervened. "No, that's not true. We are making the world safer for all people, not just children." A passionate debate then ensued as to whether the organization's vision was to make the world safer for children or for people in general. I could only sit back and watch. The emotions were real. The members of the focus group truly cared about the issue.

When the second focus group came in, I asked the same question and got the same kind of response. Either this was a truly held belief or, as I half suspected, these employees had been well prepped to give a very specific response to the consultant seeking information from them about the leaders of the group because they were fiercely loyal to their particular director. One janitor showed up in the middle of this discussion late for our meeting. He apologized for his tardiness by explaining that he had been fixing a thermostat in one of the labs. I asked him why he had to fix the thermostat now and not later, since attendance at our meeting was mandatory. He answered that despite the importance of our meeting, it was his first responsibility to fix the thermostat. "If I don't do my job, an experiment might go sour." The others all agreed and came to his defense. It was ultimately the responsibility of the facilities team, they said, to make sure that research went smoothly. Sensitive experimental processes couldn't be interrupted. Research deadlines had priority over everything else. There was simply too much at stake.

Playing devil's advocate, I exclaimed, "But you're janitors!" I exclaimed. "How does your work cleaning toilets and washing floors help the development of vaccines to solve world disease problems?"

My tardy janitor gave me a cold look. "If that bathroom floor's wet," he said, "and I don't clean it up on time, one of the researchers might fall and hit his head. If he can't do his job, then I just caused the whole thing to fall apart. We're the glue that holds this place together."

Those words and the emotion behind them are echoed throughout the message of this book. sanofi-pasteur, through a lineage of successive companies with a pride in successful research, is a company that makes a profit developing and selling vaccines worldwide. (At the time of our research, it was the number one distributor of vaccines in the world.) Behind its strategy and operations is an emotionally charged set of values and an overarching vision, which creates a meaningful culture for the people who work there. That sanofi-pasteur's janitors in Toronto feel they contribute to that vision is a powerful statement. They understand their jobs in the context of the organization's vision and make crucial decisions about their work by doing a gut-check with the organization's values and culture. It was a realization that blew me away. It was the way every company should be.

Again, let's consider the question: Do your employees work for you for love or money or something else?

I'd like to suggest that human beings think about employment as fulfilling a hierarchy of needs. At the very base level is the paycheck. Somewhere up the pyramid is dignity. A little further up is personal satisfaction. Somewhere else in the mix at most for-profit organizations (though not necessarily schools, not-for-profits, volunteer organizations and religious organizations) is the sense of earning a jackpot — money that goes beyond meeting the basics and bolsters self-worth. And at the very top comes the place where a sense of purpose connects to values, which can lead to altruism. Corporate altruism is when you can put your own advancement, needs for recognition and success (ego) aside for the greater need for corporate success.

In the last quarter of the last century Lawrence Kohlberg crafted his perception of the world from the perspective of ethical reasoning. He started as a developmental psychologist in the early 1970s and became better known for his later work in moral education and moral reasoning. Kohlberg's theory of moral development emphasizes that moral reasoning develops in stages. In this it resembles Jean Piaget's theory of cognitive development. In Kohlberg's work he started out with six stages of morality or ethics; I will focus on stages four, five and six. The final level would be reasoning. However, towards the end of his life he added a seventh which would equate to altruism, labeled "transcendental morality." After serious debate and reflection this stage was withdrawn from the theory in that it was only aspirational. As a result his theory ends with the sixth stage labelled "universal human ethics." He argues this level recognizes that human life is a more fundamental value than property rights of others or personal gratification through material ownership.

Yet, from the perspective of corporate values does that mean that we need to have a value set that extends to Kohlberg's sixth stage? Not in my opinion, it would not be realistic as most human development does not attain this level of ethical reasoning. The reality is the majority of corporations function at stage four, which is defined as the "law and order" stage. There are a few perhaps that operate at stage five, which focuses on human rights, but I would argue they are few and far between.

The link to my perspective of corporate values is that we are not going to do anything naturally that is truly a stage seven altruism. However, we will respect the rights of individuals and we will put human life before profits, and as a result, it is that connection to a sense of purpose that drives people's ambitions. It is not money. Given money being almost equal between two offers, people will go for a higher purpose for work. Ask yourself if an offer were to come to you tomorrow for 10 percent more pay at a firm you know nothing about, would you jump ship for the slight difference? If you would, perhaps you are only thinking as a stage three of conformity. The question I have asked people is what seems to be the tipping point to jump ship. The magic number seems to hover around 20 percent. In short, given the financial reward being the same, do you really work for money?

Two examples come to me. The first is a colleague at Notre Dame who had three young children and left a highly paid job in the private sector to take a position at Notre Dame. The only thing is it was a 40 percent drop in income. He thought nothing of it. In fact, he insists he did the right thing. Another colleague did the same thing some years ago. He took what equals a 30 percent cut in income to join the administration of Brigham Young University.

But picturing this pyramid with values at the top does a disservice to your organization. If you can draw people to your organization through a sense of purpose and meaning that is real because that is how people in the company act on the values, then you've got some very dedicated, loyal and motivated employees. Therefore, if the connection and engagement of employees comes through working in an organization that is aligned with their values, the values would naturally be the first item defined before your vision, strategic business plan, divisional goals or personal objectives. Money is important — nobody can survive without it — but meaning, connection and purpose form the DNA of organizational greatness.

Creating a Values-Based Organization

Johnson & Johnson describes itself as "the world's most comprehensive and broadly based manufacturer of health care products, as well as a provider of related services, for the consumer, pharmaceutical and medical devices and diagnostics markets." It says that it is composed of more than 200 operating companies, employing approximately 115,000 men and women in fifty-seven countries with more than 179,000 registered shareholders. In 2005, it was ranked number nine on *Fortune* magazine's list of Most Admired Companies, number one in the pharmaceutical category. Some of J&J's top-selling products have been among the world's best-known brand names for decades, including Band-Aid, Johnson & Johnson's Baby Powder and Tylenol. In other words, J&J is a successful company in every sense.

The company arose with a sense of purpose. In the 1870s, the British surgeon Sir Joseph Lister made a revolutionary advance in antiseptic medicine. Building on the discoveries of Louis Pasteur, Lister changed the way surgical operations were performed by trying to eliminate airborne germs, which he called "invisible assassins." Lister called for doctors to wear rubber gloves and use sterilized instruments. He also had a diluted solution of carbolic acid sprayed around the operating theater, shrouding the patient in a fog. Not many doctors believed in Lister's germ theories, and the carbolic acid spray was a cumbersome and expensive idea that limited its widespread usefulness. Robert Wood Johnson, a businessman from America, believed that finding a better way to control germs and disease would be a worthy and profitable endeavor for a company. With his two brothers, he founded Johnson & Johnson in 1886 in New Brunswick, New Jersey. The company's first successful product was a sterile gauze dressing that could be mass-produced and shipped to hospitals, doctors and druggists. Other products that followed included Johnson's Baby Powder (initially created to deal with skin irritation that came from applying plasters to wounds) and Band-Aids (created so that housewives could treat household wounds and burns).

Over the ensuing decades, and a succession of family presidents, Johnson & Johnson promoted its products as a means to reduce disease and death through more antiseptic medical and surgery procedures. The focus on pharmaceutical, medical and surgical improvements was combined with a strong socially responsible orientation. In 1932, General Robert Wood Johnson, the son of the founder, took over as president and sought to transition the company from a family-owned business to a global one. Like his forebears, he believed strongly that a company needed to be concerned with more than just money; it had responsibilities to the community and employees, too. In 1935, he wrote a pamphlet called "Try Reality" in which he encouraged business leaders to feel responsibility to customers, employees, the community and stockholders. Eight years later, he wrote the Johnson & Johnson Credo to articulate those responsibilities in more detail.

LOOK INSIDE THE BOX

Our Credo

We believe our first responsibility is to the doctors, nurses and patients, to mothers and fathers and all others who use our products and services. In meeting their needs everything

Continued

we do must be of high quality. We must constantly strive to reduce our costs in order to maintain reasonable prices.

Customers' orders must be serviced promptly and accurately. Our suppliers and distributors must have an opportunity to make a fair profit.

We are responsible to our employees, the men and women who work with us throughout the world. Everyone must be considered as an individual. We must respect their dignity and recognize their merit. They must have a sense of security in their jobs. Compensation must be fair and adequate, and working conditions clean, orderly and safe. We must be mindful of ways to help our employees fulfill their family responsibilities. Employees must feel free to make suggestions and complaints. There must be equal opportunity for employment, development and advancement for those qualified. We must provide competent management, and their actions must be just and ethical.

We are responsible to the communities in which we live and work and to the world community as well. We must be good citizens — support good works and charities and bear our fair share of taxes. We must encourage civic improvements and better health and education. We must maintain in good order the property we are privileged to use, protecting the environment and natural resources.

Our final responsibility is to our stockholders. Business must make a sound profit. We must experiment with new ideas. Research must be carried on, innovative programs developed and mistakes paid for. New equipment must be purchased, new facilities provided and new products launched. Reserves must be created to provide for adverse times. When we operate according to these principles, the stockholders should realize a fair return.

This credo functioned as a statement of the beliefs of the organization — and it was used to clarify, articulate and transmit those beliefs to a growing global employee base. The credo would have been meaningless if it wasn't grounded in the organization's actual origins and practices, and demonstrated by the leaders. But because the credo was so in sync with "the way we do things around here" it was wholeheartedly embraced by the organization. Nor did General Johnson simply frame the credo and put it on the boardroom wall (or whatever the equivalent of an internet home page might have been available in those times). Rather, he referred to the credo often and encouraged managers throughout the company to embrace it and use it as a guide in their business decisions.

The credo has remained in place over the ensuing sixty years with changes made to update the inclusion of fathers, family and the environment in the list of the organization's concerns. In principle, however, the document has stood the test of time. This adherence to the company's values has not been taken for granted. Every year, the organization takes an entire day to celebrate the values. Employees participate in a survey of how well the responsibilities listed in the credo are being covered. The feedback is provided to senior management and action is taken where shortcomings are apparent.

If values are to be really meaningful in an organization, they must be held in common throughout that organization. I have worked with two divisions of Johnson & Johnson in Canada and have seen strong evidence that they embrace the credo. The atmosphere in both sites was very positive and upbeat. People frequently expressed a sense that they are doing something of significance in the workplace and contributing to the success of an important endeavor. The credo instructs them on how to behave and provides them with a sense of security in knowing how others will treat them in the company.

As definitive evidence of how strongly the credo is held, we only need to consider the two incidents of Tylenol poisoning in the 1980s and how J&J reacted to that crisis. In 1982, someone put cyanide into Tylenol bottles sold in the Chicago area. Seven people were killed and fear spread throughout the country. It's easy to imagine a company floundering under the circumstances of such a crisis, unsure how to react, swinging wildly between concern for people's lives and concern for the life of the company and the viability of a very important brand product. Many organizations might have attempted to duck the responsibility, justifiably passing the buck to the government and law enforcement officials in the face of such extraordinary corporate sabotage, doing anything it could to avoid a financial hit while also trying to stem the flood of a public relations disaster. A host of contradictory, self-serving and ignoble decisions could have resulted, understandable attempts to safeguard the company's profits. Who could blame them? (For an example of such poor reactions to a crisis, just look at the feud that happened between Firestone and Ford over tire failure in the Ford SUV.)

But that's not how J&J responded. Within days, it voluntarily recalled the product from every store shelf in America, taking a $100-million charge against earnings. Moreover, in searching for the best solution to the crisis, J&J came out with an idea that benefited the drug industry in general by promoting anti-tamper packaging. In 1986, there was another incident of Tylenol poisoning. This time, the company promoted the use of caplets instead of capsules to decrease the risk.

The benefits of J&J's quick action were enormous. The company received tremendous credit for doing the right thing, and the brand-name product not only survived the crisis, it resumed its market leadership without lasting damage. How did

J&J manage to respond so resolutely and effectively? It didn't need to waste inordinate time weighing the pros and cons. Rather, it simply consulted its credo and understood that the right thing to do was very straightforward. "We believe our *first responsibility* is to the doctors, nurses and patients, to mothers and fathers and all others who use our products and services. In meeting their needs everything we do must be of *high quality*." By living up to its values, J&J overcame what could have been a crippling crisis and became stronger than ever in the eyes of employees, customers, shareholders and competitors. It reinforced what others already knew about the organization and made it real.

Would your company take a $100-million hit to uphold its values? Compare the reaction of J&J with the reaction of Merck when Vioxx was found to be linked with heart attacks. Merck was accused of hiding studies that showed Vioxx could be a health risk to some patients. It simply couldn't stomach the thought of losing profit from its $2.5-billion product and resisted demands that Vioxx should be recalled. Subsequent lawsuits capitalized on that failing, hitting the company's books and its reputation hard.

The decision J&J made was in line with its culture, tradition and values, as exemplified in its one-page credo. Merck claims to "put patients first" and its thirty-two-page booklet, "Our Values and Standards" makes its responsibilities clear, and those responsibilities seem to cover the same areas as J&J's. But without having had any hands-on experience with the organization, I can only comment that the booklet seems cold, as though it was put together by a committee formed of PR consultants, lawyers and Human Resources staff under the oversight of a COO. In fact, I'm not even arguing that Merck's response to its crisis wasn't the right one, given its own culture and values. The only people who can answer that question are the committed employees of

Merck. While others outside the company might feel they did not respond correctly if they acted in alignment with the company values, then for that company, it was the correct response. Did they feel the company did the right thing? Or did they feel that it did not live its aboveground *and* expressed values, but instead acted in keeping with the real Merck, drawing from the real and lived culture and values that live unarticulated and underground, known only to the employees, behind the booklet.

Just because the consequences deal with life and death doesn't necessarily make this an ethically clear argument. There are two prominent lines of thinking about corporate responsibility that form the camps of how organizations are viewed. Those who follow Milton Friedman's philosophy believe that a business organization should be responsible only to its own shareholders. In a sense, the ultimate customer of the organization is the shareholder, and everything must be done to serve his or her needs. This doesn't provide a blank check for organizations to act unethically and even illegally in the pursuit of higher profits. In fact, very strong arguments can be made that the ethical decision is ultimately in the best interests of the employee and shareholder in the long term. Nevertheless, it does put profit before principle and enables a company's leaders to rest well at night because they are within their "legal limits, not violating the laws of the land in which the company operates." Or as noted above, they are only at stage four of Kohlberg's hierarchy of ethical reasoning.

On the other hand, those in the camp of Peter Drucker, among other experts and thinkers, believe that the higher purposes of an organization are just as important as profit, if not more so. By taking care of those higher purposes (like people, community, service to others, etc.), profit will take care of itself. Put another way, profit or making money is not a corporate value; it is a by-product of living the values. General Johnson, by his credo and the corporate culture he fostered, was clearly an ardent believer in that theory. He didn't just concern himself with shareholders and community because it was the right thing to do; he did it out of his own convictions of what defined right from wrong. He focused on values because he believed covering those areas would benefit the company, too.

In terms of business outcome, it seems clear that J&J's response to a drug crisis was more effective than Merck's. Making that decision seemed easy at J&J, given its clear culture. As an individual who shares the belief that profit is a by-product of living one's values, I can imagine that it's certainly easier to walk into J&J to work in the morning following its response to a crisis, than into Merck. That doesn't mean that someone at Merck doesn't feel they did the right thing, too. Then again, maybe they feel that the actions taken to protect the company from the Vioxx crisis undermined the organization's values. If so, then the damage will go much deeper than the loss of a single super product. However, if the real, or underground, values of Merck supported the actions taken by Merck, then the employees do sleep well at night because the actions were consistent with the real values rather than with the politically correct version articulated in Merck's pamphlet.

Culture and Values

Every organization has a culture. Not every organization has a culture that achieves its vision or strategy, nor keeps its employees productive, committed and fulfilled. Nor is every culture correct for every individual. Corporate cultures, like people, vary in content and behavior, even if the headline words are the same.

Anthropologists, who introduced the modern idea of describing why groups of humans behave differently around the world, first adopted the concept of culture. Why is England different from France? Why are the Kung bushmen of the Kalihari desert in southern Africa different from the Yanomami tribesmen of the Amazon jungle in South America? From an outsider's perspective we can tell that these groups are not the same. The people dress differently, they speak different languages, they have different customs or manners, they have different social and political systems and they have different religious beliefs and different ways of viewing the world. Why do those differences exist?

As early anthropologists quickly noticed, people of a specific culture are bound by physical circumstances like climate, geography, the availability of resources and the proximity of neighbors. They develop tools, techniques and approaches to manipulate their physical circumstances and get the most out of them. Their social systems function to do the same thing. Some cultures promote large families, some small. Some feel strong kinship bonds beyond immediate blood relatives and others don't. Some cultures have complex multi-layered political systems run by hereditary authority figures; others rely on very flat and democratic systems to make the decisions that affect everyone's lives.

People of a specific culture often look alike — typically because they are from one racial group and dress and act similarly. And they also sound alike, usually communicating in the same language, dialect or accent. Along with a common history and a complex net of intertwined relationships, these factors promote a strong common identity. A culture's art, music, games, storytelling and spiritual or religious beliefs further deepen and strengthen this common identity. People of a specific culture tend to experience and view the world through a similar lens. Even though there may be many complex differences between individuals of a culture, those differences still have more in common than viewpoints and experiences held by people of another culture.

What purpose does culture serve other than to bond people together? In their quest to understand the nature of cultural differences, anthropologists decided that culture provides groups of human beings with a way of working together to survive and succeed in the world. Everything about a culture reinforces the patterns of behavior and beliefs that members of that culture need in order to thrive.

Now let's try to take the concepts of culture to organizations that mean more to us today. As anthropologists pushed their studies beyond tribes that are racially and linguistically united to larger social organizations like nations and states, the notion of culture became more complex. A nation-state like Spain has several different linguistic groups, multiple races and many different ways of life depending on geographical region and social status. Does that mean Spain has a distinct culture? Of course it does, but political and lifestyle conflicts reveal there are definitely some clear divisions in that culture. To take into account such divisions within an overriding culture, we often speak of subcultures — smaller unified groups that have more in common internally, yet still maintain strong connections to and clear similarities with the larger culture.

The idea of organizational culture stretches the definition of culture even further. In today's global business organizations, people often come from extremely diverse backgrounds. They may live in disparate regions all over the world and speak different languages. In their work, they may focus on different products in different markets. Is there anything that connects them besides a corporate logo and a paycheck?

As anyone who has experienced more than one global organization first-hand can attest, differences in organizational cultures are very noticeable. Walking through the doors of

J&J gives you a different feeling than speaking before a group at Sam's Club or lining up as a customer at the Bank of Nova Scotia. Of what are those differences composed? The same list of distinctions for tribal cultures comes to mind. People of a strong corporate culture may be racially diverse, yet a certain style of dress can predominate. People of a strong corporate culture may speak the same language or a number of different languages, but a tuned ear will pick up on subtle ways of speaking that are distinctive to the organizational culture. For instance, members of the culture may use similar phrases, intonations and terminology as though everyone is reading from the same script. People of a strong corporate culture may come from a variety of religious, spiritual and even ethical backgrounds, but their views of the way things ought to be done in the business world tend to conform also. And people of a strong corporate culture are united in their sense of common identity — they share experiences, histories, stories and heroes.

The globalization of the world economy has brought the English language to the forefront as the universal language of business. Recently the Malaysian government stopped the primary instruction in elementary and high school in English, and businesses are finding the graduates of the school system are not capable of conducting business effectively. I would suggest that while language used to reflect a culture or national sense of law and order and culture, today English as the foundation for business operations has only made communications easier, not understanding one another better.

Organizations with strong corporate cultures are more successful than their competitors. Their employees tend to bond more closely and have a greater sense of pride. The organizations have clearer alignment between strategy and execution on the job. They have more brand identification in the marketplace. The key question we need to address is this: how do those organizations do it? How do they foster a strong culture? Again, it helps to look at the dynamics of culture in the "real" world.

The how-culture-develops argument is a bit like the chicken-and-the-egg or the nature-versus-nurture debate. Does culture develop because of physical circumstances or because of shared beliefs? In fact, the answer is both. Some experts believe that culture consists of three aspects: values, norms and artifacts. By artifacts, we mean physical tools, clothing, etc, which I would argue are the least significant aspect in modern corporate culture given the wide distribution of technology and tools. On the other hand, norms, or patterns of behavior, are very distinct between corporate cultures and enormously influential. And of course, values, or what people of a given corporate culture believe is important, are critical too.

In the real world, culture ferments naturally. By this I mean that nations don't need to actively promote the development of their culture; it just happens. In the corporate world, however, organizations don't have the luxury of letting culture just happen — they need to actively promote it, maintain it and cultivate it. After all, there are many forces at play that are detrimental to the development of shared norms and values. People are moving in and out of the organization all the time. The organization may be expanding rapidly and changing at a fast pace. Communication is often from a distance with leaders of the organization never even meeting the vast majority of employees.

An organization refines and maintains its culture by focusing like a laser beam on its values and its norms of behavior within the company. Because with time and the right consequences in place, the corporate values can be taught through training and exert powerful influence over the way people act, thereby shaping what happens on the job. The work done to promote values and norms needs to be in sync, however. If values and norms don't support each other, employees won't perceive them as legitimate and real.

Values are worked on by clarifying them as General Johnson did with the credo at Johnson & Johnson. Founders and top leaders are in key positions to articulate and repeat the values of their organizations. Values get integrated into the organization's brand. And they get reinforced for generations of employees through the power of story-telling — each time a story about the corporate culture or about a hero in that culture gets retold, the values of the organization are transmitted like a secret message.

The power of storytelling is indicative of another critical aspect of values. We don't talk about values abstractly; we describe them through concrete actions. These are our norms or patterns of behavior. The founders and leaders of an organization can't simply parrot a set of values and act in ways that are discordant with those values; everything they do and every decision they make needs to demonstrate those values. Managers need to do the same thing, and they need to coach, praise or reprimand their employees for how well or poorly they act in accordance with the values. The people in the organization learn that the right behavior or the right decision is the one that best fits the organization's values. It all gets solidified and reinforced over time.

Reinforcing the Right Patterns of Behavior

In the late 1970s, in the field of education, there was significant new writing about the idea of a hidden curriculum. People realized that while every school hopefully had a clearly articulated curriculum, that curriculum didn't always rule the day. Instead, there were often other forces at play, bigger and stronger than the stated curriculum. Those larger forces were termed the "hidden curriculum." The hidden curriculum informed students how to survive and what could be done within the bounds of accepted school norms. For example, a teacher tells her students that they need to complete an assignment in a certain way and on time. But from past experience, the students know there is room to negotiate. The assignment can be shorter than required and it can be handed in late. Accordingly, even though the curriculum states that the assignment needs to be done one way, students — through the tacit approval of their teacher — figure out that it can be done a different way. And, being human, they take the easiest road home.

Corporations, of course, discover that underground culture can arise if values and norms are out of sync. A strong culture, on the other hand, is linked to an environment that enables employees to recognize what is expected of them. The expectations of the job are predictable because people know that certain attitudes and behaviors result in excellence in performance. Even in situations where clear rules or precedents haven't been set, employees can sense what's right or wrong because of how it resonates for them with the values.

Psychologist Lawrence Kohlberg built upon Jean Piaget's cognitive development work to describe the process children go through in developing the conscience of adults. A similar track can be followed in understanding how contractually bonded employees become committed disciples of an organization's values. In Kohlberg's first and second stages, children rely on obedience and punishment to determine what is right and wrong and are motivated by self-interest. In other words, they look for rewards and fear getting punished, and they see right and wrong in terms of getting caught or recognized. In the third and fourth stages, children come to rely on relationships and a need to conform to the group as they become adolescents, and they have a desire to cede to authority and the social order in guiding their thinking of right and wrong. In other words, they begin to see that their actions have an effect on others, but view right or wrong in terms of how the group sanctions those actions. In the fifth and sixth stages, adults develop an understanding that there are certain principles that are stronger than any laws or the needs of the groups, and these principles should be adhered to because they are inherently right.

An employee, like a child becoming an adolescent and then an adult, goes through similar stages. Early on, what is right and wrong is defined very dogmatically in terms of rules and regulations. As attachment to the group becomes more socially powerful, the employee worries about developing relationships, conforming and maintaining good social order by showing deference to authority. But as the employee internalizes and understands the values of the organization innately, he develops a sense of rightness that doesn't require rules, sanctions or social approval. Instead, the rightness rings true because it sets up a resonance. If you play a well-known piece of music, for example, and stop it before the last few notes, most people will mentally finish up the piece on their own. When an organization instills an understanding of its values, most employees can answer questions of right and wrong intuitively without having to resort to rules or looking around for the responses of others.

Evaluating Employees' Performance in Light of the Values

One of the most difficult things for organizations to do is to identify how people match up to the organization's values in terms of performance. Everyone knows people who are good at their jobs but detrimental to the organization. Likewise, everyone knows people who are only mediocre in terms of ability but seem to embody the spirit of the organization. If the success of an organization depends on its adherence to its own values, and not on such things as short-term profit and achievements, how can a manager or leader evaluate employee performance? In my experience, employees fall into one of four categories depending on how well they fit the values of an organization: stars, keepers, deadwood and viruses.

Stars

Stars are those employees who demonstrate your organization's values while also attaining your desired business results. They are the perfect fit for your organization and should be recognized as critical assets. Not only are they your high-potential individuals, but they also tend to be the worker bees of the company and great field leaders. They get the work done and stand as examples of the values. They are often the people who are the focus of various corporate legends that provide allegories of the organization's values. Unfortunately, because of their effectiveness, talent and reliability, managers often rely on stars too much and only reward them with extra work. They are the first people the manager turns to for help in a crisis. Eventually, the star will wake up to this Catch-22 and feel burned out and resentful because of the extra pressure — especially if deadwood and viruses are kept in the organization, exacerbating the burden that the star feels.

Keepers

Keepers, on the other hand, are marginal employees in terms of performance but stalwarts in terms of living the organization's values. When downsizing occurs, keepers are those employees who are let go because their numbers fail to overwhelm. Their presence is sorely missed, however, because they are often the people who celebrate and hold the culture together. They act as shamans and wise men and women for the organization's stories and guidelines, and serve as mentors to those new to the organization.

High	High on competencies Rethink Job Fit	High on results High on competencies Great / Recognition
Demonstration of the Values	Low on results Low on competencies Thanks for the memories / "Good-bye"	High on results Low on competencies Rethink Rewards & Recognition. Create Consequences of their actions
Low	**Achievement of Results**	**High**

Many years ago, when I was involved with the downsizing at a steel company, a custodial engineer was let go. Although well liked by all his co-workers and management, the decision to let him go made bottom-line sense. The man had a limited education, was not as physically strong as he used to be, and had accumulated so much longevity that his salary was significantly higher than it would have been in the open market. Nevertheless, people keenly felt the man's loss in a cultural sense. He was a friendly person who kept others' moods up. He had been instrumental in the firm's annual United Way campaign, and he was the key person organizing the youth hockey team. He contributed to the spirit of the firm in ways that didn't register in performance reviews. When he was let go by senior management, the repercussions were surprising. Everyone in the company became intensely worried about their own job security, as if they were thinking, "If they can fire him, they can fire anyone!" Later, one of the senior people told me that in hindsight, letting the custodial engineer go had been a mistake because he was such a good fit with the culture. As a result of his layoff, the leadership team was accused of being ruthless for having "shot Bambi." The lesson I gained from this experience was that it is better to recognize keepers' special capabilities and place them in a role where their skills and knowledge will work to success. It is more cost effective to provide keepers with the necessary training than to replace them. And it is motivating for others to see such employees retained and celebrated.

Deadwood

Deadwood, on the other hand, are those people who fail to demonstrate your organization's values and fail to achieve business results. Although it may seem a simple solution to let such people go, in reality most organizations delay doing so for various bureaucratic reasons. Often the deadwood ends up getting passed around from department to department and through attrition and perseverance even obtains a promotion or two. The damage this causes should not be overlooked. Everyone knows that a person who is deadwood is creating extra work for others. Each time such employees survive another performance review and are allowed to "live" another year, management loses credibility. When today's managers were first-line supervisors or individual contributors, you can bet they complained about their managers' lack of courage or integrity in failing to let the deadwood go. Now that they are in leadership positions, such managers need to consider the trouble caused by leaving deadwood in place.

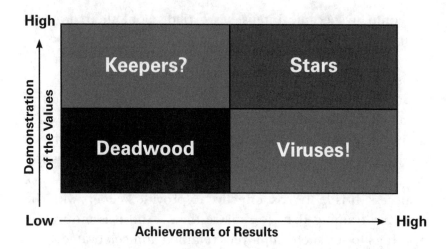

Early in my consulting career, I was conducting a focus group in a unionized environment to define the correct behaviors for the future of a frontline position. The main focus was to define the behaviors needed to provide support internally that would lead to great public service. Some people performing this work were really good at their jobs; others were frankly terrible. During the conversation, one of the veteran participants noted that "if only management would have the courage to deal with the deadwood around here that causes the public to have such a bad opinion of us, we'd all be better off." To my surprise, I learned that the speaker was the vice president of the national board of the union at the firm. I asked her if the union shouldn't be more concerned about keeping employees in place. She answered me candidly: "We all know who the deadwood are. If they were let go, we would need to file a grievance, but management would soon learn that we wouldn't fight for that person too hard because the grounds for their dismissal was bad performance. Bad performance is a reflection on all of us, giving us all a bad name." Unfortunately, managers feared the reaction of the union so much that they didn't follow this tacit advice and treated all performers, good and bad, exactly the same.

I am always curious why organizations are described as 20 – 70 – 10, meaning that 10 percent of every organization is deadwood. It seems that is the cost of doing business.

Viruses

Viruses are the most difficult people for an organization to know what to do with. They are talented individuals who achieve desired business results, sometimes even at top levels of performance. What's wrong with them? They don't exemplify the values of the organization. They are black holes taking all of the attention and rewards that go with top performance and negating the impact because anyone who tries to follow their example will be going down the wrong path.

In an age in which high-priced talent can work anywhere they like, it may seem picky to require a top performer not only to get results but get them in the right way. We often hear middle and senior management argue that the virus is a star in the eyes of the executives because he or she makes the numbers that make the boss look good. Yet, before you let viruses stay on for selfish reasons (they are making better results than anyone else in the company), consider two hard realities.

First, each time keepers and deadwood see a virus receive reward and recognition for the right outcomes and the wrong behaviors, the deadwood learns to focus, for the short time, on results over values, and keeping their job until someone notices again. The potential impact on keepers and perhaps your emerging stars is to think why work so hard because the end seems to justify the means. You are giving them permission to abandon the values your organization stands for and pursue results any way they can. Second, by letting a virus succeed, you are saying to the rest of your people that your organization's values are not actually meaningful. Moreover, that message is also getting out to your customers, suppliers and partners.

Dealing with a virus shouldn't scare a manager. Time and again, I've seen that when the viruses are provided honest and clear feedback, they often realize that they are not a good fit for the firm and decide to leave on their own. Although there's a fear that performance drop will occur as a result, almost every time a virus is finally released from a firm, the person taking his or her place meets or exceeds that productivity within a short period of time. Alternatively, when provided with clear feedback, some viruses decide they want to change. With time, effort and proper support and positive recognition, they can modify their actions to comply with the culture of the organization. This can have a great impact on reinforcing your organization's values. You probably have many more keepers than viruses, and your viruses probably have some degree of celebrity or highly visible status. Whatever happens to them gets noticed by almost everyone.

A number of years ago, I worked with Jos Opdeweegh, the CEO of TDS Automotive, to help his global organization articulate and spread its values. In our recent conversations, he let me know that he is even more convinced now of the importance of that work based on the impact he has seen. As the CEO, Opdeweegh says that it is his job to ensure that every important decision in the organization is discussed and measured according to the values. He's also come to understand the importance of acting on removing even top leaders who do not fit the values. I remember one of those leaders well.

I was in Europe at the time, teaching behavioral interviewing based on the values. The session with TDS's regional plant managers generated much interest because using the values they could easily make the connection between hiring the right person versus hiring any warm body. The manager at the factory where we were meeting, however, treated his staff in a way that was contrary to the values. At noon, this person who was not in attendance came in and said he had arranged for a tour of the plant to be followed by a brainstorming discussion about increasing operational efficiencies. His colleagues immediately protested that they would rather continue with the behavioral-interview training because turnover was their biggest problem, and understanding the values was showing them a better way. The plant manager evidently didn't see any value to our work but retreated under their unified protest and left us to continue. The plant manager's attitude turned on a light switch for Opdeweegh, however, who realized that the manager didn't demonstrate the firm's values at all. Soon, he decided to let the plant manager go. It was one of the leadership experiences that helped him realize the importance of being consistent with values in order to align the firm's people to the business results.

A second virus story provides a more positive example. An insurance firm was in transition and sales for the group benefits division were not going well. My firm was asked to create a behavioral profile for the sales team. We took a full circle view of the job. We conducted focus groups with the best performers on their sales team, the managers who grew successful sales people, the manager's manager, as well as the support staff. In addition we consulted a range of clients outside the firm, from their support staff right up to the executive vice president making the final decision on whether the insurance company would get the benefits contract. Once the behavioral profile was concluded and validated, we conducted a 360-degree-feedback process and asked each salesperson to seek feedback from at least four of his or her clients.

The results provided a wake-up call for many people. Because we'd validated the behaviors, we realized that the standard training materials were teaching the salesperson the wrong behavior. For example, salespeople were taught that following up meant hand-delivering a proposal. But in the field, hand-delivering a proposal actually aggravated the decision makers; many felt obliged to interrupt their work day and have coffee with the salesperson, even though a decision couldn't possibly be made yet. Clients actually wanted salespeople to courier the proposal and follow up by checking to see if the paper had arrived, then make an appointment two weeks later when they could intelligently discuss the proposal. On the other hand, clients were also disappointed because there was no additional follow-up after the initial and unwanted follow-up. As a result, the sales team came across as uncaring and arrogant.

One of the client firms had been doing significant business with the insurance firm for seventy-five years. During our 360-degree review process, the executive at that firm informed us that they would not be renewing their business because the behavior of the sales rep was not to their liking. It would be an understatement to say that this sales rep went into shock when he received his feedback. But understanding the reasons, we focused him on two specific business objective behaviors to modify how he followed up and communicated with the client.

The sales rep worked relentlessly on his new action plan. His manager was aware of the behaviors he was trying to develop and provided a great deal of support in making those changes. They had short weekly conversations about how it was going. Three months later, the manager made the effort to collect anecdotal stories to gather perspective on whether the sales rep was succeeding in changing his behavior. He discovered that some clients had noticed the positive change, while others hadn't. The manager decided to let the sales rep only know about the positives, which helped keep the sales rep motivated to continue working on the change. This had a domino effect in that it reinforced the right behaviors and encouraged him to demonstrate them more frequently.

Seven months after the project started, I met the senior vice president of Group Benefits on the street. He quickly mentioned that the client whose business the group had written out of their planning objectives six months before had actually renewed their business after all. When the senior VP asked that firm's CEO why they decided to renew, he was told that the sales rep's efforts to do the right thing had been so apparent, it had restored faith, and the insurance firm's courage to act on negative feedback from a client had reaffirmed why the relationship had already lasted seventy-five years.

Your Culture Captures Your Values

Even your customers will help support you when you're living up to your values. A strong culture is like a warm home or a solid foundation. It provides a steady sense of stability and security in an often confusing and disconcerting business world. Imagine if a CEO articulated and put into motion a very public strategy, but was actually trying to move the organization in a different direction, using different incentives and rewards and measures of success, through a secret strategy. You would hardly expect employees to be able to go out and execute that strategy flawlessly. Aligning your employees with your firm's values helps them connect meaningfully to the reason you're in business. The execution of your strategy follows. Values are set by the founders, fostered by the top leaders and safeguarded by managers, but without employees, there wouldn't be any such thing as corporate culture. Without the right employees, your corporate culture is in danger.

CHAPTER FOUR

Inside-the-Box Management Tools

❑ Values and behaviors become the basis for the people process system.

❑ Top performance must be defined in terms of those behaviors that best demonstrate your values.

❑ Hiring and firing decisions have to be consistent with values.

❑ Values must be incorporated into performance reviews.

❑ When values are real, they support employees' emotional commitment to the organization and make it a place worth fighting for.

❑ The manager is ultimately responsible for the consistency of the organization's values.

Good marketing and good strategic planning will help your organization achieve its business objectives. But unless you have the right people in the right jobs at the right time, your success will not be sustainable. The road is too long, the obstacles too difficult to predict, the forces of change too disruptive.

The best strategy in the world will fail unless it is executed well. Some think that this means focusing on the individual performer rather than the role itself. Jim Collins describes this as "getting the right people on the bus" and letting the nature of the work involved take care of itself. But it's not as simple as that. By selecting people and building positions around them, you limit your corporate capabilities to the possibilities of the individual. Are those people in line with your strategy? Who knows? On the other hand, if you first define the roles you need to fill in order to execute your strategy, then you are focusing on long-term organizational success that goes beyond the individual. The downside is that you might find that the talent you are able to get and the talent that you actually need is far apart — a fact that keeps food on the table for leadership development consultants.

In the real world, there's no chicken and egg; we've got both at the same time. Organizations that discover the need to clarify their values and mission can't take a competitive time-out, figure out what they're all about and jump back in the game again. They need to do it on the fly. When they discover that they need jobs done certain ways, they're not allowed to hit reset and hire an entire new batch of employees. They need to develop the people they have, while also steering the ocean liner in a new direction. Questions arise. Will values stick? Can you teach old dogs new tricks? Will new employees be more influenced by the new approach or the old ways of doing things? Can you get all your managers on board, or will they secretly resist?

As pressure points go, the manager is key. The manager is most directly responsible for the individual employee's performance. An organization can say whatever it wants about the importance of values, but if those values aren't modeled by the manager, few employers are going to adopt those values. Rather, the employee's instinct for survival and the desire to please the single most influential force in his or her career will inevitably pressure the employee to do as the manager does, not as the organization says. But if a manager is on board, then he or she will view well-articulated values, carefully linked to job behaviors and integrated in a people system that supports the organization's goals in the areas of productivity, quality, customer service and safety as a godsend. Managers, in my experience, are desperate and grateful to get support for doing their most distasteful jobs. Above everything else, managers find four critical tasks difficult to do right:

- Hiring new employees.
- Conducting performance reviews.
- Disciplining employees or giving them bad news about performance.
- Firing.

They dislike those responsibilities because they lack the tools or system for analyzing situations, making the right decisions and conveying the information in a way that it can be received. Without support, those discussions are often based on subjective interpretations of events the manager may not even have witnessed. Moreover, the outcomes of the discussions vary greatly, depending on the personalities involved.

Values are the fulcrum that gives managers the leverage to hire the right people, assess their performance and guide their development in accordance with what the organization stands for and what it aims to do. But how do you use something as intangible and idealistic as a value in making concrete managerial decisions that affect the ability of the organization to meet its strategic goals? In this chapter we'll look at turning values into meaningful tools.

The Fundamentals of Defining Performance

What does performance on the job really mean? Peter Drucker once said, "We know how to identify specific physical traits which render an individual more or less likely to perform a specific manual activity like laying bricks ... We know nothing, however, about configurations of character, personality and talent such as come into play in knowledge work, especially work as a manager (it could even be argued), that in the case of rote physical labor, job performance is a complicated mix of motives and values, skills and abilities applied to a task." So how do we talk about performance in a precise or meaningful way?

By dictionary definition, performance is:

1. The manner in which somebody functions, operates or behaves.
2. The effectiveness of the way somebody does his or her job.
3. The actions taken in order to achieve a task or specific result.

Notice that the first definition talks about how a task is done, or the behaviors involved. The second definition focuses on how well that job is done. And the third definition focuses on the outputs of the task. In those three definitions, we have all of the elements and contradictions inherent in the problem of assessing performance. Some managers and organizations consider only the outputs of performance — they want to examine sales, seat time, productivity or some other quantifiable measure. Some managers and organizations rank performance by measuring it against some other variable. But, in fact, it is how a job is done that is essential to examine when considering performance.

We call the "how of performance" behavioral competencies. A behavioral competency is the smallest unit of on-the-job action that is observable, measurable and capable of change over time when the correct consequences are in place. In other words, when we talk about behavioral competencies, we're focusing on activities that are both observable and teachable. Fifteen years ago it was tough selling decision makers on the link between on-the-job success and the right behaviors. The real concern, people felt, was business results. But as behavioral competencies became better understood, leaders came to see them as a chance to gain an edge through people.

LOOK INSIDE THE BOX

Behavioral competencies are one of the most misused tools within the corporate world. Not because they don't work but because they are not actually behavioral.

If a behavior is an action, then you need a verb and/or adverb in the statement. A commonly used competency is: "Open to innovative ideas."

The statement is too vague, enabling the manager and employee to come to two different interpretations. One might

Continued

say they are open because they listened to it, even discussed it at a meeting; but no action was taken. The other would say verbal support is not enough; providing time and money would display openness.

Also you can be open to many ideas but not supportive. As this statement stands, it is only an outcome of an action.

To state the behavioral competency you would:

- Ask questions about the innovative ideas of others to test the depth of their support for the idea.
- Provide time and resources when a new or different approach should be tried.
- Take the time to help others clarify why an effort was not successful.

Another example taken from an often used competency dictionary is: "can facilitate brainstorming." It leaves me thinking I can, but will I?

The problem is that the majority of companies have not been able to develop a behavioral competency system that really does the trick. Few organizations understand the need to link behaviors to organizational values and culture in order to really drive towards the business objectives. A good competency system can also cost a lot to develop in terms of time, money and resources. Too many organizations are eager to use off-the-shelf systems of competency terms and descriptions as an easy way out. This leads to language that is so generic that it obviously comes from someone outside the firm. The lack of homespun authenticity to the statements lowers credibility, even when those statements are actually good definitions. You can't take what has proven to be a sound behavioral statement at one company and successfully impose it on another. Competencies come from the historical roots of the organization and have to be aligned to the organization's culture.

So let's look at how to identify behaviors and write behavioral statements. Clearly defined behavioral statements support what is key to being successful in your organization. In order to come up with those criteria, I recommend that they be developed through detailed employee and key stakeholder input, and be based on a clear understanding of the organization's values. The best way to develop the behavioral profile of a specific job is to invoke a full-circle perspective of people who interact with someone in that role. This should include the person in the role itself, as well as peers, direct reports, internal customers, external customers, their direct supervisor/manager and human resources. Use the behaviors of top performers who demonstrate the right values as a guide. Don't focus on status quo performers or get dazzled by outcomes that weren't arrived at through the correct behaviors. The behaviors you decide on must be positive and realistic, truly valued by the organization and not just wishful thinking. By creating widespread understanding of the concrete language of success, you're developing a deep knowledge of what the organization needs to accomplish in a language that everyone can speak.

Getting that language right is one of the toughest aspects of the process. Behaviors describe what a person is doing. They can be observed, heard or experienced. Don't focus on outcomes — even though bottom-line thinkers believe that the results of a behavior are the most important aspect of performance. Outcome statements hint at behaviors, but they are so vague or general about how the work should be done as to be open to broad interpretation. When you talk about behaviors, always use an action verb such as *asks, applies, follows* or *creates*. Also, use concrete terms to describe what can be observed about someone doing a job. You can rely on simple language that is clear and understandable to convey that picture. Your statement should be free of qualifying words like *sometimes, always, never,* and you should avoid using negative terms. You should avoid compound statements that combine more than one behavior in a single statement. The key to creating a good behavioral statement is to discover some essential basic activity in the job that can be worked on to help employees achieve better results within the context of the company's norms and values. The statement also needs to be inherently ratable by others providing feedback. This is not an easy task; in fact, it takes a unique combination of art and science to do well.

LOOK INSIDE THE BOX

Creating a clear behavioral competency is about defining the specific actions or performance a person would have to take in order to do the right thing, in the right way, to achieve a result that is acceptable.

A common pitfall is using language that seems trendy but says little. Phrases like *business acumen, conceptual thinking,* and *learning on the fly* are usually accompanied by a general definition. However, that definition sheds little light on actions necessary to demonstrate the behaviors within the context of the organization's culture and business plan. For example, communication might be listed as a competency category, with a corresponding definition such as: "Adopts a win-win approach to negotiation, argues skillfully and uses a range of techniques to influence, persuade, or gain the support/co-operation of others." While this sounds good on paper, it doesn't describe how one acts in a way to consistently achieve excellence in communications in that particular organization. Here is an example of definitions for communication that do a better job:

Communication

- Fully shares with others across the organization the rationale behind a decision in order to ensure buy-in.
- Keeps direct supervisor informed of major information so there is a clear understanding of the current business circumstances.
- Asks questions to seek information.
- Listens carefully to understand before trying to be understood.
- Provides information to direct reports in a timely manner.

Once those behaviors are identified and turned into a collection of behavioral statements that describes a role, the resulting profile must be validated for clarity, language and content. Does it really depict the job accurately? Does it get at the heart of what distinguishes an adequate performer from a top performer? Does the behavioral profile lend itself to the future development of the person in the role? The number of competencies should be short — no more than five value statements common to everyone in the company, and no more than four or five additional competencies for the specific role or job function. You must also ensure that all behaviors described in the profile are aligned with the values and vision of the organization. And remember to use your organization's own language.

The following profile for an executive or senior management role at VanCity, a Vancouver-based financial services company, will help to make the above concrete. When VanCity developed that profile, it drew on behavioral competencies it believed to be essential to the success of current and potential people filling those roles. VanCity needed their people to drive change and lead the organization. VanCity also focused on behaviors that the organization believed would truly differentiate top performance. In other words, it didn't create an exhaustive list of all the skills required to be an executive; rather it created a subsection of behaviors that were particularly critical. VanCity believed that having an executive or senior manager demonstrate these behaviors would show their commitment to the organization's values and business plan.

The senior management group competencies are:

- Leadership/Strategic Thinking
- Communication
- Corporate Social Responsibility
- Continual Learning (self and others)
- Innovation/Creativity
- Relationship Management
- Teamwork
- Coaching and Feedback
- Self-confidence.

On their own, such a string of words doesn't tell us very much. They need to be broken down into the critical behaviors that make them meaningful. Let's look into how the executives at VanCity provide coaching and feedback.

Coaching and Feedback

- Uses a consistent and predictable approach (a set of guiding principles) when dealing with people; treats people fairly but not necessarily the same.
- Agrees upon clear success criteria (qualitative and quantitative) with direct reports, then steps back from the day-to-day decision making.

- Provides latitude for direct reports to reallocate priorities and resources as needed, all the while remaining available to assist where value would be added.
- Asks questions and discusses issues (rather than providing solutions) to ensure that direct reports maintain ownership and accountability.
- Uses everyday business interaction as practical opportunities to coach and guide colleagues.
- Expresses genuine appreciation for and rewards high performance and accomplishments, thus motivating others and building their sense of worth.
- Regularly gives honest and candid feedback to direct reports to let them know how they are doing.
- Deals promptly and honestly with poor performance, providing guidance and support while explaining what the consequences would be for continued poor performance.

Are these behaviors consistent with VanCity's values? On paper, I think they are. The company states its values as follows:

LOOK INSIDE THE BOX

Values of VanCity

- **Integrity** ... we act with courage, consistency and respect to do what is honest, fair and trustworthy.
- **Innovation** ... we anticipate and respond to challenges and changing needs with creativity, enthusiasm and determination.
- **Responsibility** ... we are accountable to our members, employees, colleagues and communities for the results of our decisions and actions.

The only people who can validate whether these values are actually being adhered to or not are the employees and customers of VanCity. As evident on its website, the organization has done a lot of work capturing the stories and legends that bring its values to light. The organization has also pledged to audit its values performance every two years through an external report. At the very least, if VanCity does not live up to its values, it will be possible for people to hold the organization accountable. They have stated what they are about clearly and openly, and put systems and processes into place to make it real.

An Integrated Talent Management System

How do you use values to get the right people on the bus? Every organization is interested in getting top performers, but if values are really important, how does one determine when the talent and culture fit provide a good mix? To better understand, let's consider the difference between someone who is merely capable in his or her role and someone who is actually competent in a behavioral sense.

LOOK INSIDE THE BOX

Differentiating between capable and competent

- You are capable within your company when you have the skills and knowledge to do a job (Technically proficient).
- You are competent when you are both capable and consistently perform the desired behaviors.
- You have integrity when you live the values of your company every day.
- You demonstrate high performance when you do all the above.

We all know people who are technically good at their job but still don't have what it takes to be an outstanding organizational contributor. It's not their fault; they just lack the right fit. Someone who is capable in his or her job has the skills and knowledge to do the job technically, but may or may not do the job in the right way (according to the norms of the company) or do the job consistently enough to be considered a top performer. This is one of the most difficult distinctions organizations need to make. Almost everything about the system of hiring, rewarding and firing employees in most organizations is oriented around technical ability. In fact, people are hired for their knowledge (or their technical ability), promoted for their innovation (or their ability to take their technical ability to another level) and fired for their personality (or how they demonstrate that personality through on-the-job behaviors). So, if we're just looking for technical capability, we might hire someone who could do the job; but the chance that the new hire will wow us through innovation is low, and the chance that he or she will disappoint us through behaviors that cut against the grain of the organization's values is higher than we'd like.

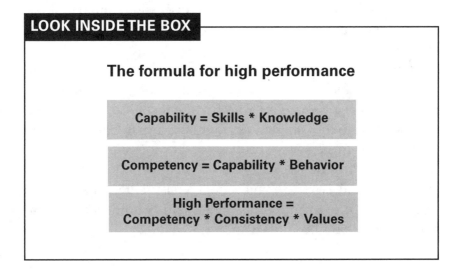

LOOK INSIDE THE BOX

The formula for high performance

Capability = Skills * Knowledge

Competency = Capability * Behavior

High Performance =
Competency * Consistency * Values

The three most important people activities for an organization are:

1. Hiring.
2. Performance management (which involves setting performance goals, providing feedback and coaching to support achieving those goals, and assessing progress).
3. Selecting who to further develop and promote.

We'll take a look at hiring and performance management in this chapter, and look at leadership development and succession planning in chapter five.

The important thing is that values stand at the hub of all of these talent management activities. Values become tools for talent management when we articulate them in terms of concrete behaviors. They are the basis for what you look for in new hires, and how you assess whether those people will fit your culture. They also become the basis for assessing whether someone's on-the-job performance meets organizational expectations, and whether they are top performers worthy of promotion. By using values as the key for all people-related discussions and decisions, you reinforce the values each time you hold conversations about the values.

When an employee lives the values of an organization everyday in every situation, we say that he or she is a good fit. A star employee is someone who has the technical ability or the capability to do the job, but also demonstrates the behaviors the organization prefers — its values — and does all of the above at every opportunity without exception. Superior performance, then, is defined as performance that is consistently displayed and aligned with the organization's values and that helps to achieve the organization's business plan.

Hiring to Fit

But how do you go about finding someone who fits? The answer is to define the job by developing a behavioral profile and then to conduct behavioral interviews to fill the role.

Creating an Integrated HR System

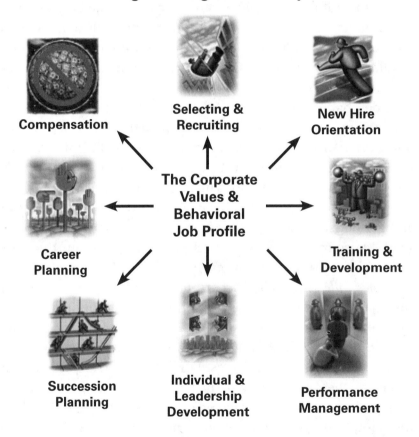

As anyone who has done traditional question-and-answer interviews knows, the process is woefully inadequate at predicting who should or shouldn't be selected for a job. Traditional interviews go something like this: the candidate arrives and shakes the interviewers' hands. If the candidate looks good, has a firm grip and makes the right joke about traffic, the weather, the parking lot or the big game last night, the interviewers know they've got their new hire. The rest is all theater. The interviewers ask leading questions that telegraph what they want the candidate to say. The candidate follows the script by providing those answers in his or her own words. If the interview goes into depth, the candidate's resume gets hauled out and the interviewers discuss the candidate's technical skills that apply to the position in question. They might even discuss some of the candidate's achievements and how they compare with the goals of the organization.

Does that sound extreme? Many managers talk about making gut decisions, and one of the areas in which they're most proud of doing this is the interviewing and hiring process. They just "know" when someone is a good fit. In fact, research shows that it only takes about ninety seconds for a manager to decide whether or not to hire someone. Are they right? People who believe in instinctive and gut-decision making will argue with that such decisions are solid. Malcolm Gladwell writes very persuasively about the basis for making instinctive decisions in his book, *Blink: The Power of Thinking Without Thinking*. According to Gladwell, human beings who make snap decisions based on limited information do better than those who spend an inordinate amount of time collecting, assessing and weighing large amounts of data. I don't have the expertise to judge all decisions, but I strongly disagree when it comes to the area of hiring. In fact, the traditional interview only gives you a one-in-five chance of making the right decision. Behavioral interviews, on the other hand, give you a 70 percent chance.

Why is that the case? No matter how insightful or probing the manager is trying to be, a typical traditional interview provides very little structure to collect the data needed to make a sound analytical decision. Instead, the manager relies on his or her nearly instantaneous impression. Of course, we think we are relying on data, but let's consider the sources. The traditional approach to hiring relies on the job description, the resume and the interview itself. There are big holes in each of these areas.

The traditional job description is a weak place to start since it tends to focus on the technical requirements of the position. As I've mentioned, although we may hire people for their technical knowledge, we usually end up firing them for their personality and lack of fit with the organization. Firing represents a failure of hiring and performance management as much as inadequacy of employee performance. If a person fits an organization's culture and demonstrates the behaviors that lead to success in that culture, there should be no reason to fire that employee. In fact, every time you hire or fire someone, you send a message to the rest of the people in your organization as to who is valued and why.

Few details uncovered by thinking about the job description actually get at the attitudes, approaches and behaviors that are essential for success. In fact, focusing on years of training and education and other technical credentials can eliminate candidates who might exhibit everything you really want in a candidate; they can learn the technical skills you need them to know once they are on the job. Meanwhile, the job description provides a road map for the candidate who wants to tailor his or her resume to the needs of the position. The smart candidate uses that map to highlight or mask his or her technical credentials. Not to be cynical, but outright lies about technical abilities, years of experience and educational credentials are far more common than you would think. Imagine how much more unreliable a person's description of his or her own attitudes and personal beliefs can be when that person is trying to impress you by matching his or her education and life experience to the job posting.

During the interview, we spend an inordinate amount of time going over the concrete details of credentials, accomplishments and experiences, even though those facts are written in black and white on the resume before us. We also try to probe attitudes, motivations and goals, but we have no system or sound basis for how we ask about those things. We tend to ask our questions and get our answers from hypothetical situations. Again, this provides more of a test of how someone interviews than how he or she will perform on the job.

Behavioral questions, on the other hand, provide high-yield information. Behavioral interviews are based on the idea that, as Lord Byron once put it, "The best prophet of the future is the past." In other words, what we have done in work (or related) circumstances in the past is the best indication of what we will do again in the future. Think about it this way. Over time, our values dictate how we will act more consistently than any other force such as pleasing a boss, responding to circumstances or trying to live up to guidelines. This is because our values are strongly held beliefs that are emotionally charged and highly resistant to change. We hold them truly and deeply because they mean something; they really matter to us. Naturally, this influences how we behave. Behaviors are the expression of our values.

LOOK INSIDE THE BOX

Behavioral questions help the interviewer to find out if the person has the correct behaviors to match the company values.

Traditional Questions:

What are your strengths and weaknesses?

If you were in a situation and had to choose between A or B, what would you do?

Behavioral Questions:

Tell me about a time when you feared you could not get the project completed on time.

Tell me about a time when you had to choose between quality or quantity.

In order to properly conduct a behavioral job interview, we need to understand what values are important for our organization. We also need to have determined what behaviors (or expressions of the values) are done on the job by top performers. We then need to turn those behaviors into questions that will elicit information that tells us whether job candidates will act the way we need them too on the job. For example, to find out whether a candidate has the same values about customer service as we need, we first must determine how those values are manifested on the job, create questions that relate to the information we need and ask the candidate to tell concrete stories about how he or she provided customer service. Through further questions, we can develop a picture of how consistently and frequently the candidate exhibits such behavior. From that behavioral information, we can analyze whether the candidate has the right values fit with our organization — as well as the right skills and knowledge.

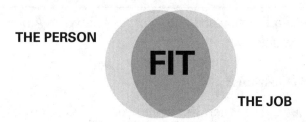

THE PERSON

FIT

THE JOB

The best fit occurs when a person's capabilities — his or her skills, knowledge and behaviors — match the requirements of the job and the culture of the organization. Interviews that only determine whether someone has the skills and knowledge needed are hit or miss when it comes to hiring someone who will really have a positive impact on the organization. When the fit is solid, there is a much better chance that the candidate will provide outstanding service to the organization and receive strong job satisfaction in return. A good cultural fit, who also performs well, is someone who will thrive inside an organization that is clear about its values, maximizing both the return on the organization's investment and the individual's long-term commitment to the organization. (For detailed information about the process of developing and conducting behavioral interviews, please see my book, *The Talent Edge: A Behavioral Approach to Hiring, Developing, and Keeping Top Performers.*)

The Performance Management Blueprint

Performance reviews are like the spring cleaning of the managerial world. Everyone knows it needs to be done, but no one wants to do it. Most managers assess performance based on the last complaint they had about the employee within the last four to six weeks. In other words, they haven't kept track of how their report has performed or developed since the last performance review.

Performance appraisals don't equal performance management. Performance management is an ongoing series of conversations that enable open and frank discussion between manager and employee. These discussions are based on actual events from situations in which the direct report has direct knowledge. Most often the manager is in the dark as to how his or her direct report actually acted in any given situation, because how much of the manager's time is spent with the direct reports, when the direct reports are doing their job? In reality the manager is holding a conversation about performance which that he or she did not observe first-hand. No wonder people chuckle when I say most performance reviews are based on the most recent information the manager has from someone else. It seems they focus on the negative when they hear things about direct reports.

A performance review is the end-of-the-year stage of the performance management cycle. That cycle starts with setting out expectations and goals, followed by frequent conversations in which both parties assess how those goals are being met and what development work is needed to achieve the business goals. The performance review is just a meaningful summation of all the work that has gone on during the course of the year. It takes into account the business objectives, or numbers aspect, of the job and the development plan, or the path whereby the employee grows in ability to attain those numbers. In some companies, performance management is a series of missed appointments and avoided discussions. Development plans are a random assortment of trendy workshops or skill-building courses on which the employee or manager is keen. The actual performance review ends up being a trade-off between excuses and blame.

Objectivity is Possible

One of the most difficult things a manager can do is be objective about a direct report's on-the-job performance and prove that objectivity while teaching, guiding, rewarding or disciplining that person. In the same way, it is very difficult for an employee to be objective about his or her own performance. Behavioral competencies based on organizational values create the important factual basis for solid performance assessments. This greatly clarifies how employees are rewarded and recognized in the organization, and that transparency, in turn, increases the degree of perceived fairness for all people decisions. It ensures that all employees get measured by the same transparent and widely understood criteria, regardless of a manager's biases.

Defining behavioral competencies enables us to know in concrete terms what successful performance looks like. For employees this provides a blueprint for success. A person seeking a promotion, alternative job or a completely different role than the one they currently have only has to find the behavioral competency model for the role they are seeking to attain and begin a gap analysis between the behaviors they currently demonstrate with regularity to the behavioral competencies of the role they seek to fill. Giving self-motivated employees the means to be their own career planners in line with the organization's vision is a tremendous asset. Well-defined behavioral competencies encourage people to take charge of their jobs and their careers by making decisions and behaving in ways consistent with the organization's values and what it believes is important. Every employee wants to know what it takes to be successful, just as every manager wants a language and set of measurements to provide that kind of guidance and assess how well people are living up to it.

The Process

In the real world, there are complications, however. It can be difficult for a manager to assess whether an employee is using the right behaviors consistently and frequently, particularly when the manager may not even be present when the direct report carries out his or her job. So how can a manager make those kinds of judgments?

Step One: At the very start of the year, the manager and all the direct reports need to have a conversation about the way people in their group and the company, in general, demonstrate the values. This meeting serves notice to both sides that they have a mutual understanding of the behavior of the values and the job behavioral competencies. This meeting also helps to ensure that the manager and his or her direct reports see things from the same perspective. This meeting, if conducted annually, will help calibrate the understanding between all parties.

During this group meeting, the manager needs to set consistent expectations and tell his or her report exactly what he or she needs to do to be successful. It helps to explain the organization's vision and strategic plan while discussing how the employee can contribute to that meaningfully. Holding the conversation at the start of the performance cycle allows the manager to say, "This is what success will look like twelve months from now." This takes the guesswork out of expectations.

Step Two: When the manager and direct report meet to set the individual objectives, they also fine-tune which of the behavioral competencies will be the specific ones to ensure success. The purpose of this meeting is to enable the direct report to set the development plan without being told by the manager what the plan should be. The engagement or commitment of the employee will have a better quality and chance of success if the direct report is making choices, not being told what the objectives and the development plan are for them. At the end of this meeting, the direct report now has the capability to share with the manager when he or she believes they have been successful in achieving the results while demonstrating the correct behaviors.

Step Three: When discussing the progress during the year with the direct report, the manager uses the same techniques as in the behavioral interview. Getting the employee to discuss the concrete details of the actions they perceive they have taken on the job provides the manager an understanding of how the direct report thinks they are acting out the required job behaviors. By using behavioral questions and following up with additional probing questions the manager builds a clear understanding of how the employee perceives they are doing on the job. This then affords a starting point for the next step, based on the direct report's definition of his or her reality.

Step Four: Once equipped with the employee's perception of how he or she worked in a particular situation, the manager can also ask others who were directly involved in those circumstances with the employee to ensure that they perceived the same behaviors. This is not intrusive or even difficult to do when the behaviors are known. They're very self-evident, even when seen through the eyes of others. Yet, by using open-ended and behavioral questions, the manager is not asking the other person to pass judgment; he is only asking the employee to share the story of the interaction as he or she perceived it. This helps the manager maintain objectivity and clarity, thus avoiding the issues of likes and dislikes.

Step Five: Now the manager can close the loop by providing the employee with meaningful, first-hand knowledge of how the person performs on the job. In turn, the manager can positively reinforce the correct behavior with acknowledgement of it. On the other hand, if the direct report's perception of the employee's behaviors is at odds with other people's, the manager can probe as to why that difference exists. Remember that behavior is a function of consequences. If that is true, there are positive and negative consequences. When the behaviors of the values are correctly demonstrated, you need to point that out to the person. When the person receives positive feedback, he or she will seek additional positive feedback by making greater effort to do the right things. In fact, I would suggest, that without too much attention to the inappropriate behaviors, the negative behavior will be reduced or eliminated.

One of the obstacles to providing feedback is the manager might believe that the employee will be resentful. As the manager you may also believe that the direct reports might not like you. The manager also fears that if he or she tells the truth that the employee will become defensive. None of this need occur. Following this outline, the manager has never passed judgment. You have put the employee in a position of making his or her own decisions on how the performance review at year end will read.

You let the employee understand what has to be done and demonstrated along the way to meet expectations. You gave them permission to provide you with knowledge of situations and how they understand they acted in the situations. By doing so, they also provided the manager with meaningful information for positive feedback or corrective assistance. In the end, they become the masters of their own destiny. It reminds me of when I taught grades seven and eight. I always would capture the class's attention when I announced they all were starting with an "A." Many never saw an "A" on a report in their lives. I would lay out the expectations and get them to tell me what they needed to do to meet those expectations. At the end of the discussion, I told them that if they ended up getting a grade lower than an "A," that would be their decision, not mine. It works for students and it works for adults in the workplace.

Such performance discussions need to take place at least once every couple of months in order to really reinforce the right behaviors and support the employee in attempting to use those behaviors on the job. When I tell managers that, their most common refrain is, "We don't have time to do all this." I've often been tempted to ask in return: "If you don't want people to be successful, then why are you managing them?" No one has enough time to do everything they need to do, and managers are no exception. But is there a more critical activity for a manager than providing supportive feedback? If for no other reason than personal survival, consider the vicious cycle. Yes, you may dread providing frequent follow-up on development goals and performance management, but as a manager you are only as successful as your direct reports.

You need to give feedback on a continual basis, not just in negative situations. Progress must be measured along the way so that people have time to adjust their behavior before the end of the performance cycle. Creating a supportive environment where people know what they need to do to be successful builds momentum towards the business objectives. At the end of the period, both the manager and the direct report share the same understanding of performance and the same interpretation of events, both positive and negative.

Increasing the manager's role in creating and assessing expectations actually helps to change the paradigm of performance management, moving it from the manager's burden to the employee's responsibility. By sharing in advance what is expected of the employee and providing clear positive and negative consequences for doing or not doing the behaviors, the manager is telling employees the choice is theirs. As a result, opportunities to provide positive feedback for the right behaviors become a routine conversation. Learning theory teaches us that when you provide positive feedback, people actively seek out more of it. We also know that when you discuss something with someone, you are drawing their attention to what is important to you. Managers also have the option of providing feedback when they observe employees doing the wrong thing, but this is not always as effective. By finding employees doing the right behaviors at the right time and sharing your observations of their improvements, you can often get employees to self-correct their less desirable actions. If they do not, at least the manager will have observed positive and negative actions closely and provided feedback on them from a position of objective assessment.

In this way, managers let employees know they are reaching out to them to make them successful. This establishes a positive cycle of performance improvement. The end result is that the person, the manager and, ultimately, the company all move towards achieving the strategic business plan with less pain.

Assessing Values Fairly

The cry from employees is: how can the behaviors of the values be fairly and objectively assessed. Can you objectively measure something that is based on perception? Most organizations have tried to address this issue by providing employees with a continuum ranging from inappropriate to exemplary behaviors for the role or position. This typically creates a five-point scale with the highest rating labeled, "Exceeds expectations." The idea that someone can exceed expectations, however, perpetuates the belief that what's important is how well you do the behavior, not how frequently you demonstrate it. It is only when the opportunities occur to live the values that the person must, without exception or excuse, live the values. Anything less would not be meeting expectations. As a result for values and for behavioral competencies, we send an inappropriate message via the scale because you cannot exceed what you are supposed to do whenever the opportunity presents itself.

But how do you really know whether an employee has mastered a behavior? It's not when an employee's results are outstanding, but when an employee shows total consistency in using the right behaviors all the time. The right behavior is not something an employee selectively demonstrates depending on the time, location and people involved. Rather, only when a person uses that behavior in every situation — when it has become second nature — can he or she be said to be meeting expectations. The employee's ability to perform the behavior is not the most important thing; more important is his or her ability to do it well all the time. Many years ago the vice president of operations for a major grocery chain said he learned from his first manager when he began in the business cutting meat that "you can only expect that which you are willing to inspect." If you discuss the behaviors and values associated with them at the setting of the objectives, the mid-year point and the end of the performance cycle, you can be assured that the individual is not likely to change his or her behavior. If you follow up frequently, you will realize positive changes that will impact the business results.

Consistency is king. You measure performance by comparing the frequency of the opportunity to demonstrate the right behavior against the times that the behavior is actually demonstrated. The only way for a manager to know when a direct report feels they have done the correct action is through conversations initiated by the direct report. I suggest a simple four-point scale, allowing the manager to simply tick off the appropriate box. Please note that the definitions are not based on how well the person does the behavior but by the frequency the behavior is done when required:

LOOK INSIDE THE BOX

Exceptional Performance	Based on the definition of business and work objectives at the start of the performance review cycle, the individual has achieved results that exceed expectations as defined at the start of the year. This person requires no guidance and, in fact, finds time on his or her own to help others be successful.
Meets Expectations	Based on the definition of strategic business objectives and work objectives at the start of the performance review cycle, the individual has met the range of performance that falls within meeting his or her commitments. This person applies a high standard of skills, knowledge and behavior in almost all situations. On occasion, this person will provide coaching or training support for peers.
Satisfactory/ Needs Development	In areas identified for development (skills, knowledge or behaviors) this employee has made some progress, yet there is room for further development. This person has met the minimum commitments, but requires occasional support or direction. Alternatively, this person is too new to the company or to the particular job to determine his or her capability in the job fairly.
Unsatisfactory	While this person is meeting the basic requirements in some activities, the consistency of the application of the skills, knowledge and/or behavior is in need of immediate attention. The employee's performance is below standard, and he or she did not reach the commitments made at the start of the year. This lack of results is due to poor performance, not lack of training or experience. This person requires constant support or supervision.

Values should be rated differently than behavioral competencies. The best and most accurate scale for numerically measuring the demonstration of values is, in fact, a two-point scale. An employee either demonstrates his or her commitment to the value all the time, or doesn't. He or she either does the right thing when called upon to do it or doesn't. Since the values are the DNA of the corporate culture, some might suggest that the feedback on them is yes or no; a two-point scale. I believe that would be correct. However, even with the values you will find that some people will sometimes find it difficult, in certain situations or with particular people, to live up to them. Consequently I would suggest that the values be rated on a three-point scale: don't demonstrate them when they should, demonstrate them but with inconsistency, or demonstrated them without exception. Further I would suggest that even if the person were to exceed all their business and job targets but fall short on the values, he or she should not make bonus or at best only a percentage of bonus.

In general, whether values or behavioral competencies are involved, if the employee doesn't demonstrate the behavior or value consistently, then the manager needs to coach, lead and teach the employee to become more comfortable with the behavior. Again, positive reinforcement is key. People respond more to positive feedback than to negative. If a boss is always finding fault, the employee will start to flinch. If the boss is always encouraging and clear about how to do better, the employee generally wants to learn how to do more and better to receive more positive feedback.

I'm not suggesting that a manager can never let employees know that they are demonstrating the wrong behaviors. However, such feedback needs to be offered to the employee using detailed behavioral terms. If a manager is going to tell employees that they are not team players, or that their communication style is lacking, he or she must provide concrete examples. As a manager, you need to explain your perceptions of employees' behaviors and the impact of those behaviors on the organization.

Further, you must suggest concrete ways that they can change their behaviors so that they will do better next time. No boss, no matter how forceful, can tell an adult to do something and expect wholesale buy-in. An effective manager lets employees know that all behaviors have consequences, whether positive or negative. In the end, this makes employees accountable for their own actions. If they choose to the do the right thing, they choose to become better performers. If they choose not to do the right thing, they choose to lose their job.

LOOK INSIDE THE BOX

Using 360° feedback in a meaningful way:

1. Tailored to the behavioral statements of the values of the firm.
2. Used for employee development only.
3. Controlled by the employee meaning the employee determines who provides the feedback and who sees the feedback.
4. Accountability of the employee to clearly state one but not more then two development plans that are linked directly to achieving the business results.
5. Accountability of the manager to provide support and feedback to the employee.
6. Get the direct reports engaged in a conversation on how to improve demonstrating the desired behaviors more frequently.
7. On-going conversations between the employee and his or her direct reports on how the employee is doing in demonstrating the right behavior at the right time to the right people.
8. Follow-up with both the manager and with the direct reports for suggestions.

In the real world, however, a manager is not always present when the behaviors are being demonstrated. We have come to realize that this process of multi-source feedback only works effectively when the feedback receiver (employee) controls the process. In the end, the report is not anything more then a catalyst to behavior change. As a result when the employee is the first and only person to see the feedback, the opportunity of the feedback providers to be more direct and honest is increased significantly. The employee can choose to share the report but that should be the employee's choice, not the company's or the manager's.

So how can a manager prove that objectives were achieved using the right actions? What evidence is the manager using? Multi-source assessments have proven under certain circumstances to be very accurate and powerful tools for getting the message to employees about how others see them, but they are not effective when used directly for performance reviews or succession planning. An executive at a company where we gave a 360-degree feedback once referred to the process as "weeping in the woods." He explained that at an executive off-site retreat, a facilitator once gave each of the executives the results of his feedback in a sealed envelope and then told them to find a quiet outdoor place in the resort to review it. The news was so devastating for everyone involved that they later referred to the experience as "weeping in the woods."

Feedback as to how a person is perceived by others can be a gift, but there are certain guidelines that need to be in place. First, the person who receives the feedback, that is, the employee, should feel control over the process. The feedback receiver must be the one who selects the feedback providers. In some cases this is academic. We can't select our own boss, for example, and our peers and direct reports are also limited. The only real choice might be which customers, suppliers, etc., are selected and which are not. Another aspect of control is who gets to see the final report. If the manager is allowed to see the report, then when it actually does come time for a performance review, it's a little like telling the jury to ignore the previous evidence of guilt or innocence. Feedback providers who know that the boss will see the results will deliberately refrain from providing damaging criticism and will often inflate their positive opinions rather than tell the subject what he or she really needs to hear. Similarly, when the multi-source assessment process is used for rewards and promotions, the results are also inherently biased.

The second major concern is that the feedback providers must feel safe in the knowledge that the process is anonymous and confidential. Once, when I was involved in providing feedback to a group, the rules suddenly changed. Initially, anonymity and confidentiality were respected. The feedback receiver was meant to share the learning as desired in order to develop an action plan to modify a select few behaviors for more consistency and better business results. Then the corporate office introduced the idea of showing the feedback to the manager and human resources in order to feed the succession planning process with good candidates. Over night, feedback changed to reflect the new stakes. It was no longer about helping the individual develop — careers were on the line.

Human Resource professionals frequently debate all of the activities discussed above. Many of them would suggest that to add the values to the process and to make it that you can not exceed expectation around behaviors would further complicate the reality of contact between supervisor and direct report. These human resources people might suggest that managers need to control things to "manage." The paradigm of control has not worked for most people in most situations. Let's take a look at two situations in two major organizations where the above process has taken hold. Where in previous years most employees would exceed expectation and after implementing the above process those same employees are engaged and committed as they now understand doing a good job is meeting expectations when it comes to behavior around the values.

Creating a Legacy of Values

Boehringer Ingelheim is a global pharmaceutical research business. The parent company in Germany remains a family-owned business. In 2003, I worked with the Canadian subsidiary, Boehringer Ingelheim Canada Ltd., when the company wanted to develop a performance management system based on its values. It proved to be an opportunity to make values a living reality that affected the way work was done in the organization, supporting and reinforcing the culture and vision at the same time.

Ten years before, Boehringer, the parent company, had launched its values with much fanfare. While it was very successful in capturing what was unique about the organization, there was a feeling among the rank-and-file employees in Canada that the statements were too detailed, lengthy and complicated. They needed to be simplified and brought down to the local level, using everyday language in order to articulate the values statements in a meaningful way to the employees. Ruta Stauskas, the vice president of human resources, began the conversation with the executive committee by focusing on how the values could be used in a performance management system. She asked the committee to consider the importance of that system as a means of identifying the fundamental things the organization needed from employees day in and day out. Laying those concerns onto a foundation of clearly expressed values seemed like a good idea to everyone on the diverse management team, even the president who was by inclination a numbers-oriented leader.

Stauskas and the executive group spent considerable time coming up with a short and simple list of four fundamental values.

LOOK INSIDE THE BOX

Values of Boehringer Ingelheim (BI)

Caring for People

1. Supports fellow employees and their families through thick and thin.
2. Asks people who they are, not only what they do.
3. Provides others with positive feedback about things that they have accomplished, both within the business and in their personal lives.
4. Takes the time to assist others in their efforts to help them develop beyond their current capabilities.

Respect

1. Treats others the way in which they themselves would like to be treated.
2. Listens openly to others' points of view that may be different from his or her own.
3. Judges each person only on their demonstrated capabilities (skills/knowledge/behavior).
4. Puts in the effort and time necessary to keep a promise.
5. Gives praise to others in a manner the other person appreciates.

Honesty

1. Takes the initiative to promptly admit to his or her own mistakes directly to those impacted.
2. Has courage to provide direct feedback in private about behaviors that are contrary to BI values.
3. Shares with other employees all information they need.
4. Takes responsibility for his or her own actions, accepting both positive and negative consequences.

Continued

Trust

1. Keeps full confidence of others as requested.
2. Supports, both privately and publicly, the final decision following a full explanation or discussion.
3. Discusses with others the agreed-upon objectives with full disclosure of expectations.
4. Seeks out understanding from multiple areas of BI to ensure that the objectives contribute to the strategic plan and values.

The values felt true to the company, which was still very much rooted in its family-owned tradition as a place where caring, respect, honesty and trust were the critical means by which results needed to be achieved. As a result the values and job specific behavioral competencies were integrated into the performance management process.

Stauskas then led the initiative to apply these values to a variety of human resources initiatives, including a performance management system. The BI process focuses on four dimensions during the performance management cycle. At the beginning of the cycle, the manager and the direct report clarify the expectations of what is to be accomplished and how that needs to be done. Throughout the cycle, there are frequent discussions on how those expectations and results are being met. In addition, the manager is charged with identifying and providing support to help employees achieve results and to help them further their development. Finally, at the end of the performance management cycle the manager provides a performance report that assesses the individual's work throughout the year. When this report comes out, there should be no surprises — manager and employee have been in frequent conversation to assess progress and figure out what kind of support is needed to achieve the goals. Employees' performance is ultimately judged not only on the results they achieve, but on how they have achieved them in keeping with BI's values.

Putting the values in place as performance measures generated enthusiastic responses from the rank and file. As Stauskas puts it, "People like the values because they feel that they are attributes they bring to the workplace everyday, and that being acknowledged for that in the performance review is a good thing." The problem before the performance management system got upgraded was that performance assessment and reviews were vague and unspecific. By sectioning off each value, competency and job skill in the review process, there was a greater likelihood that managers and reports would talk about specific areas the report could focus on for development. Previously, managers tended to give open-ended performance appraisals without having clearly targeted objectives. Without clearly delineated objectives managers would be able to "adjust" evaluation as they saw fit to give the rating they wanted to give the employee. The new form forced a conversation where managers acknowledged areas that were a strength for the employee and areas that needed work. Employees, in turn, truly wanted to hear about the areas they needed to work on developing. Such specificity and clarity helps focus on very targeted areas.

The values became embedded in the ongoing performance process and began to show up in the course of everyday issues. People began to understand that the organization is not looking for results at all costs. "They've come to understand that if we follow the values," Stauskas notes, "the results could even be potentially better." They understand, also, that behaviors have consequences and that those employees who violate the values will be called out for such actions. In meetings where touchy issues have come up, someone will put the brakes on to do a values check. According to Stauskas, "They'll say, 'Wait a minute, what do our values tell us here?' And everyone else around the table will know what the right answer should be, making the decision much easier."

It helps that the president of the firm has embraced the values so openly and consistently. "He just lives by them, talks about them openly, uses every opportunity to remind people that they are fundamental. He assures people that they can make mistakes in their job and can expect support for improving their performance in the future, but violation of the values will not be tolerated." It also helps that the values developed locally in Canada turned out to be consistent with those of the global organization, a major concern when the process was initiated. The board members of the parent company have been impressed with the fit of the values and the simplicity with which they were expressed.

But it takes real events and stories to validate whether values are truly alive within the organization. Stauskas notes a demonstration of the value concerning caring for people. "Caring for people is a Boehringer Ingelheim worldwide trait. As a family-run business, the parent group is a very caring company. They always have been and always will be. But we needed to define caring and make it more open, more universal to the company, not something you just do with someone you're close to, but with everybody." Specific programs also helped support the value and make it real. C.A.R.E. is the name of the company's "absence management program." It brings tools, requirements and ongoing touch points between manager and report when an employee is out sick for an extended time. "We all know, unfortunately, that the longer a person is off work or disabled, the less likely they will come back after recovery. Providing that feeling of 'we need you' and figuring the best way to accommodate you to get you back was fundamental to our value," says Stauskas.

Stauskas tells a very touching story of how this played out with one employee. "There is one example in particular where the company had an employee who became ill with cancer. The individual showed such strength that it was incredible. During the very difficult treatment process, the individual had the wish and the will and the desire to continue to work even though she was seriously ill. It would have been very easy to adopt the attitude that 'We know you are ill, it's okay, you can stay off work, that's what disability is for,' but everybody knew that the sick employee really needed to keep busy — that was part of her emotional need to stay on top of the disease."

For a company where caring was a supported value, helping her manage her illness through work wasn't even a question. "You could see the company rally behind her, doing whatever we could to give her the work she needed and letting her have the time off when she needed that. When she finally did succumb to the cancer, it was very difficult for the company because we all got to know her better. People are still amazed at how much she did in her last couple years during her illness and how much the company was there for her." A year after her death, a group of women joined a breast cancer run in her memory, a legacy of the meaning behind caring.

Those are the kinds of corporate legends that give a corporation heart and soul, and provide meaning and support for the people who commit their lives and best efforts to them.

The Manager is Responsible

Human Resources is not responsible for the organization's values — the managers are. Although situated at the hub of the talent management wheel, HR is a partner in hiring, performance management, firing and so on, but values are in the domain of the manager. After all, who do employees look to when it comes to confirming or modeling how to be successful in the organization? Their manager. The impact of this can be observed in the implicit rule of the employment contract. Despite everything we've learned about organizational fit, people don't leave organizations; they leave managers. They leave good organizations because of bad managers, just as they often stay at bad organizations because they feel personal loyalty, commitment and support for their manager. The truth is, a good manager can provide a supportive environment for meaningful work even in bad circumstances. A manager is the face of the organization's values — or the embodiment of its hidden curriculum.

Once values are articulated and set, the management team becomes the passionate champion, defender and auditor of those values. Using values allows managers to do it right. Instead of giving performance reviews on subjective issues, managers can use concrete value-based behaviors as the basis for having a meaningful discussion about performance, development, goals and expectations.

If everyone in management understands values in the same way, they all measure knowledge, skills and abilities correctly. When values are not clear, the organization hires wrongly, develops wrongly and promotes wrongly. For an employee to be recognized, rewarded or promoted, values and the right behaviors need to be demonstrated consistently, not just once.

Money doesn't motivate a workforce. Culture, a sense of belonging and the chance to grow through the job are what really matter. People hunger for job satisfaction. If they are treated like adults, they act like adults, taking responsibility for their jobs and performance improvement like CEOs. Such an environment is not built through an autocratic management culture or a hands-off approach. People need limits, support systems, accountability and confidence to thrive. They have a hierarchy of needs ranging from security, certainty of expectations, consistency, structure, sense of belonging, respect and a standard of top performance. Only by meeting these conditions can an organization create an environment in which people are capable of giving and becoming their best.

Your Employee Brand

One of the great myths of employment is that compensation matters more than anything else. In reality, as long as people receive pay that they consider fair, they are content with the money. We all want to work in a place that feels right — one that is a fit for our values and provides us with a sense of community, meaning and purpose. How, then, do you attract prospective employees to your organization when values-fit, not money, is the deciding factor? You do it by projecting your employee brand.

In the marketing sense, brand is the face you present to the world, the promise of a particular kind of experience. A winning employee value proposition arises by tailoring a company's brand to its products and the jobs it has to offer to appeal to the specific people it wants to find and keep. It also means paying whatever it takes to attract and retain strong performers.

An employee brand requires an appealing culture and inspiring values — qualities that apply to every activity and function within the company. When interviewing candidates from the outside, you learn to sell them on joining the firm based on your employee brand.

Employee engagement is actually the other side of the same issue. When you measure employees' commitment and engagement, are you actually asking them if they are working in a place where they have a clear view of the company's vision and believe they are being treated according to the values you promised at hiring and orientation? If you are, then your employees are engaged. If not, they are disengaged.

Being an "employer of choice" means you treat your employees the way they want to be treated. Your employees will stay or leave based on those values and the way their direct supervisor lives them. Do you know what those values are? Do you use them as your guide in all business decisions? Do you hire and fire based on those values? Are your values part of your review process? Are they measured and celebrated in the performance management process? Are they clear — defined behaviorally — so that everyone has a consistent understanding of what they mean on the job?

Have the courage to ask your employees whether your efforts at becoming an employer of choice are meaningful or not. If you are imposing values that don't fit, or are not living up to them, they'll let you know. If you're having a retention problem, analyze who is leaving and why. Where is the breakdown in values occurring? Is there a virus in the organization? Do what is right according to your passionately lived values, and you will authentically express your employee brand.

LOOK INSIDE THE BOX

Meaningful conversations. Getting information from others is about asking the right questions.

Step 1:   Share with us one of the times you or one of your co-workers lived the values or missed an opportunity to live the values.

Step 2:   Tell me how working with these specific behavioral competencies will ensure your business success.

What are the situations you might be in when the values might be challenged?

Step 3: Describe for me a recent time in the last month when you believe you demonstrated the behavior you chose for development. How has making the behavior improvement impacted your ability to get the job done correctly? What was the situation and who was involved with you at the time?

Step 4: When meeting with someone who was involved in the particular situation the employee described, you can simply say to the person: Take me through your perception of what happened at that particular time and place. If there is no reference to the direct report, ask specifically for what they remember was their involvement.

Step 5: Meeting again with the direct report the conversation can begin with: Congratulations on the continued efforts and improvement, keep it up. Or you can say: Remembering the situation you described tell me, if you were someone else in that meeting observing you, what would they say?

CHAPTER FIVE

Selecting Inside-the-Box Leaders

❏ There is no one and only correct definition of being a good leader.

❏ Values are the anchor for measuring fit between a leader and the firm.

❏ Values of a corporation don't change by simply changing the person at the top or changing the name on the door.

❏ Values can evolve over time.

❏ Don't confuse strategy with a culture shift or change in values.

❏ Followers will allow leaders to take them on a journey as long as there is trust.

❏ Take care of your people by living the values and your people will take care of the business.

In many ways, leadership is where the impact of clear values really comes into play. Leaders, after all, serve as role models for the organization, even as they steer it in new directions. Without consistent alignment between the values of the leader and the values of the firm confusion reigns. In this chapter, let's look at how leaders are typically developed to see why this is such a persistent problem for organizations.

When Warren Bennis wrote his classic treatise, *On Becoming a Leader,* he drew from the experiences of having interviewed and shadowed a number of famous leaders from a variety of walks of life for approximately three months. In his book, he said there is no one and only formula for defining leadership. Instead, it's a combination of factors that can be divided into five broad characteristics: vision, mobilization, communication, coping with change, and relationships.

Bennis affirmed that no particular leader has or should have all the characteristics in all the five components and all of their sub-components. He also implied that characteristics that are right for some leaders might be wrong for others. In other words, leadership is a many splendored thing, grown from the personal experiences of the leaders and inspired by the situations in which they find themselves. Because each leader's experience is individual, leadership is difficult for others to emulate.

While this was not exactly a rallying cry for mass-produced leadership development programs, consultants have still managed to capitalize on the swell of business interest in leadership by offering packaged approaches in saleable products. All those products purport to have the right answer for helping a corporation develop leaders for the twenty-first century. For a not insignificant extra fee, such consultants will come to your organization and customize their materials for you. They don't explain the disconnect between promising an approach that's universal and providing a solution that's site-specific. Instead, they make you believe they are doing something that's uniquely suited to your needs by fitting your experiences into a mold that's been predetermined as correct. Perhaps this is what Chris Argyris, author of *Flawed Advice and the Management Trap*, meant when he wrote:

> ... one of the biggest traps managers fall into is embracing the newest "Wow!" advice from brand-name gurus on how to build employee commitment. ... when they do, they lose credibility with the employees ...

How do they pull the wool over your eyes? First, if you're a potential client, they talk about the success of their "unique" leadership approach and present case studies of renowned companies that benefited from the work. Then they show you their tools and measurements — because everyone wants tools and measurements. If you show interest, they cite massive amounts of research and data indicating that the leadership characteristics they discovered are vital for success in the new millennium. If you sign on, they further support their argument by putting your people through a multi-source (360-degree) feedback process and showing the individuals who are tested how their specific scores match up to the massive amounts of normative data. Of course, you know what they say about statistics — they can be interpreted to prove anything you want.

A few years back, a world-renowned manufacturer brought a highly recognized and championed leadership program into its firm. The consultant convinced the executives that they needed leaders who were emotionally balanced and effective team players who communicated extensively and empowered employees by engaging them as partners in decision making. This would result in making everyone more passionate about the work and vision of the firm.

The program sounded good, if a little familiar. But the manufacturing company began its leadership program with great fanfare, putting managers through a four-day program that included feedback, action learning and team assignments. Everything seemed to be going well. The consultant unearthed anecdotal stories of how effective the training was and proved noticeable changes in behavior. Yet, despite these changes, people did not become more passionate about their work. Instead, turnover increased significantly.

The manufacturing company conducted a series of follow-up interviews to check on morale. It determined that while the new leadership behaviors were in fact resulting in their leaders demonstrating the desired new behaviors, employees weren't happy. One employee described the change as follows: "Before we had leaders who knew what had to be done. Now they are not making decisions. We don't really feel comfortable anymore." Managers, according to the normative indicators, were improving in their communication with staff, but to staff they were overcommunicating, searching for consensus instead of being decisive. The result? The new management style made everyone feel directionless.

While it may not sound politically correct, the employees of the firm wanted to be led, not empowered. The long-standing culture of the firm was to cut to the chase and be decisive. Leaders communicated only to the point where employees knew what they needed to make a great product and be successful. The new humanistic leadership approach was proving to be a mismatch with the old benevolent dictatorial leadership culture. Imposing a leadership style that was not aligned and consistent with the firm's culture actually caused leaders to lose credibility with employees. The result for employees was profound anxiety and discomfort with the company's operations and future direction — stress that had real bottom-line impact.

When the wool was finally pulled back from everyone's eyes, the manufacturer made a dictatorial decision. Without consulting any consultants, engaging any employees or over-communicating their thought processes, the directors of the firm decided to abandon the new way and return to the company's roots. Despite calls to launch the firm into the twenty-first century, success for this company required going "back to the future" — to the leadership behaviors that had been successful in sustaining a significant competitive advantage for the firm's products in the marketplace.

If there's a field of endeavor flooded with more trends and theories than leadership development, I have yet to encounter it. People are always eager to jump on the latest leadership development bandwagon in the hopes of reaching nirvana, but they end up seriously distracting their organizations if the program is not a good fit. Any change in the role of the manager and the employee, or even the language that gets used to discuss performance, disturbs the culture of the organization, making everyone confused about what's really important going forward compared to what used to be important in the past.

In this chapter, we're going to look at how to deliberately weave the development and selection of leaders into the cultural fabric of the organization. The key, as should be no surprise by now, is to focus on values alignment.

The Top Leader

The decisions an organization makes about leadership are among its most critical because nothing influences the culture, direction and operations of the firm like the people in charge. This is true throughout the management ranks, but the merit of leadership decisions are never so exposed as at the CEO level. To be a top corporate leader, you need strong technical abilities, but you are prized because of a combination of experience and soft skills. Top leaders are considered valuable when they can engage and motivate others through charisma and communication, provide a compelling vision and a competitive strategy that achieves results. There's growing recognition, however, that a top leader also needs to have values. The problem is, we confuse a leader's commitment to personal values with a leader's commitment to the organization's values. A leader can be morally dubious personally and still be a great fit for the organization. A top leader has to be an embodiment of the organization's values. If he or she is not, then either the organization will have to change — a difficult and unlikely event — or the top leader will be rejected like a foreign invader, a much more familiar occurrence given the high churn at the CEO level.

Few companies have a better reputation for developing leaders aligned to the organization's values than GE. In chapter two, we talked about how companies have tried and failed to imitate GE's values. But they have also tried to hire GE leaders to their own top jobs in the hope that the development path such leaders took at GE will provide them with the background necessary elsewhere.

Bob Nardelli, the CEO of Home Depot, is one such leader. As a former GE executive, Nardelli was, by all accounts, an extremely effective and valuable leader — "the best operating executive I've ever seen," according to super-CEO Jack Welch. He grew up in the GE culture, only leaving it for a few years in mid-career because he was frustrated with his level of advancement. When he returned, he made his ambitions clear: one day, he wanted to be CEO. When the time came for Welch's retirement, Nardelli was short-listed as one of three possible candidates to succeed to the top post. Boards of directors all over corporate America should take particular note of the fact that all three candidates for GE's leadership were found within GE itself.

In the end, Nardelli didn't get the job, and Welch never explained why. Nardelli took the news hard. Becoming CEO of GE was his dream, and GE values were in his bloodstream. He didn't even consider leaving before being turned down, even though companies like Lucent, Ford and Kodak had put out feelers to see if he would. Another failed CEO candidate for GE, Jim McNerney, quickly accelerated his talks with 3M to become that company's CEO. Left hanging, Nardelli was then approached by a GE board member who also happened to be a director at Home Depot. He let Nardelli know that change was afoot at Home Depot. Soon, Home Depot's board had deposed CEO and co-founder Arthur Blank and hired Nardelli to be their new CEO.

3M and Home Depot felt pretty lucky to get GE's cast-offs. In particular, Nardelli seemed like the answer to a lot of Home Depot's growing problems. Home Depot is a company with a short history but a strong culture. Bernie Marcus and Arthur Blank founded it in 1978. Both men had been senior executives at a California hardware company called Handy Dan. They didn't like the way the company did business, so they started their own company, Home Depot, in Atlanta. Right away, and in no small part because of the passion and energy of its founders, Home Depot developed a distinct cultural feel and strong sense of mission. It was conceived as a no-frills, do-it-yourself warehouse that scrimped on fancy presentation to offer low prices and knowledgeable service. The service culture seemed to be embodied in the distinctive orange store signs, popping up all over America as Home Depot grew beyond anyone's expectations over the next twenty years — faster than any other retailer including Wal-Mart. It was said that the store employees "bled orange," meaning they were totally committed and faithful believers in the vision and values of the founders.

There was, however, one significant and looming concern. Despite its remarkable growth and success with the customer, Home Depot was hurting financially. Much of the pain could be linked to operational inefficiencies. Home Depot had invested in new stores all over the continent, but failed to support that growth with an appropriate investment in the logistics systems needed to supply and manage its network. It didn't have an automated inventory system. It allowed managers tremendous leeway in evaluating and tracking store employees. It bent over backwards for the customer, priding itself on offering cash back for returns, no questions asked. To some, Home Depot's "do-it-yourself" management style and decentralized operations were undercutting its own success.

To fix those problems Nardelli seemed like the perfect choice. Although Nardelli had no retail experience, GE was known for operational discipline and Nardelli was GE's most operationally disciplined executive, a details-oriented manager who never missed a target or made a mistake. What better leader to bring a similar discipline and rigor to operations at Home Depot? At first, the choice of Nardelli looked good to outsiders. The stock price continued to rise over the next six months as he introduced reforms, strategic plans and new processes. Within a few years, however, the overall share price dropped 50 percent as Home Depot lost significant ground to rival Lowes Home Hardware. Lowes offered a distinctly different experience than Home Depot with its bright lights, well-finished interiors, clean aisles and friendly service to attract customers (in particular, women) who were less macho about "do it yourself." Since the two stores were direct competitors, the success of Lowes can't be considered in isolation from what happened at Home Depot. So what went wrong at orange?

LOOK INSIDE THE BOX

The Home Depot Values

Taking care of our people	The key to our success is creating an environment where all associates feel that they are respected, their contributions valued and they have equal access to growth and development opportunities. By surrounding our associates in this environment, their personal and professional growth are inevitable!
Excellent customer service	Along with our quality products, service, price and selection, we must go the extra mile to give customers knowledgeable advice about merchandise and to help them use those products to their maximum benefit.
Respect for all people	In order to remain successful, our associates must work in an environment of mutual respect, free of discrimination and harassment. Everyone has value, regardless of gender, ethnic or educational background.
Building strong relationships	Strong relationships are built on trust, honesty and integrity. We should listen and respond to the needs of customers, associates, communities and vendors, treating them as partners.
Doing the right thing	We exercise good judgment by "doing the right thing" instead of just "doing things right." We strive to understand the impact of our decisions, and we accept responsibility for our actions.
Giving back to the community	An important part of the fabric of the Home Depot is giving part of our time, talent, energy and treasure to needs in our community and society.

Continued

Entrepreneurial spirit	Home Depot associates are encouraged to initiate creative and innovative ways of serving our customers and improving the business, as well as to adopt good ideas from others.
Creating shareholder value	The investors who provide the capital necessary to allow our Company to exist need and expect a return on their investment.

Home Depot's values seemed to fit its decentralized, customer-focused, independent culture. On the other hand, Nardelli and his operational philosophy was alien to Home Depot. In his first nineteen months on the job, twenty-four of thirty-nine senior officers either left the company or were fired. To replace them, Nardelli brought in many ex-GE people and other outsiders who also lacked retail experience. As a leader, Nardelli instituted a more-work, less-play atmosphere at the top. He arrived to work early and left late, established weekly meetings with his direct reports (versus the quarterly meetings of his predecessor) and even had weekend meetings, something that had been unheard of before his tenure. He squeezed inventory, payroll and other costs, and got rid of Home Depot's cherished cash-return policy, long considered sacred by the employees. (See The Home Depot Values, "Excellent customer service" and "Doing the right thing.") He centralized buying from nine centers to one, eliminating many local suppliers in the process that had long benefited from good relations with the mega-store. (See The Home Depot Values, "Building strong relationships.") His number of part-time sales associates rose from 26 percent to 50 percent. (See The Home Depot Values, "Taking care of our people.") Meanwhile, rival Lowes continued to stick to the idea that full-time salespeople provide better customer service, maintaining 80 percent full-time employees.

Not all of Nardelli's innovations can be considered draconian. Although he put a GE stamp on performance appraisals, ranking all salaried associates from the CEO on down, he does not institute GE's famously harsh rank-and-yank policy of firing the bottom 10 percent of performers each year. Taking his own pain of being rejected at GE to heart, Nardelli carefully considers all sides of the issue before letting senior people go, and meets with them personally. He's self-effacing, eager to learn and fosters transparency — all admirable qualities that any leader would do well to emulate. He's also trying to institute a coaching culture throughout the organization, starting a leadership institute like GE's Crotonville that will focus less on training store employees and more on building leadership. And he has an aggressive growth strategy, geared less to individual consumers than professionals and major corporate accounts like General Motors, Disney and Staples.

I'm not claiming that Nardelli is a bad CEO, or that he's not doing what Home Depot needs, or that he won't ultimately be considered successful. I have no ability to judge any of those questions. Rather, my point is that GE and Home Depot are two different companies with different markets, different types of employees and different values. When Nardelli came on board, he brought a different culture with him. Why should he have felt connected to the values of Home Depot? For most of his career, he bled for GE, caring deeply about what happened there. When he jumped to Home Depot, it almost seemed as though he kept GE in his sights, hoping to prove they made the wrong decision. It's a tough way to run a company that needs your passion and belief as much as your hard work and strategic acumen.

As a frequent Home Depot customer, I have noticed the decline in customer service and it feels directly related to the company's change in values. I'm certainly not surprised to see the impact of that change. When the leader's own values and vision are in tune with the organization's, employees feel confident and certain about the direction in which they are going. When the leader's values and vision are out of sync with the organization's, employees feel distressed and confused.

Consider GE as a counter-example to Home Depot. Succeeding Jack Welch could have been an impossible task, but selecting Jeffrey Immelt from within the organization created a straight line running through the heart of GE's values. Immelt has put his individual stamp on the CEO position, but all of his changes have been within the realm of expectation, meaning they did not assault committed employees', customers' and shareholders' sense of what is right and wrong for their company.

The same could not be said at Home Depot. Some would argue, as no doubt the board of directors did, that Home Depot needed the kind of shake-up that could only be provided by an outsider. This implicitly meant that Home Depot had no worthy successor within the company, a sad and demoralizing comment in itself. It also, less directly, implied that Home Depot's values needed changing, an equally demoralizing idea for those who cherished those values. Eventually, Nardelli might succeed in morphing Home Depot's values into ones that more closely reflect his own (or GE's). But the transformation won't happen quickly and it won't be painless. The company that results may resemble the old Home Depot in name only. I wouldn't be surprised if the orange brand changes, too. Somehow, the color just might not seem right anymore.

Keeping Leadership a Family Affair

It's easy these days, with the number of new CEOs, to come up with examples like Nardelli. Many of these high-profile CEOs function like a superclass of executives without homegrown roots, circulating between situations. Take Carly Fiorina. Did she ever feel at home at Hewlett Packard (HP)? Did the employees, customers and shareholders of HP ever feel at home with Carly Fiorina?

Her years at HP were tumultuous and stressful. She was hired as the first CEO to come from outside the company and was assigned the task of shaking up what seemed like a stale culture to improve performance. She brought panache and charisma to an organization that was relatively faceless since the passing of its co-founders. From the very beginning, she made a concerted marketing effort to connect the firm's brand with the legend of its early founders and the ordinary car garage from which they had worked. But at the same time, she struck against those founders' famous credo, described as the "HP Way," which fostered organizational community, team spirit, trust, innovation, entrepreneurial spirit and respect for employees.

In her attempt to turn HP around, Fiorina was willing to step on a lot of toes. She asked employees to take a pay cut, then announced layoffs soon after. In the old days, firing was a last resort, only after reassignment was deemed impossible. Fiorina made managers lay off people from departments other than their own to minimize strife — a practice that seemed heartless. She tried to centralize and control a very decentralized and loose organization. The co-founders, Dave Packard and Bill Hewlett, had been famous for using management-by-objective techniques in which employees were given the freedom to achieve mutually agreed upon goals in whatever ways they thought best, an approach that fostered freedom and creativity. The management style at HP was very practical and oriented to solving problems; it was based in solid engineering. Fiorina was more about marketing and mergers. Inclined to flashy presentations, she flew around the world in a GulfStream jet with an entourage of top executives and security. She tried twice to merge HP with another sizable company, a failed bid with accounting firm Price Waterhouse, and a contentious but ultimately successful bid with computer manufacturer Compaq. During the lead-up to the merger with Compaq, Fiorina fought a proxy battle with a powerful board member who just happened to be a direct descendent of one of the founders and a self-appointed steward of the organization's values. Fiorina dismissed him as a dilettante who had never worked in the business. She was finally ousted in February 2005.

Fiorina had plenty of success as a leader and is one of the most impressive top executives of her generation. On the other hand, it seems apparent that she didn't mesh well with the culture of HP. Long-term employees of the company held the HP Way with almost cult-like devotion. Fiorina seemed to view the HP Way as an impediment to progress. Because of stale performance, the company clearly needed to alter its business practices. But the blow to the culture which that change brought seemed to bring strife and a further deterioration in performance. Notably, Fiorina's successor, Mark Hurd, also came from outside the company, but he brought a much more low-key engineering-focused style of leadership to the firm. He sold the GulfStream jets, reduced the flamboyance of the CEO position and concentrated on the basics.

As anyone who has experienced it can attest, a company with a strong culture is like a family. I have observed such complex emotions in large industrial manufacturers, ruthless financial firms, and high-tech start-ups. Deep friendships form. Members of the same company intermarry. They celebrate and mourn together. The company can change and go through crisis, the members can come and go, but the family feeling is very strong and can survive a lot of strife.

What makes that feeling of family resilient? The common connection arises from a set of common values and behaviors.

As in a close family, members of a company with a strong culture can anticipate each other's actions and thoughts; they talk the same language; they share stories about legendary events. Despite differences of personality and opinion, they share a common purpose.

LOOK INSIDE THE BOX

Changing Strategy Doesn't Change Values

When organizations are under stress, they often come up with big changes or a new strategy. Usually that comes with new values. Long-term employees know to hide until the fad has faded. Newer employees begin to get palpitations and dust off their resumes.

Is a shift from quantity to quality a values shift? Is moving from an audit and process strategy to a customer-focused strategy a change in values?

With this change will the organization's leadership and employees leave their values behind? Not a chance. In fact, they will find opportunities to celebrate their values in order to make the change easier.

Ambassador Adlai E. Stevenson said of Eleanor Roosevelt when introducing her at the United Nations that she is a person who would rather light a candle than curse the darkness. Many corporate leaders should take heed.

We wouldn't expect the new leader of a family to come from outside the family unit. So why do corporations, in their succession process, so often look outside for help? Perhaps it's human nature to turn to a stranger when rescue is needed. Boards hire

CEOs from outside the organization, particularly when they need someone without too many emotional attachments to turn things around and set a dramatic new direction. More often than not, however, the only thing that gets turned around is the sense of common purpose and shared expectations. When a company is stagnant, in crisis or underperforming, shaking things up is mighty tempting, but perhaps we should also consider what gets lost.

A company becomes a family when its leaders live up to the company's values and hold others to those same standards. A company with a venerable tradition like HP was proud of its history and credo. Changes to strategy and approach might have been necessary to compete in a changing world, but changes to values as demonstrated by behaviors are extremely disruptive and disheartening. When morale goes down and anxiety goes up, performance usually suffers.

Companies and families outlive their leaders. Values outlast individuals and are passed on to the next generation. The biggest threat to a company's values comes from its leader. When a leader is selected without testing that person for fit with the organization's values, trouble is likely.

The Serious Responsibility of Succession Planning

Consider McDonald's in contrast to HP. In less than a year, McDonald's went through four CEOs. A sign of a company in distress? Usually, but not in this case. When McDonald's was stumbling in the early 2000s, it avoided the knee-jerk instinct to pluck some celebrity CEO from the ranks of another company. Instead, it looked to its own culture and asked Jim Cantalupo, a retired executive, to right the ship. Significantly, one of Cantalupo's first acts was to put a successor in place who would lead the company in the future. The future came more quickly than expected when Cantalupo died of a heart attack a few months later, hours before a major speech to McDonald's franchisees. The succession plan was so solid, however, that Cantalupo's successor, Charlie H. Bell, was able to give that speech as the company's new CEO. Bell was a lifelong McDonald's employee from Australia. A few months after his appointment as CEO, Bell stepped aside because of cancer. Bell's own carefully chosen successor, James A. Skinner, assumed the position without confusion. A *New York Times'* article "New McDonald's Chief Vows to Keep Strategy Unchanged" reported that Mr. Skinner said he would continue with the strategies of his predecessors.

Few firms could handle such tumult because few have a real plan for executive succession. Most companies don't experience the tragic end of their leader while on the job. Instead, the proof of the general failure of succession planning can be seen in the frequency with which the revolving door spins at the top of organizations. New CEOs seem chosen for trendiness or popularity rather than by any consideration of the long-term strategy needs of the organization. Naturally, they don't last as long as they used to. In choosing a CEO, it behooves the search committee to first screen each candidate's recent past on the job behaviors to ensure the person is aligned with the values. If they do not pass the values interview, their consideration should be dropped.

Generally, the best candidate for succession to the throne comes through the family line (or rather the employee line), and perpetuates the ruling family's (or company's) values and stability, etc. The end result is a kingdom that trusts the leadership and supports it in good times and bad. Employees recognize the necessity of continuity and consistency in values and, in return, the leaders receive high performance and loyalty.

In fact, most organizations hire their CEOs from inside the company, although the number of CEOs chosen from outside is growing. Hiring from inside is considered the safe choice, except when the past CEO has messed up, and the board of directors feels the organization needs a change. But is it the organization's culture that needs a change, or was the wrong person hired in the first place? There doesn't seem to be as much debate about this nuanced consideration.

LOOK INSIDE THE BOX

The CEO Effect

For a long-term investor, the CEO is absolutely the key to the whole thing. He's much more important to me than the business itself. I base my evaluations on personal contact. I believe that if you come to the right conclusions about the CEO's character, intelligence and expertise, you will make the right investment choices. Why? Because a company is almost the exact inverse of a democracy, and whereas a democracy's strength comes from its breadth and depth, a corporation's strength is driven from the top down. Every company comes to mirror its CEO over time. Whatever the CEO cares about will be reflected throughout the corporation.

— Herbert Allen, Allen & Co., "The Best CEO's," *Worth*, May 1999, pages 102–148.

When the wrong CEO gets hired, the blame for that failure lies with two groups. First, the current CEO and second with the board members who should be holding the current CEO accountable. Making sure that either a few potential successors have been selected and are being groomed should be one of their top three areas of concern from day one. As time evolves, the successor of choice should emerge.

Let's look at the board's responsibilities first. A board that has been in place for a few years should have gotten exposure to internal high-potential candidates and become fully aware of their capabilities. As with any time a promotion is being debated, the first task is to identify the knock-out factors that will allow the anointed candidate to hit the ground running. In this regard, the most important issue is culture and values fit. Unfortunately, values and culture are occasionally seen as something to run from, not embrace. When companies are underperforming, people are quick to say that the culture of the organization needs a shake-up. Accordingly, the boards will often turn to high-profile CEOs from other firms, or "turn-around-artists" who have a reputation for delivering instant results. But is the culture really to blame? Improving delivery systems or customer service or otherwise changing strategy and operations will not change an organization's culture. If you want to change the performance of an organization, the place to start is at the middle with the layer of management that is closest to implementation, not the top. Improving the quality of middle management pays great dividends for the organization's future leadership since such people have time to learn the corporate norms and values before emerging in leadership roles.

The other issue to realize is the business' worth from the human capital perspective. Traditionally this is defined by the intangibles. The intangibles are such things as copyrights, patents, research in progress, etc. But too often the other intangible is overlooked — the character of the corporation, the nature of the collective whole. While the markets might consider person A more capable of running the company than person B, the initial bump in stock price will be short-lived if the person in charge doesn't recognize the importance of the history and legacy of the firm.

In fact, it's often the head that gets cut off, no matter how sick the body may be, and so boards often choose outside CEOs instead of revamping employees. The level of disruption this causes needs to be considered. During times of competitive crisis, cultural continuity is probably even more important to minimize emotional stress and focus on the business of turning things around. With something so tumultuous as a change in CEO, business continuity means keeping the people of the organization aligned to the values and purpose that has given them a sense of meaning in the past. Take that security away from them, and they will feel lost. A firm being run by a CEO who does not respect or model the organization's long-standing values will flounder. Nothing will help a CEO hit the ground running better than ensuring the morale of employees is high — something that's more stable when the values and culture are not under threat.

LOOK INSIDE THE BOX

The role of the Board of Directors should be:
1. Checks and Balances.
2. Assembling candidate slate and assess regularly.
3. Getting involved early.
4. Creating small, dedicated committee of outside directors.
5. Planning in case of emergency.
6. Taking lead in choosing successor.

Moreover, what typically happens when an outside CEO takes over? Chances are they will soon call on their old friends and cronies to join them while rejecting, isolating or blocking the leaders who were in place and served as keepers of the corporate memory before the newcomer's arrival. Losing that corporate memory has a big impact on employees and customers alike, and when a company within a year or two has all new faces leading the organization, it's a disturbing message.

All in all, it should be the board that takes the lead in the CEO succession process, not the outgoing CEO, and it needs to drive that process from a grounded understanding of the organization's culture. Board members should be involved early by assembling and assessing the slate of potential candidates regularly. They need to plan in case of emergency. Even if an outside CEO is the favored choice, the board should assure that there's also a viable internal candidate there for comparison during the final selection decision.

In too many cases, however, it's the CEO who has the most control over the choosing of their own successor. Too many CEOs seem to worry that an "anointed" successor represents a threat to their authority and ego. To leaders like Michael Eisner, former CEO of Disney, grooming a replacement means relinquishing control — an inconceivable act for him and many CEOs. When I worked with the chief of police in Calgary, Alberta, I learned how differently succession planning could be viewed. This person believed that the chief of police in any major metropolitan area should step aside after five years. Accordingly, the chief began the succession planning process soon after assuming command, and when five years were up, she stepped aside despite a contract renewal offer. To say that the vacating chief was a saint who lacked ego would be ridiculous. But this chief did take pride in knowing that success can be measured by judging the quality of those who continue the legacy by ensuring the continuity of the culture of the Calgary Police Services (CPS). That attitude now permeates the organization's culture and top administrators. The greatness of leadership should be measured by how you leave the organization, not just what you have done for the company up to the point of departure.

While the responsibility and accountability for CEO succession belongs to the board, the CEO has the obligation for orchestrating the succession planning throughout the remainder of the organization. Yet, the obligation for assuring a good process is in place is too often given over to human resources. The problem with that, however, is threefold:

1. Human resources rarely has the power or capability to execute a succession plan effectively.

2. Mandating human resources with the process sends the message that succession is not a business tool.

3. There is no one right way of doing succession planning anyway.

There are a number of benchmark studies on succession management, but the reality is they contradict one another. Succession management is more than a program unto itself; it functions best when it is an integrated aspect of the firm's human resources activities, aligned and supporting the corporate business strategy and rooted in the values of the firm. In other words, a firm can't choose its path to succession from preset options like a customer chooses food at McDonald's. This reality supports the reasons why succession works best when appointments are made internally. In effect, succession planning is actually the culmination of effective and successful talent management.

To give human resources the power and capability to make a difference in partnering with the CEO and board in facilitating succession management, some important shifts have to be made.

Succession planning has to be seen as a strategic business tool for which the CEO has full accountability, responsibility and ownership — not to be consigned to anyone else. Every effort should be made to hire from within. Hiring outside often means that the firm has not identified and groomed the right talent. It's also a message to core performers of the limitations of their future within your organization.

Succession planning should be one of the CEO's and board's key objectives. The process of succession should be reviewed by the board at least twice a year for the top two levels of the organization. You will know when succession planning is really integrated into the organization's strategic mindset when promotions into key management and executive positions, regardless of business unit, are made only with the approval of those responsible for succession planning.

Boards and CEOs must realize that corporate culture is greater and stronger than any one individual — even the best CEOs. Changing culture by choosing a particular CEO is an arduous, thankless and probably quixotic task. Most CEOs who are forced to leave organizations do so, not because of simple performance issues, but because the culture rejected them as a poor fit.

Talent Management, Not Replacement Planning

If a truck ran over one of your senior people today, who would replace that person? Having someone in place to do that person's job equals replacement planning. But replacement planning does not take into account the growth, strategy and future development needs of the entire organization.

LOOK INSIDE THE BOX

If succession planning is truly to be considered a business tool, it has to embrace the potential of those who might be leaders in the future and go beyond the few that report to the leaders today.

Succession planning means focusing on ensuring those in the talent pool are forever living the values. You need to identify at least three people who can be selected at any time for similar opportunities. This is the organization's responsibility.

Replacement planning is simply the traditional identification of who could replace you immediately if you were to leave your role. This is too often the decision of the current manager.

Many organizations confuse replacement planning with succession planning. In some cases, they even develop elaborate systems for identifying and grooming leaders who serve as mirror images of the current regime. Genuine succession planning is a different animal altogether. It involves determining the capabilities that your organization will need in the future, then identifying a pool of candidates who have high potential to develop those capabilities. The leadership development plan that those high potential candidates are guided through will involve learning and skill-building opportunities commensurate with their development needs, as well as assignments and new experiences that test fit in increasingly challenging situations. In recent years, such old-school approaches as job rotation, cross-silo management experience and the fulfillment of outrageous requests (special challenges that go beyond the expected to test the mettle of a candidate) have come back into vogue because they combine learning with real on-the-job experience. Having a series of programs, workshops or external courses is not a development plan in and of itself.

A true succession plan means that you have a group of candidates who are currently in roles whose challenges they have mastered or nearly mastered and who also demonstrate some of the behaviors, skills and knowledge for other roles in the organization. That pool of high potentials is matched up to the pending anticipated vacancies over the next three to five years. But first you must start by looking closely at those jobs and how they will evolve according to the organization's future business needs. By knowing the strategy and the future, you can determine and validate what skills, knowledge and behavioral competencies will be needed at what level in the future. Before even beginning to develop learning plans for your high potentials, you must know where you are headed. If you allow the high-potential pool to determine this, you will be dealing from a very limited perspective. Whether you have the right people waiting to fill those positions in your high-potential pool and whether you have time to develop them will also determine if you have to acquire the talent by hiring it from outside. By recognizing years in advance that the necessary talent needs to come from the outside, you are able to bring that person into the organization prior to them reaching higher levels of responsibility. In doing so, you ensure the fit required to lead through values.

It's vital that you identify the characteristics of the future roles prior to reviewing your current talent; otherwise you will be biased toward their makeup versus what you really need. Further, by knowing what you need in the future, you also discover what you might have today that you don't need in the future. This will help you avoid having to work with a person who may be high potential today but who is not going to fit into the plan tomorrow. Succession planning is about the positions first, then the people.

You then map out what behaviors, skills and knowledge each of your high-potentials have and what it will take for them to close the gap to fill three or four potential openings in the coming three to five years. The person who takes on the role should already be able to consistently demonstrate the key behaviors of the role beforehand. You can't afford to let him or her learn on the job. No one in the high-potential pool is promotable until there is an opening for which they have already mastered the minimum requirements. If, at that point, you realize that you have an essential role to fill but don't have anyone internally ready to step in, then you must go outside the company to find a person to hire.

In other words, not everyone in your high-potential pool is going to be promotable. This is something that many talented and driven people have difficulty accepting. One of the most misunderstood concepts in talent management is this issue of promotability. Who's at fault for the skewed expectations? If you're that person's manager, then you are. Funny, but employees actually take it seriously when you state in their performance reviews that they exceed expectations. In their minds, that means they're doing well enough for promotion. No wonder they think they are ready for a higher role. The reality is that the current performance review has little to do with identification of high-potentials let alone selection of those to be promoted.

Next thing you know, you've got a bunch of disgruntled top performers. The salesperson who broke all records, the team player who lifted the performance of everyone on the team, the customer service representative who can handle the most irate customers — all come to believe that they should be moved up the ladder. Unfortunately, nothing about being a top performer in one role means that a person will be a top performer in a role that involves a promotion or perhaps even a lateral move that requires different skills, knowledge, behaviors and experiences. The requirements of the new role can be quite different.

The best indicator of future success is past success. But that does not take into account the idea that people must grow, develop and learn new behaviors to be successful in another role. Even if high-potential candidates are not ready for a new role, their hard work in personal development should be recognized. They should be applauded, showcased, rewarded and given the respect, prestige and esteem of a top performer. You want these people to stick around, even if a promotion is not open to them. They are your best role models for inspiring top performance in others. They are the backbone of your organization. These people are not "B" players. They are you masters or role experts without whom you cannot be successful.

LOOK INSIDE THE BOX

Specific Behavioral Indicators for Everyone at Every Level

The company values are the foundation of the rite of passage. Without role modeling the specific corporate values, the individual should not be even selected as high potential let alone promotable.

Integrating Values and Capability

If talent management is a business tool that will ensure achieving the strategic plan, it has to be recognized as a business process. The organization that promotes based on performance over

carefully measured potential pays a price. Let's look at each level
of responsibility in the organization to understand this better.

Moving from Individual Contributor to Supervisor

The Generic Behavioral Indicators of a Supervisor

- Communications
- Teamwork
- Providing Feedback to Others
- Results Orientation

As people become managers of individual contributors,
they must demonstrate some of the key characteristics of what
differentiates a line manager from an individual contributor.
This involves a transition from motivating yourself to motivating
others. The ability to handle multiple priorities that take time
to complete is also critical. Managers must learn to hold others
accountable for their work and learn how to give praise as well as
provide meaningful and constructive criticism. They must learn
how to set meaningful consequences, draw boundaries and fire
people when necessary. Frontline managers also have to know
how to select candidates during the hiring process. All of these
characteristics are behavioral, not technical, though some are
governed by local laws and others by corporate policy. Many
such decisions are highly emotional. Few individual contributors
have experience in these activities. Moving the best technical
contributor to this role without prior opportunity to learn and
practice the behaviors is a formula for failure. In the transition
from individual contributor to frontline supervisor or manager,
people are often put in these new roles without any training
or required experience that will enable them to be successful

at the tasks they will encounter — until it's too late. Training in interviewing, performance feedback and the like should be part of the knowledge an individual would need prior to actually moving into the position.

Moving from Supervisor to Manager of Supervisors

Generic Behavioral Indicators of a Manager

- Selecting people (fit to values)
- Coaching
- Strategic Planning
- Team Leadership

Often, despite having struggled in the role as frontline supervisor, many still get an assignment as a manager of supervisors. They move up the organizational chart because of other relationships they've built in previous roles, despite having never mastered the requirements of being a first-level supervisor. Since the behaviors needed for promotion are predicated on mastery at the current level, the negative effect is cumulative.

In some cases the recently minted MBA student who is being fast-tracked is thrown into this role without having been able to get his or her legs wet as a supervisor. Those who are not good supervisors are not likely to become good managers. This creates a resume as stable as a house of cards. Often, as you ascend in the ranks, your capability to move beyond that role decreases. Of course, such people can still be successful if they are trained somewhere along the way. If they run into a manager who finally tells them what they need to hear, not what is easy, they can become good managers. Going back to learn what needs to be learned can help a leader gain the behavioral requirements of other levels of management. Too often, however, we avoid dealing with the issue and wait for such people to fail rather than ensuring they succeed.

Becoming a Manager of Managers

Generic Behavioral Indicators of a Manager of Managers

- Influencing through others
- Business acumen
- Risk taking/Creating Innovation
- Networking

As managers progress to the second level of management, they become a manager of managers. This requires further development of new behaviors they need to demonstrate prior to moving into the position. The issue for most second-level managers is that they are too often moved directly into that role having only been individual contributors. This ensures that they have not mastered the first-line managerial or supervisory behaviors required for managing managers. It also shows that people are being promoted, not for how they do things, but for the results they achieve. This can build into a managerial and leadership crisis within the organization. If it's clear that an individual contributor's results matter more than his or her behaviors, employees will quickly pick up on this and follow that easy path.

New behaviors emerge at the level of managing managers. The individual now has a wider and more selfless role in the organization. He or she has to put aside the individual or team good for the good of the organization or business unit. Managers of managers also need to coach managers on how to coach. If the manager of managers isn't ready for his or her position, you end up with the blind leading the blind. Few organizations invest in training firstline managers to coach and hold others accountable. By default, these individuals often turn to the behaviors that made them successful in the past as individual contributors. Firstline managers who are doubting themselves begin to micro-manage. Now the actions of micro-management are reinforced as a positive habit when they are promoted to manager of managers. The habit of micro-management follows them up the career ladder as a behavior they perceive to be a winning strategy. In turn they role-model micro-management for the supervisors to follow as the correct behavior.

Another behavior that the manager of managers needs to acquire is the action of giving people opportunities to do things they have not done before. Managers of managers need to put people into roles and situations in which they can learn new skills, knowledge and behaviors. For example, if the person has never been a project manager they need to build that capability in the person. If the person has always had line responsibility, perhaps he or she needs time in a staff role. Managers need to see the development of others into leadership roles as a key responsibility. They need to provide others with time for learning and provide them with feedback that furthers their growth. How many managers of managers do this in your organization?

Another important activity is the need to hire and promote new staff. Here, the issue of corporate values hits a crossroads. Since most people receive little or no training in soft skills until they become a manager of managers, they usually learn these skills by example from those around them. Managers of managers then interview new hires based on what they have done to be successful, rather than hire for job-person-role fit according to the skills, knowledge, behaviors and values of the firm. Consequently, when managers of managers need to move people from the role of supervisor to manager, they often find that there is no one who fits the organization.

Some people might criticize the development approach I've just described since I do not recommend bringing outsiders into leadership roles at the executive level. Where, then, do you get new ideas and new blood in the organization? The best opportunity for bringing in fresh outsiders is at the level of managers of managers. The new hire can focus on values alignment and then give people time to adjust to the norms and culture of the firm. The risk of failure is greatly reduced, since the newly hired employees will either learn to live within the values successfully or will be outed prior to moving further up the organization. The critical issue for being promoted into the manager of manager role and all subsequent roles either vertical or horizontal is the values. Not having a person who first hold themselves accountable for the values at this level enables that person to bring along others who also don't live the values. In fact, the manager who doesn't role-model the values might even block someone who does for fear of being "outed" by that individual.

Running a Business Unit

Generic Behavioral Indicators of a Business Unit (BU) Leader

- Future thinking
- Holding people accountable
- People development
- Focus on long-term results

Now that the successful have mastered the skills, knowledge and behaviors in the functional area they know best, the next move up the organizational ladder is to manage a business unit. This step means that while they have already successfully accomplished major challenges they need to add a number of behaviors to their quiver.

First, they need to add to their teamwork activities an ability to work with people in other areas of the business unit whose objectives and expectations might be different from the business area they know best. To do so, they must refine their listening, influencing and negotiating behaviors. They need to move from fact-based decision-making to more intuitive decision-making. Furthermore, they must learn how to deal with multiple senior managers from other areas of the organization as well as the forces governing internal political winds. At this level, business unit managers take on a greater accountability for results that impact the bottom line, including full profit and loss responsibility and accountability. The business unit manager must put the needs of the business ahead of his or her own personal success.

As just noted, the major obstacle the manager from one area has as they emerge as a leader of multiple business areas is the difficulty of working with managers of multiple functional units. The common tendency is to be perceived as showing favoritism to the area from which they "graduated." We also need to consider the poor manager of the functional area from which the business unit manager comes. He or she is likely to experience great pressure because the business unit manager is having trouble letting go. At the same time, the new functional manager is seen by other functional managers as the golden boy who is getting all of the attention. The new business unit manager must learn how to let go of the specific knowledge area he or she knows best and see the bigger picture from a view that integrates business units for the greater good of the organization. This requires taking a step back and listening to people in order to see the impact on short- and longer-term objectives.

LOOK INSIDE THE BOX

Ninety-day plans lead to little actually being accomplished in ninety days. Continual rapid course adjustments to the ninety-day plans only frustrate business unit managers and confuses employees.

Eric A. Mendelson, CEO of HEICO Aerospace, recently proudly announced to his leadership team that of the forty-one people at the leadership meeting thirty-seven of them were internal promotions.

He further expressed that he doesn't look at short-sighted planning but wants his leaders looking at long-term ways to sustain the company. That growth has been an average of twenty-plus percent year over year since he took over the leadership just over ten years ago.

Perhaps the business unit manager's most critical task is ensuring that the manager of managers is accountable for people in the organization living the values, not just getting the results. Sometimes this means taking a loss in anticipation of a long-term gain — something that requires courage and conviction. Business unit managers get that courage from their passion for the values and vision of the organization. They want to be seen by those above and below them as a role model of the values and a champion of the vision.

Long-term thinking coupled with new ideas around strategy can have a major impact on a person's capability to lead the business unit. As a leader, a business unit manager needs the functional manager to understand the competition and understand how to make business decisions that are in full alignment with the values and vision of the organization. When the functional manager *fails* at living the values, especially in organizations where the values are clearly articulated, you end up with individual contributors and first-line supervisors who become cynical about the organization because of the discrepancies between what is said and how work is really accomplished. When this happens, the business unit manager will grow out of touch with individual contributors and lose the pulse of the organization. They need to acquire new means of communication with individual contributors, or their micro-manager persona will be amplified.

The business unit manager is perhaps the last role in the organization's hierarchy into which people from the outside can be transitioned into the organization and still have time to learn the values and the culture prior to becoming an executive. If the organization is in rapid growth and/or a de-layered or flat hierarchy, then this level should be drawn from within the employee ranks to ensure values and vision continuity.

A Manager of Multiple Business Units

Generic Behavioral Indicators of a Leader of Multiple Business Units

- Strategic thinking
- Celebrating success of others
- Holding others accountable for the development of others
- Identification and development of high-potential employees

At this level the air begins to thin considerably as you have reached the upper rungs of the organizational ladder. Focus turns from the business unit to the entire business.

Here is where the chickens come home to roost. If you have not been a team player and learned the behaviors of compromise and negotiation and of putting the organization's needs ahead of your unit's needs, you will soon find yourself sitting in the office of an outplacement councilor. If your self-worth is derived from having clearly set goals and objectives that you can orchestrate for success, you will find that your potential for development might remain after mastering the elements of this level. At this level you need to be focused on future thinking and the fair deployment of human and other capital resources.

Being successful as a manager of multiple business units should mean that you have mastered or become an expert in the previous role level. Prior to moving up in the organization, you should have successfully demonstrated some of the key behaviors required for the next level. The higher up you go in an organization, the less skill and knowledge you need, but the more your behavioral competencies become critical. As a result, a failure to adopt the right behaviors really starts to impact organizational performance. Values must be consistent at all ranks. From your first appointment as supervisor through all successive levels, you should have lived the values of the organization as a prerequisite for promotion. If you haven't done so, the impact of that will be felt at this level. If you are a virus in the organization — a highly effective producer who does not live the values — then the damage you can cause will be considerable. An organization that goes down that slippery slope will find it hard to recover.

The Pitfall of Using Behaviors from Competency Models that Don't Fit the Values

I have worked with two different organizations that backed themselves into the position of promoting viruses. While they intellectually knew they should stop the practice, they perpetuated it because of the difficulty of judging results below values. One of these companies asked us to help it define the behavioral competencies for becoming a high-potential who would eventually be promotable. We met with a number of managers of managers whom the company considered highly successful and whom it had already put on the high-potential list. We conducted focus groups with them and looked for the behaviors that would sustain the firm's competitive advantage into the future. We soon realized that this was an empty human resources activity to which the executive team was not committed.

As the profile emerged, the participants were excited about having an opportunity to define the characteristics of success. The participants knew very well that the organization's current culture was not healthy. They characterized the culture in terms that were anything but endearing. It was clear to everyone that the company was run by an owner who appointed CEOs to run the firm, while maintaining control and treating people as physical assets who could be easily replaced. In fact, every three years the owner made a habit of replacing the leader who, in turn, would replace the leadership team. As a result, the culture was filled with fear and anxiety. The characteristics of someone who was considered to have high potential could, and usually did, change frequently — whenever the leadership team changed.

We articulated our concern about the project to the head of human resources. We also articulated our concern that the leadership team clearly did not support the effort. For example, not one of its members was willing to take an hour and a half to two hours to participate in an interview to articulate the characteristics of a high-potential leader. Soon we found ourselves calling a meeting with the senior person in the human resources department to express our realization of the futility of the activity. Soon after we withdrew from the project, the company decided that going with an off-the-shelf personality test coupled with an off-the-shelf behavioral competency model for 360° feedback would make the hollow exercise as painless as possible. The reality is many of the behaviors used in the model were counter to the organization's values or not relevant to assisting managers in achieving their respective business plans.

While the firm's business results have remained stellar in the short term, the organization has yet to define itself in a way that is meaningful. New MBA grads are not known to seek it out as a firm of first choice even though the firm has managed to become listed in magazines as an "employer of choice."

The Pitfall of Focusing on Shareholder Values

In the second company example, the CEO was focused on shareholder value. When we began to work on values with one of the business units, the members of the business unit were thrilled to be building a better future. The 100-plus-year-old firm was moving into a new field and setting the business unit up as a separate entity with its own culture. But setting out to create a new culture means thinking long term, not in results-focused ninety-day plans, which the CEO was noted for demanding. Unfortunately the CEO's almost single-minded concern for shareholder value caused most business unit leaders and their direct reports great frustration. He constantly put pressure on the president of the new business unit to cut costs at a time when they should have been losing money today to make money in the near future. While the business unit has continued to function, the dream of building a set of values to make the unit unique from the parent company was canned in order to save money in the short term. Financial results have not improved, and many of the senior managers in the unit have left for new work. Those that have stayed are frustrated and are not operating at peak capacity because they're not being properly supported and their authority is being usurped. This has forced a mentality of circling the wagons. Instead of building a vision, the remaining managers are looking out for themselves.

This is the ruination of many a wonderful organization. Dallas Mavericks owner Mark Cuban says it best. His comments reflect clearly that many of North America's business leaders who are focused on ninety-day plans are in it for themselves because they are provided outrageous amounts of short-term wealth by being granted obscene amount of shares. Cuban noted:

> Most shareholders are in for the long term, their philosophy is: "I've invested in your company for the future and the future of my family so don't screw it up." But CEOs know they can score big if the stock shoots up in the short-term future. So the ownership of shares divides CEOs and shareholder, rather than putting them in alignment.
>
> — Harvey Schachter, "Monday Morning Manager," *The Globe and Mail*, Business Section, April 3, 2006, page B2

Moving into the Executive Level or "C" Suite of Offices

Generic Behavioral Indicators of a C-Level Leader

- Stewardship of the corporate culture (values)
- Development of future executives (succession planning)
- Visionary thinking
- Passion

Once you have mastered running a business unit, the next step up the career ladder is to run a group of businesses. The air is so refined that few reach this level. Those that do have all their strengths and weaknesses greatly amplified and on display. The responsibilities of the business, of employees and of the long-term future of the firm all weigh on these individuals at the same time. Their single-minded focus becomes the legacy they leave behind.

At this level, you must have refined your capability to think into the future, to evaluate recommended strategy, to pull together information from a diversity of direct reports and to make ultimate decisions that have an impact on almost everyone in the firm. At the same time, you have the responsibility of developing business managers to be leaders as well as looking into the capabilities needed to run the business in the future that are not present today. This means developing successors to be more successful than yourself and putting your ego significantly in check. When the organization's talent is not being developed to move into key roles, it is because of a lack of leadership at the C-level.

Those in the executive office must be living the values of the culture of the company. Any deviation is amplified if the firm has espoused the centrality of the corporate values. Employees who work in an organization where the top executives don't model the values will become cynical and disenfranchised.

Unfortunately an example of this recently came to my attention at a financial institute where we helped define the values fourteen years ago. Back then, the CEO and his direct reports created the value-set that the CEO modeled consistently. Those values became the foundation for all hiring and promotions and were the basis for the 360-degree feedback process for all senior managers. The corporate memory of this young firm was formed around behaviors that reminded people of the importance of the values for individual and collective success.

Two years ago the CEO announced his retirement. The board members did their search and found a person who had successfully run a similar financial company to come on as the CEO of this firm. The outgoing CEO realized that the collective corporate memory of the stories that defined the values was important for the incoming CEO to learn and understand. So he told the board he would like to overlap with the new person for about three months to ensure cultural continuity and see that those who were "raised" according to these values would recognize the new leader as a steward of the corporate culture. When the board informed the incoming CEO of the outgoing CEO's wishes, he said if his predecessor were to remain even for one day he would not take the position. I thought it was a tremendous lost opportunity, but not surprising given politics and ego. The situation reminded me of an old expression from the Bible that goes something like this: "Now there arose a new King over Egypt who did not know Joseph."

Not surprisingly, this outsider, who did not fit the culture but nonetheless came into the role of CEO, shook the organization's identity down to the level of individual contributors. The impact was almost immediate. The new person replaced some of his direct reports straight away; others from the old team soon resigned. Those at the manager of managers level called the former CEO to ask for advice. A company once heralded as being a great place to work was soon withered by a new regime that did not celebrate the corporate legends because they simply did not know them.

At the level of CEO, and his or her direct reports, it is imperative to hire someone who lives the values of the organization in every situation without exception. The easiest place to find such a person is most often within the organization.

Planning for Leadership

In a values-driven organization, leadership is a process of growth and development. C-level executives represent the culmination of that process, rather than magical visionary figures who step in to show others the way. Executives are not exceptions to the values and standards of the organization but the embodiment — they are role models for everyone of what it takes to lead and succeed.

As such, a firm that recognizes the need to live by its values can start at no better place than with its talent management system. Organizations need to define a hiring and promotion process that is aligned with the values of the organization. They need a performance feedback process to correct anyone not living the values, even if those people are generating strong business results. Meaningful consequences need to be in place for those who don't live the values in all situations.

As an employee progresses from individual contributor to top management, he or she grows in technical abilities even as values alignment and the right behaviors become increasingly critical. Organizations that pay attention only to the development of their top executives are missing the point of talent management. All leaders and managers need to concern themselves with the development of others. But the first thing many organizations cut from their budgets is training activities. While training is best learned on the job, many growth and development activities are often cut to save money in the short term at the expense of the longer-term health of the organization. By maintaining budgets that allow for professional development of the softer skills, you foster a culture of learning in which leaders at all levels serve as internal trainers for other employees. In fact, this is the best form of training since it comes on the job and invokes the desired behaviors.

To create a talent management system that culminates in meaningful succession planning, the organization starts with a clear articulation of the values and the behavioral competencies required for success at each level. It then focuses on people development that is in line with future needs. By clearly defining the role profiles with behaviors that are aligned with the values and define success into the future, your organization will grow dynamically, not just repeating the same old processes every year. By holding fast to the values and the profiles for the position a person is promoted into, you create an objective and defendable set of criteria taking the subjectivity or favoritism out of the succession or promotional process. There must also be a fair way of recognizing and rewarding those who are experts or masters in their current roles, and who are the backbone of the organization so they feel they add value without the necessity of a new title or promotion.

Clearly defining the criteria at each level creates a road map for success. When an organization defines the behaviors of a role concretely and is transparent about those requirements, managers can have simple discussions about why someone is or is not qualified for promotion. Indeed, employees can — and often do — take it upon themselves to direct their development towards a promotion they want, even if they haven't been identified as a high-potential candidate. No organization that's geared to success and growth can have any problem with that.

Many executives say that they are concerned by the lack of emerging leaders in their organization. Some surveys note that up to 70 percent of executives asked said their number-one issue was finding leaders on time. Yet, many of those same leaders, thinking in ninety-day blocks of time, refuse to invest in human capital. They wouldn't dream of letting their equipment become dated or their machines go unserviced, yet they do little or nothing to support people maintenance. The CEO is responsible for making talent management and succession planning a business tool. As with any business tool, he or she must invest in these processes in order to produce a positive ROI — return on intangibles.

The CEO and members of his or her team have a responsibility for putting the needs of the business first. They have to provide opportunity for future leaders to be nurtured and developed. They have to channel their egos and design the architecture of the firms longer-term sustainability; they have to focus on leaving a legacy. They also have to hold others accountable for how they role-model the behaviors for others within the firm. They have to ensure the future is based on the values they inherited or built the company upon. They must provide positive feedback to those who demonstrate the desired behaviors and they must remove those who don't, despite personal relationships or enviable results. Values are the temperature check for the health of the corporate environment. Think outside the box all you wish as long as the behaviors are inside the box.

CHAPTER SIX

Does One Box Fit Forever? Organizational Growth: New Strategic Directions are Pursued but do the Values Ever Change?

❏ Values are ingrained in corporate culture and resistant to change.

❏ Most efforts at change that involve a shift in values fail.

❏ Celebrating the values is a positive action that leads the way to calibrating an understanding of the values among employees.

❏ Values without action are only beliefs.

❏ One set of values will always be dominant in a merger and acquisition.

Edgar Schein, values expert and author of *Organizational Culture and Leadership*, has said that 80 percent of companies that attempt to change their values fail. Yet change is the one constant in today's organizations. Leaders change. They also like to formulate bold new directions for their organizations — new visions, new operational strategies which catalyze organizational change. With or without grandiose visions, companies merge, acquire, shift product lines, enter new markets, downsize, reengineer and rebrand all the time. Change and adaptability, if not a necessity for survival, are certainly a common experience. What about values? Do they still hold true in the throes of constant change? Can they be changed to adapt to changing circumstances, or are they an impediment to a nimble organization?

LOOK INSIDE THE BOX

Values, while they evolve over time, remain constant. As a result, once the founder of the company establishes the values, in all likelihood the values will remain throughout the history of the firm.

Values are like curbstones along the road. While there might be some room to move, employees need to know the limits are clearly defined.

Defining the behaviors of the values is the responsibility of the executive team, especially upon their appointment to effect a smooth transition.

The introduction of new values is a receipt for disaster, while celebrating the existing values creates continuity and ensures stability.

Values, as we have defined them, are deeply held beliefs that are highly impervious to change. While it's true that many of society's values have changed over the decades, it's also true that those changes have come slowly and painfully. Think about gay marriage. Once it was an unimaginable event; now it is legal in many regions throughout North America and Europe. But the change was not easy, nor is it a done deal. People with contrary values are fighting that change tooth and nail. To them, it's just not right. Consider whether any of your own deeply held personal beliefs have really changed over the years. Most of us struggle to make any significant change — even to our diet or lifestyle. But if you have gone through a major change in values, what inspired it?

LOOK INSIDE THE BOX

The continuity of values from generation to generation:

The genesis of the values set is started by the founder of the corporation and those that were the first generation of employees.

Corporate leaders who lead through values must define for themselves which actions they — and others — must take to be perceived as living the values.

Caution: Too often when reading what has been created, the values and codes of conduct read as an "employee bill of rights." They seem to be written with managers in mind. As a result rank-and-file employees feel that managers, and not employees, need to live up to the values.

Often, such shifts come about because of life-altering experiences, something as traumatic as a death in the family, an illness, a divorce, a serious health issue, a crisis of faith. One CEO whom I know went through such an experience. He was a hard driver who expected all his senior executives to burn the midnight oil, even though many of them had young families. He would take vacations but "check in" two, three and four times daily. After his own grandson tragically died of cancer, he shocked the entire team by not coming to work or calling in for almost a month. Upon his return, he stunned the entire executive floor when he ordered the executives to go home early on a daily basis and do more for their families. The gravity of what he had gone through led everyone to believe he was serious. His follow-up actions confirmed it. When they saw that he now left the office before 6:30 p.m. every day, they knew that change had come to that particular value of the organization. The change became real when the senior executives decided to follow the CEO's lead and make family a new priority to be embraced by all.

Some organizations believe that a change in values is necessary to recreate a brand and revive a sinking fortune. Some companies believe that a change in values is necessary when scandal or strife has deeply marred the organization's image and pride. To me, it is likely that both incidents are less about re-creating values than returning to the real values — and changing strategy, operations, regulations or leadership as need be. Regardless of the reasons, there will be tremendous resistance to changing those values inside the company and even among customers and shareholders. The pain of value change is the acid test of the values' importance.

In fact, organizations rarely make a change in values, but sometimes they have to. There are two major circumstances in which I have seen companies forced into changing values in order to survive. The first is during a significant merger or acquisition. The second is when an industry itself undergoes rapid forced change, as during deregulation or a change from a controlled market to a competitive one. Both circumstances are extremely trying, difficult and fraught with danger. But focusing on values and knowing precisely what about those values needs to change and be translated into action is the best way I have seen for organizations to survive and thrive under their new circumstances. Rather than being a hindrance to such change, values are in fact the lighthouse guiding the ship safely through the storm.

Mergers and Acquisitions

An unwanted value change will not occur without a fight, no matter how spectacularly and enthusiastically a change is announced and embraced. Rather than going away, old values tend to lurk below the surface and reappear at the first sign of strife or stress. If new values have not been firmly and vigilantly inculcated, as soon as people are unsure about what to do, they revert to the "way we do things around here." That's the story behind many failed mergers and acquisitions. After the honeymoon, problems set in because the cultural side of the equation has not been given as much weight as the financial and market considerations.

LOOK INSIDE THE BOX

Getting the word out:

The leaders have to make the values real and they have to be willing themselves to judge by the values. A general broadcast or webinar, or a meeting with all employees present is not the way to get the word out and ensure it is understood correctly.

Continued

Step 1: There was a television program in the early days of TV called "To Tell the Truth." In this corporate setting you might call it "Whom do You Believe?" The answer for most employees is their manager. As a result you will pay more attention to the values and their meaning if you hear it directly from your manager who has heard it from their manager.

Step 2: Ensure that these manager and direct report conversations are held jointly with a manager and their direct reports from another department. This reduces the chances of not having the values properly presented. It also sends a message that the values are for everyone, not jut one department.

Step 3: As the values discussion trickles down, the stories of where people perceived others living the values and the stories of them contradicting the values has to *role up* (move up the hierarchy) to senior managers as well.

Step 4: The more you repeat something, the more you understand it and act accordingly. Plan on the meetings of Step 3 to be repeated from different perspectives for eleven consecutive months between managers and direct reports.

Is there any force that wrenches a culture more violently than a merger? The statistic I have heard, and I don't know whether it's based on fact or just anecdote, is that if a merger is going to fail it will do so within the first eighteen months. I wish I had a dime for each time I have heard someone say that the merger failed not because of business issues but because of a lack of fit between the two firms.

Recently, I was introduced to the CEO of a highly recognizable breakfast food company. He had just been appointed as the company CEO after it was purchased by his company, a global food, beverage and restaurant conglomerate. He was experiencing a lot of trouble getting the breakfast firm to fit in with the new owners, the global firm. The irony was that many years prior, at the start of the CEO's career, the CEO had worked for the breakfast food company. His "return" to his old company was seen by his colleagues from those many years ago as a kind of homecoming. He had many worries in this regard. The culture of the conglomerate parent, where he had thrived, was the antithesis of the smaller breakfast food company. For these reasons, the returning CEO's welcome back was accompanied by a huge sigh of relief as the executives and employees at the breakfast firm thought he would "protect" them. The people of the acquired company looked upon their new boss as a returning friend. Indeed, many of the executives of the breakfast food company had worked with the new CEO earlier in their careers.

Unfortunately, this feeling of relief amounted to a false sense of security that their culture would remain intact. The employees of the breakfast food company had solid reasons for wanting to keep that culture intact: it had served them successfully for several decades. The working knowledge of the culture of the company the newly appointed CEO was returning to would protect his direct reports from the aggressive culture of the acquiring conglomerate for an initial period. Eventually the new CEO had to introduce the more aggressive and confrontational culture of the new parent firm. Infusing the parent company's values led to great tension between him and his direct reports; those who could not make the transition had to leave.

When I talked with the CEO about this conflict, he came to realize that the people aspect of the merger, the intangible assets, were just as important as the financial and tangible assets, which had long been under so much scrutiny and due diligence. The parade of auditors had never once discussed the intangibles like culture and values. Nothing like that could find a spot on the balance sheet. After reinterpreting his experiences in this light, the CEO understood that he would have to communicate the need for change much more clearly. It took a year of hard work before the people who had been happy in the old culture came to terms with the new reality.

How often do acquiring companies try to soften the blow by labeling the acquisition a "merger of equals"? In my view, this only complicates and confuses the change in values that might take place. Merged companies may dole the top executive roles out relatively evenly, but in the end one culture tends to predominate over the other, and that tends to be the culture that is in power in terms of the balance sheet.

LOOK INSIDE THE BOX

Mergers and acquisitions are in reality always acquisitions. They might even be the smaller overshadowing the large firm. Either way it has to be stated clearly and concisely what are the ground rules of the dominant culture.

This will light the candle that prevents the employees from fearing the dark.

Don't be surprised if some of the employees at a variety of levels leave once you have clearly outlined your belief system. Their early exit prevents you from having problems with these same employees and eventually letting them go at great expense down the road.

Employees notice this power struggle right away. Unlike auditors, the first thing the people in an acquired company think about are the intangibles like their working environment, friendships and alliances, and the "way we do things around here." Soon after the merger begins, they form a very rapid opinion about how they are being treated and draw positive or negative conclusions about their fate. Intangibles may not hurt if you drop them on your foot, but they are very painful when a powerful corporation tramps all over them. The merger is attractive because of its potential return on investment, but employees will be measuring it by the return on intangibles. In the end, the merger may go ahead because of the return on investment, but it's the return on intangibles that will really make or break the best plans.

When Values Collide: The Battle of Red versus Blue

Once upon a time, not so long ago, all airlines flew the friendly skies (not just United). Business was good, markets were filled with opportunities, customer service was a priority. For a lot of different reasons, times got tougher and things began to change. Some airlines thrived, but most suffered. Then things got much worse after September 11, 2001. The impact on the airline industry was immediate, and the pain kept getting worse as the price of jet fuel began to skyrocket.

LOOK INSIDE THE BOX

Return on Intangibles

For those who are of the school that says "if you can't count it, you can't measure it" and therefore you can't prove return on investment, consider a statement attributed to Albert Einstein:

"Not everything that can be counted counts and not everything that counts can be counted."

Return on an intangible is not easy to calculate because people and events don't happen in a vacuum.

During this time of turmoil, some airlines considered forming alliances with once bitter enemies. But in the airline industry, such unions are difficult to manage since airlines have very strong cultures and their employees are fiercely loyal. Although it's generally a low-paying industry, employees care passionately about which team they play on.

The Red Team, as we will refer to them in this case study, had a long proud history that began with the advent of commercial flying in the 1930s. They were identified closely with their home country as an airline that had spread its wings to fly the world, especially to routes in Europe and some key destinations in the Far East. The airline's employees were proud to be in aviation and prouder still to be with the Red Team. Many had taken advantage of the company's share incentives over the years and felt as though they had an ownership stake. They provided efficient and friendly service and had a reputation for top safety and were recognized within the industry as having the best maintained aircraft in the world.

Company Blue, on the other hand, had a shorter history; they were less than a quarter century old. Their base was in the mid-west and western part of the country, with lucrative routes to the Far East. As an upstart competitor, Blue (not Jet Blue) was often in dire financial straits, but their foothold in the West was so solid that the Red Team couldn't seem to find a way in. The Blue Team wasn't satisfied with just holding on to this advantage; they wanted to fly in the Red Team's markets too. As a result, they purchased one of the strongest small upscale airlines in the industry and became a better competitor.

As the last century came to a close and the airline industry realized it was in big trouble, the Blue Team struck a partnership with a larger airline that had a positive image and a strong financial foundation. The integration of these two companies helped Blue even more. Soon, Blue's position was further improved by some bad luck in the Red Team. The Red Team's union went on strike, grounding the airline for some time. This forced Red's most loyal customers to fly the Blue skies during the strike.

Of course, Blue took advantage to try to convert the flying public to their team. They did everything they could to acquire more of the highly profitable frequent flying public supported by Red. The tactics became quite ruthless. The Blue Team decided to recognize all of the frequent flier miles that customers had accumulated with the Red Team. They sent out upgrade certificates to make people feel comfortable. Nevertheless, the pull customers felt by the Red Team was strong. Six months after the strike ended, both sides realized that brand loyalty was stronger than the outreach Blue had attempted through great service and hospitality.

Both Teams said the other team would not survive in the new competitive reality. Observers agreed and corporate raiders swept in to plunder the fortunes. The corporate raiders were rebuffed, and the two teams were left to their own devices. Soon the newspapers were rife with speculation that one team would buy the other. Both teams were involved in different worldwide alliances. Rumors also spread that these outside partners would purchase them or provide badly needed cash, but nothing happened.

The next event was the head-on attempt by the stronger Red Team to buy the Blue Team. Despite flirting with the financial danger zone, the Blue Team would not give in. Out of left field, the Red Team was subject to a hostile takeover launched by a takeover specialist. The Red Team now had wolves at two doors. Emotions became more intense, but rather than help each other, both sides only dug in deeper.

Finally, in 2001, the Blue Team went bankrupt and the Red Team was named the winner, allowing it to purchase Blue. So began the final merger battle. Management was eager to integrate the two sides, despite the fact that only months before they'd been calling for the other group's downfall. In the free market, management has the power to clean house in order to reduce the largest fixed costs of a corporate entity — salaries, benefits and pensions. But the victorious Red Team was thrown a curve. The government protected the Blue Team's employees from being laid off. Management had to keep those employees in their current roles for five years.

The airline employees, now working side by side, were less than civil to one another. Both sides felt that they had the better planes, service and management. In order to create the image of a smooth transition, everyone was sent off to participate in transition team meetings. It didn't work and animosity remained strong. Daily business continued, but management put strategy and performance issues on hold. In an effort to stem the bitter words, a memo was sent out banning people from talking about certain subjects. Meanwhile, the two unions were trying to work out their differences, even as the lines in the sand got more sharply drawn.

About a year into the merger, 9/11 hit, followed by the skyrocketing cost of jet fuel, the increased cost of maintenance and landing fees, and the decrease in the flying public. Times were worse than tough. If ever there was a need to come together, this was it. But the Blue and Red Teams remained sworn enemies, the Hatfields and the McCoys of the airline industry. As a customer, the lowest depths for me occurred when I boarded a plane and clearly heard a former member of the Blue Team's flight crew, in the company of the captain, bitterly complain about his treatment at the hands of the Red Team's leadership. The captain traded his own bitter ridicule of the new employee policies. It was not a pleasant experience to board a plane in the care of such disgruntled employees.

Fast forward five years. You might imagine things have improved. And it's true that the Red Team has been able to re-emerge from reorganization and receivership as one of the financial stars of the industry. And yet, despite new wolves at the door, whose tactics make Blue Team's prior actions seem almost endearing, the divide between Blue and Red has only narrowed slightly. You still have flight crews identifying themselves with their original airlines. You still have seniority issues within the unions. You still have two cultures within one airline, even after thousands of hours of change management efforts and programs.

It's amazing how strong and enduring a culture can be. The mindsets of Blue and Red held distinct views on the correct way of behaving, despite functioning in the same industry and serving the same public. From an outside perspective with some inside insights, I can assure you that neither culture was better than the other. They were both right — each from their own side.

Yet, financially and in terms of the market they were serving, the merger itself was inevitable. So what could the two companies have done differently to make the integration smoother? I believe that three things hampered the likelihood of easy success.

- The first was out of management's control. Government-enforced restrictions on firing and union agreements on promoting employees severely limited how the new entity could deal with their cultural problems.
- The second problem was similar, in its way, but self-inflicted. The memo banning certain topics of discussion put a lid on dissent but only created a worse build-up in pressure. Employees still bitterly refer to that memo today.
- Finally, the third problem was one of political correctness. As in so many mergers, the executives of the dominant company understood that to the victor go the spoils, but they believed they needed to be quiet about that fact in order to maintain a façade of equal partnership. They shied away from telling it like it really was: we are all one team now — and that team is Red.

Values need to be consistent throughout an organization. A company cannot function well under two sets of values because those values dictate how the organization behaves, how it rewards employees, how it reinforces performance, how it talks and thinks, hires and fires. The discord between two competing sets of belief systems is a distraction few organizations can handle, let alone one that is struggling to come to terms with a new identity.

LOOK INSIDE THE BOX

The underground values:

- Underground values are the daily actions that are rooted deeply in the organization that ultimately define the culture.
- They are taught by one generation of employees to the next in showing them ways to be successful.
- When values are articulated and they don't reflect the underground values, the values exercise is most often met with cynicism.

The Red Team should have made their own values eminently clear, celebrating them so that Blue Team employees could begin to understand the difference. Those values needed to be put forward as the ground rules for the engagement of all employees. I believe that when the Red Team made the effort to find stories and legends in the Blue Team's history to celebrate and eventually build a common joint values set, they made a critical mistake. In effect, such an effort showed that similarities were few and the differences were amplified.

Symbols are also very powerful signs of value change. I believe that the Red Team's logo should have changed immediately. While painting planes is no simple task and more expensive than one might think, the simple emblem on the fin gives employees an important sense of pride. Waiting three years for a new look for that fin was too long. The Red Team also waited six years to design a new uniform. When the merger initially took place, the Blue Team frontline staff were forced to wear Red Team uniforms — a difficult prospect to swallow. By launching the newly integrated firm with a new symbol and a new uniform, they would have created an important sense that values were also united. This needed to be combined with reinforcing those values behind the scenes by clearly articulating those values, defining them behaviorally through actions and rewarding and recognizing people who lived the values and demonstrated adherence to the true culture.

LOOK INSIDE THE BOX

Consistency is key to success:

In values-based organizations there should be no tolerance for deviations from the behaviors that define the values. Like a child who pits mother against father to get what they want because they know the parents lack consistency, the same is true for employees.

No matter how difficult it might be, some very difficult decisions have to be made in terms of whether to invest in coaching and getting a very senior person on side with the right behavior or recognizing that person will always be a virus and despite their ability to get the results they will never fit. Not dealing with these decisions sends a message to everyone right to the shop floor that the values are not for the senior people. Why bother making the effort!

Such inconsistent or mysterious behavior can only create "above ground" values that state an aspiration, while the underground values thrive as the values an employee must live to be successful in the culture.

Instead, because the Red Team tiptoed around this value change, they sacrificed clarity. In addition, because the government mandated that no one could be fired, the Red Team had no chance to rid the organization of the viruses and deadwood who were holding the merger back. There were too many employees for too few jobs. The Red Team desperately needed to refine its team to a core group who celebrated their values.

While each merger takes its own idiosyncratic path, it's my experience that many fail for similar reasons. The return on investment is clearly understood. The return on intangibles remains a hopeless mystery. Some firms do cultural audits in advance of acquisitions. But often those audits are pro forma attempts to justify the acquisition or smooth the early bumps and lose focus in the medium term once the executives have moved on to other concerns. The fact that values are poorly articulated in the first place and are expressed in similar terms in nearly every company does not help. Without a deep understanding of what makes one culture different from another in terms of behaviors, culture looks like soup made of the same broth.

LOOK INSIDE THE BOX

Ways in which the values exercise fails:

- Too often these exercises are orchestrated by an external consultant who knows little to nothing about the corporate culture.
- They miss the point that values are for employees and no one else because the employees are the only people living in that box.
- Committees often design value statements, and as a result, the above ground statements try to be too many things to too many people.
- Values have to be lived and rewarded in good times and bad.
- Putting the values on the wall, website or the back of business cards does not make the values understood or real.

Even the successful firms suffer from not having clear values, or worse, having an above ground set of values that look good to the employees of the new firm but when the new employees are imported into the new company they discover the real culture. A long-term telecom employee once told me that he was once proud of working for his company and understood clearly what it stood for. The success of the company had been outstanding, and it had gobbled up many smaller competitors over the ensuing fourteen years. But with each acquisition, the employee felt that the company had lost something. Everyone assumed that they'd be getting the best of both worlds, but with each acquisition the sharp edges got rounded a bit, the terms of what was and wasn't acceptable got loosened and widened to accommodate a more diverse set of employees. As a result, the values of his firm became less emotionally powerful to him. He told the focus group I was leading that if management were to once again treat people like the values really demanded they treat their employees, then his job at the telecom would become a career again.

The ingredients for being a values-based firm:

Step I: The first step is to ensure that the senior leads themselves clearly articulate the values. I have seen senior leads put their hearts into the values exercise. They come up with clear statements that employees who get it understand. Then the leads turn the wordsmithing over to a public relations or communications firm or internal team. As a result, the process loses its flavor and even the executives don't recognize what they have said. One other word of caution: when the executive team meets to define the values so that the values are meaningful and behaviorally articulated, they need to have an outside person facilitate or, as one client called it, "animate" the conversation and dialogue. If an internal individual who is not a member of the team leads the conversation, you will have issues of trust. If a person on the team leads the conversation, the issue is that that person has to exclude him or herself from participating and valuable information and ideas are lost.

LOOK INSIDE THE BOX

We know that as a student you assimilate enough to learn the material to get by. As a teacher, you are forced to learn the material in-depth and be knowledgeable in order to be successful. Similarly, having each manager hold regular conversations with their direct reports forces the manager to learn more prior to presenting the information.

Step 2: Communicating the values in a way that is meaningful means having the manager at each level speak to the values with his or her direct reports. While fancy celebrations with laminated business cards are nice for some, they have little meaning to most. In the real work world employees are looking for approval of their results and behaviors from their manager, peers and direct reports. When you trickle down the values through meaningful conversations, each person gets to calibrate them through conversations with his or her own boss and team.

The cynic in me says, however, that you will always run into a manager who will not conduct the conversation with passion and meaning. They will at best go through the motions. In turn their direct reports will pass the values on with the same ambivalence. To ensure success you have to have a checks and balance to the process. You need to provide the managers with a "discussion guide" or old-fashioned lesson plan for them to follow. You also need to have the discussion between the manager and direct reports in groups that mix two teams from two different departments together.

Since each level of the organization is looking up to see what might be flowing down from above, it is essential that those at the top have their values act together. The members of the leadership team have an obligation to live the values without excuse. If they waiver from the path and move beyond the curbstones, they grant permission to others to do the same. If the leaders don't do what they say is right, they begin to build animosity among the employees when they try to hold employees to operate within the curbstones.

Using the values as the abettor of the correctness of a decision keeps the values forever present when making business judgments. This results in exchanges that are driven by the available facts or are being made because it is the way others in the industry operate. These exchanges can prevent the firm from taking an action that would prove to violate the cultural norms and be seen by the employees as "the wrong thing to have done." I have seen executive teams use the values as the cornerstone for decision-making; this helps cut short an otherwise potentially prolonged discussion and can prevent otherwise inappropriate action.

It's Not about the Money

It is possible for an organization to undergo major change successfully, but values need to be the cornerstone of that change. KMV, the company I'll describe next, used its values to choose a merger partner that made sense for its long-term goals, rather than choosing the partner with the most money on the table. By giving up some of the money, it made a more profitable decision in every sense.

Although in an entirely different industry, KMV was founded about the same time as Team Blue, described above. Both were the continuation or outgrowth of previous organizations. KMV began in 1989, the tapestry of two different sets of threads. One set started in the early 1970s with Dr. Oldrich Vasicek and John Andrew McQuown. At the time, they were both working at Wells Fargo on a number of finance-related evolutions, which included equity index funds and some early attempts to use options-pricing theory in the context of credit analysis for corporations.

The second thread, which came later, really occurred when Vasicek and McQuown and a number of other people formed a firm in 1984. In 1986, a third future partner, Stephen Kealhofer, joined as the head of research. Although that firm went out of existence two years later, it created a set of ideas that were too good to drop. In the summer of 1988, Kealhofer approached Vasicek and McQuown to persuade them that they really needed to continue the concepts they had been developing. In February of 1989, the three men, along with two additional partners, started KMV from scratch.

KMV began as a bootstrap operation. The founding partners continued to work other day jobs rather than capitalize KMV with outside dollars and gain a source of income. Each partner devoted extraordinary energy to the business, growing the revenue by 20 to 40 percent per year and the number of employees by 20 to 30 percent.

By the middle of the 1990s, it was apparent that KMV had hit upon a niche that was in high demand. Nevertheless, a variety of managerial issues had come to the fore, and it was necessary to regularize a variety of managerial processes. It was also important that the partners confirm and articulate the raison d'etre of the firm in terms of values. In navigating such discussions, it helped that the partners had worked with each other before and had strong relationships and a lot of mutual understanding.

McQuown describes those formative decisions: "For example, we needed to convey some equity in the firm to a significant fraction of the people that were there, the senior people especially. We had to compartmentalize responsibilities in more coherent ways. We had to kind of give up on the partnership model and invoke a more hierarchical model to some degree. We wanted a flat organization, but we wanted a communicative organization, and the way we looked at the discussion around values was as a way to have the eighteen or twenty people in the senior positions express themselves on a broader array of matters, including 'Why are we in business?' and 'What human components do we need to deal with?' In other words, we were interested not just in economic outcomes but things like quality of life and responsibility and clarity of purpose and quality of feedback and all of that kind of stuff. We wanted to make our values an explicit component of our discussion."

By this time, the leadership team included eleven people — diverse in age range and geographic origin but extremely passionate about what they were doing and committed to growing success. The values discussion took place off site in Sonoma, California, and revealed a number of things about each of the individual members of the leadership team. As McQuown says, "We used the discussions as a lightning rod to get opinions out on the table and examined, whatever was on their minds, which in turn gave us, the more senior leaders, the opportunity to say what was on our minds, and for all of us to adapt to a more narrowly shared set of views."

At the off-site meeting, the team expressed a variety of views on the business and the longer-term strategy. There were some relatively new players in the group who had only recently joined the firm. The group used the time together to also conduct some of their strategic business planning. They used their values discussion as a cornerstone for the correctness of going in one direction or another. They also began to realize that some of the newer members of the team might not have the same values, or at least not feel personally comfortable with the way the values were being described behaviorally. This would have a major impact when the time came to expand the firm's capitalization.

After the off-site, the leadership team finalized the first draft of the values and the explanatory behaviors. I met with a number of smaller groups of employees to run them up the flagpole and get their feedback. In conducting the focus groups, we were very careful not to reveal the values or the behaviors until the group had the opportunity to articulate them for themselves. As each group discussed the values, it was abundantly clear that the small employee population had a firm grasp of the values. To me, this meant that the underground and explicit values were one and the same.

The executive team met again to receive the feedback on the values and to fine-tune them for themselves. The attempt to formally articulate the values was stifled, however. One of the members of the executive thought that the wording needed to be "jazzed up" and asked an advertising and public relations firm to present their version in their own words. Seeing the results, the team quickly realized that the new wording was not authentic. Looking back as chairman, McQuown maintains that the exercise was critical.

"The fact that we didn't nail down six big values, etch them in stone and put them on everybody's desk shouldn't take away from the fact that people in general (even beyond the leadership team) got quite a lot out of the discussions, and we homogenized our views. Other than turning our values into a hymn and singing them every morning … the process worked. I think we reached a level of agreement among the senior people about what our shared values were, and once we reached the agreement, I don't think we needed to do any more than that. It was worth the effort for sure."

The team realized that everyone in the firm had had an opportunity to be involved in the process of developing the values and that they needed to be integrated into the hiring and the performance feedback process as well. There was enough clarity among the leaders to model the values with consistency and hold others accountable for living the values, too. They were already using the values to talk with each other about important business issues, without actually describing them as values conversations. So, in the end, the values were never posted and the exercise became a part of the oral tradition of the firm. People knew if a person fit the firm depending on whether they behaved consistently with the values. The values became the basis for behavioral interviewing and then a part of their performance management process.

The values also clarified some critical fissures in the firm. During the development process, it became apparent that one of the members of the leadership team was not aligned with the values and their behaviors. In retrospect, it was at the initial off-site that it became clear one of the newer leaders was not a good fit. He did not have the same aspirations or the same belief system. Ultimately, they decided to let him go, and as McQuown noted: "I think some of the reasons that we did, surfaced in our value search."

Soon, KMV was facing another kind of challenge — they were being pursued by a suitor. The founders decided that if it made economic sense to sell the company, they were willing to walk away, but they believed in the mission and culture of the firm as part of its success and felt that it was worth protecting and supporting. I was engaged to facilitate a discussion with the executive team on the fit of the suitor to the values of the firm. I asked the team members if in their interactions prior to this point with the people that were interested in taking them over they perceived that those corporate leaders had the same belief system. The answer was a resounding no. I then asked them, based on how they articulated their values and behaviors, whether they could sell their firm to the suitor, knowing that the employees they hired and the clients they fostered would be treated differently than they had been treated to that point. Would they, as the sellers, sleep well at night? Deep inside, the KMV team didn't like what the buyers represented and were apprehensive about their motive for the acquisition. They decided not to go ahead with the sale. The concern for values overwhelmed any interest in capitalizing on the value of the enterprise.

Two years later, KMV was sold to Moody's. The need for capital to accomplish their long-term objectives was still critical, but they made a decision to go with a new suitor based on values fit. They examined a number of alternatives from that perspective and chose the best option.

At the new firm, four members of the original leadership team remain. The cultural continuity is strong and seamless. Because the values alignment has been so evident, the people of the firm still react and treat one another and their customers the same way as they always did. The values that were created by the three founding partners remain their legacy for the organization. That legacy only exists because they put values ahead of money and personal gain.

KMV understood that submitting to a merger and acquisition did not imply a merger of equals. They had no illusion that they would have the power to decide their own culture in the future. So they actively sought out a merger partner who fit their values. They had the courage and conviction to complete an audit of the intangibles and measure them with the same scale with which they measured their need for capital and their desire for personal profit. As a result, the great change the company went through felt like an evolution rather than a cataclysm that stifled the beating heart of the firm.

The Aspiration to Change

Sometimes an organization has to change from within to deal with a changed world. Leaders who are quick to attempt a values shift may not understand the extent of the change they are seeking to make. Indeed, quite often, a company's new direction only needs a new strategic plan or a new structure or a new way of operating. Despite the extent of the work that goes into such transformations, they are relatively minor compared to a values overhaul. When values really do need to change, the strategy for making that transformation happen requires the foresight and persistence of a Napoleon. Take the case of Union Gas, located in Chatham, Ontario.

By 1999, Union Gas had been in business for eighty-five years and was in charge of the distribution and transmission of natural gas operations for the province of Ontario. As in many other energy monopolies, deregulation was looming. According to Grace Palombo, vice president human resources and general counsel, Union Gas had a very strong culture and work environment. "But we were at a point where the landscape and the market were changing." Deregulation presented a severe challenge to the operations of an old company, which had long had the market for gas cornered. Suddenly, consumers were going to have a choice about who to buy natural gas from. Union Gas knew it would have to learn how to compete in that market. On the good side, this change in regulation would also give Union Gas greater flexibility in the way it operated and marketed. As Palombo says, "The things that were happening made us realize that we had to become a different kind of company, more customer-focused, more into marketing. We had to become much more efficient and less wasteful. And we had to think differently. We really had to change our approach to work."

The company president spearheaded the change, and the support from that top position was critical in seeing the arduous and complicated work through. Because the organization was about to enter a deregulated marketplace for the first time in its long history, the entire purpose and function of the company was about to shift. Accordingly, the first thing the president and the top team decided to do was to articulate the new vision or mission of the organization. What would Union Gas be in business to do when the markets changed? How would it distinguish itself from the new competition? From that point, two initiatives were launched simultaneously. The first was to uncover and articulate the values of the company, not only as they had existed in its eighty-five-year history, but as those values would have to become in order to function in the new environment. The second initiative was to redesign the organization by flattening it and defining accountability and work processes through behavioral competencies at every distinct job level.

LOOK INSIDE THE BOX

Union Gas Values and Behaviors

The Union Gas Values and corresponding behavioral statements were written as a means to help the organization evolve from a regulated utility to deregulation. The values did not represent a radical change.

Integrity
- We deliver on our commitments.
- We welcome diverse opinions and treat everyone with respect.

Continued

- We express our opinions openly and are able to disagree without being personal.
- We support decisions, once made, both publicly and privately.

Valuing Our People
- We practice open and direct communication.
- We set shared goals.
- We give direct and frequent feedback on individual performance.
- We support our employees' efforts to develop their skills and competencies.
- We celebrate our successes.

Focus on Customers
- We actively seek feedback from our customers and act on it.
- We make it easy for customers to do business with us.
- We treat every interaction with a customer as an opportunity to reinforce their preference for natural gas as a fuel and Union Gas as a supplier.

Passion for Growth is our commitment to increase shareholder value.
- We focus on results — growing revenues, reducing costs and achieving good returns.
- We are innovative and learn from our mistakes.
- We value all employees' ideas in looking at business opportunities.
- We find opportunity where others don't.

Operationally Excellent is delivering consistently excellent service while constantly seeking ways to do things better.
- We deliver consistent repeatable processes at targeted service levels at the lowest cost.
- We put safety first.
- We are reliable and ensure that natural gas is there when our customers need it.
- We continuously seek to improve.

As the head of human resources, Grace Palombo recognized that it was important to do the work of articulating a changing set of values very carefully. "We did not criticize the past because the company had been successful in accomplishing its mission [in the regulated environment]. What we did was focus on the future, and values became the starting point for us. We said, 'Okay, effective six months from now, when the prices of gas and electricity converge and there is lighter-handed regulation, we're going to be in a competitive marketplace and we need to be different.' So we spent some time describing what that would be, and articulating what we were aspiring to become in order to continue to be successful."

After describing what the new Union Gas would look like, the top leaders articulated what the new culture would need to look like to be successful. Based on that description of the culture, the top leaders articulated the values the organization would have to have. My own work with the organization began at this point, helping to determine the values and spread them throughout the employee base and beyond.

Jane McCreadie joined the organization in March 1999, as director of learning and development. Her first assignment was

to oversee the changes being done to the organization's structure
in flattening it out and defining the competencies for each job
level. As a newcomer, in the midst of such tremendous change,
she faced great challenges but met them by doing what few in
human resources do: she got her hands dirty in the field and was
not afraid of taking a stand when there was a critical business
case to be made.

McCreadie was not only new to Union Gas but new to the
industry as well. Union Gas in particular had very little turnover,
and new faces were rare, particularly at the top levels, since
managers and senior managers were almost always promoted
from within. Knowing that the level of respect she could expect
to receive was limited, McCreadie was determined to find out
what people thought of her once she'd been on the job for six
months, and to listen to their feedback. So she created a select
group of people and had a 360-degree feedback assessment of
her performance done. One theme that came through clearly
was a general wish that "it would really be good if McCreadie
understood our business better, and knew what happened on the
front line, in understanding how to build our HR programs."
McCreadie recognized that this was a criticism she needed to
face immediately, so she decided to go out into the field to see
what the work was like. As she puts it now, "I was a little hesitant
about what value walking along a pipeline with a wrench would
offer, but if this is what garners respect from these folks, I knew I
needed to do it." When she asked a district manager to arrange for
her to join an actual work crew, he suggested putting off the task
until the spring because of the bitter cold of winter. McCreadie
knew, however, that work crews needed to work eight- to ten-
hour shifts even on the coldest days of the year, so she said to go
ahead with the arrangements.

A week before Christmas, she visited the district, and it was indeed the coldest week of the year. The district manager and his team were tickled that someone from head office was visiting. They couldn't believe that someone actually wanted to see what kind of work they did. They took her to a workman's clothing store the night before and got her the proper clothes, such as long underwear. The next day, McCreadie went out with a crew to do a set of regular calls, scheduled maintenance work and responses to gas leaks. She walked the line, checked valves, tightened connections and cleared snow away. She asked if she could do some actual work, if it didn't violate the collective agreement, and got permission to shovel away some snow.

On the surface, picking up a shovel wasn't such a revolutionary act, but McCreadie views it as the single most effective thing she did in her first year. The word spread that someone from the head office had actually gone out in the field, and that head office was interested in how people worked, rather than just pushing changes on them from afar. She would tap that new group of allies repeatedly in the years to come to help her sell the ideas of human resources to the larger operations.

Back at her own job, McCreadie encountered a serious problem. While there was values articulation work being done at the top levels of the company, and much work being done in the field to flatten the organization and define job levels, there was less coordination going on between these two initiatives than she might have expected. The gap had developed because the internal people running the project did not have a direct line to top management. They didn't understand the new vision, "so in essence, what I saw happening, was that they were creating a competency model based on what was successful in today's organization, as opposed to tomorrow's." Operating as the bad cop, McCreadie had the courage and business acumen to put a stop to that work, mid-way through its development, and lead everyone in recalibrating before going forward again. The internal people doing the work were shocked at first, in large part because they had been doing such a good job in developing competencies that seemed to fit the (current) organization so well. They also took offense that someone as new as McCreadie could know what competencies the business needed since she had just joined them. But McCreadie was able to talk to those people about what the top executives had shared with her in terms of the mission and vision of the new organization. "They needed to understand that this was a much broader change strategy than just defining a competency set to support new HR programs. This was bigger than HR, and it was essential that we connect into that larger plan and get aligned to it."

McCreadie found that over the next few weeks, as she repeated her message and talked with more and more people about the situation, the respect for her position grew. People understood that she was plugged in at the top, and while she might not have known in great detail what the employees did on a daily basis, she did understand more about how the future was shaping up. Some of those discrepancies were quite problematic. The internal work, for instance, had come up with a competency system that had seven levels of expectations. Meanwhile Jane knew that the organization was flattening to five levels, so only three levels of competency expectations would be necessary. Using such examples, she was able to convince the group that while the work they were doing was good, it was a little off track. They decided to put the brake on any such changes until the vision, values and organizational restructuring work was completed by the top executives, then align the internal competency work and the redesign of HR programs accordingly.

Back at the top, Grace Palombo was struggling with determining values for an organization that was undergoing great change.

"If you have the culture you want, and you don't have your values yet, you can go through a process of accurately describing what you do have [in terms of values], and put that up on a poster. [In theory] employees will then say, 'you know you're right, that is how we live and that is how we do business.' But my experience has been at most companies, what goes up on the poster does not accurately reflect the day-to-day life." To go forward and put up the new values of the company and say "this is what we believe and this is how we are now going to do business," regardless of how poorly they fit with the actual work, would invite employees to shake their heads and view the entire values exercise cynically. Palombo knew that employees would even be able to point out times that the president had not acted according to such stated values. Her solution was to list the new values as "aspirational statements." As she puts it, "I positioned us by saying in some cases we do demonstrate these values throughout the company and in some cases we don't. We need to keep in mind that these are the desired states that we should all be striving towards. There are times when we won't meet those expectations and we'll fall back, but we need to have constant reminders of how we want to be." For Palombo, this made it even more critical that the new values be integrated into the HR programs under development so that, for example, every performance review in the future involved a discussion of the organization's values and how that applied to an employee's work performance.

Describing the new values as "aspirational statements" limited cynicism, Palombo found, because it allowed them to be positioned as non-critical. "It removed the ability for someone to say, 'that's not how we are today' or 'you're my boss and you don't act that way.' The only disagreement we found was when someone didn't agree on what we needed to become."

Still, Palombo was concerned with how to communicate these values to the organization en masse in an efficient way to impact all employees. "It wasn't necessarily the 'what' of what we were going to tell them that concerned me, but I was struggling with how to do it in an organized, contained way," she says. I was at hand as an external consultant at this point to put together values workbooks describing the new values and a plan for implementation that carried forward the momentum that was building and would quickly cascade the values throughout the organization.

In my first session with the top executives, I talked about how the values of the organization needed to be constant. The challenge going forward was to ensure that if the world changed significantly again, the values that they had come up with would still be relevant. This forced them to really debate the importance of the values they had chosen. For example, customer satisfaction is one of the highest concerns that regulated energy-monopolies typically have. It was apparent to me after convening a number of intense focus groups, and already apparent to many of the top executives, that customer satisfaction was no longer going to rule the day the way it once had; it needed to be debated. This was an incredibly touchy subject, and I was warned not to even raise it because the CEO would "throw me out of the room." Knowing that values had to be real or they would be nothing, I brought the issue up in the meeting with the CEO, who reacted viscerally to the idea.

The CEO showed courage, however, in being open to a discussion. I asked the senior vice president of operations about the stated company policy on response time to a call from the public about a smell of gas. The VP answered that it was twenty-four hours. If the caller was a babysitter or an elderly person who could not deal with the danger on his or her own, the response was sooner. But otherwise, in a competitive market, it was impossible to respond immediately to all such complaints without having a service technician waiting on every corner. In the old environment, only immediate service would have constituted living up to the value of customer satisfaction. This vindicated my position and opened a conversation about what the new value should be. Collectively, the executive team came to the realization that its primary responsibility was to educate the customer at every opportunity, not just say yes to service demands and fail to come through. This did not sound exactly like "customer satisfaction"; instead, it sounded more like "customer care," which is the value we settled on.

The decision to use customer care and the corresponding behaviors had a major cost-saving impact. The pursuit of customer satisfaction would have translated into behaviors that required responding to customer requests without clarification or hesitation. Customer care, on the other hand, meant that call center employees were trained to ask customers who wanted gas connections when their building contractor would be working on their property. Many were calling thirty days or more before the event. The customer service representative could then negotiate the fact that the customer did not need the service for another twenty-nine days. As a result, they were able to deploy staff with greater success, reducing the need for overtime and enabling the use of third-party contractors, while also determining friendly windows of time in which the service person could show up at the customer's residence. The net result was a significant cost savings and customers who felt as though they were treated with respect and integrity according to the stated value of the company. The only downside was that the software designed under the old value of customer satisfaction to prompt a response needed to be changed.

Everyone found it amazing how a discussion about values had such a real impact on business and performance. There was renewed enthusiasm for the importance of the exercise, and everyone was committed to making it real.

When the values were finally rolled out to the organization, the employees had been working with new competencies for almost two years. They had undergone performance reviews and created development plans using those competencies. Accordingly, there was an initial sense that the values were just another progressive initiative that probably wouldn't mean much in reality. Employees knew, on the other hand, how tangible competencies played out in their daily jobs and performance assessments.

LOOK INSIDE THE BOX

Hiring for skills and knowledge will not a good employee be! If the differentiating factor is fit to the culture, then you need to conduct a behavioral interview that focuses on fit. You only have one time to get this right. Asking questions that might make the candidate a little uncomfortable is not a bad thing. They will not be uncomfortable if they live the values and have demonstrated living the values in their recent past experiences.

Sample Values-Based Behavioral Questions:

1. Tell me about a time when you had to make an immediate choice in production between quantity or quality.
2. Tell me about a time when you were asked by your manager to work beyond regular hours.
3. Tell me about a time when you were caught off guard by the actions of other employees in your firm.

In order to counteract that feeling of "yet another HR initiative," the top managers like McCreadie and Palombo decided to have the values come out through the public affairs department rather than through human resources. This would help promote the idea that the values were a company initiative. In broadcasting those values, public affairs did a very interesting thing. They first talked about how important the Union Gas values would be from a branding standpoint in a new marketplace. According to McCreadie, "They talked about the benefits of the values in dealing with external agencies, and telling other organizations that we operate this way. And then as a secondary point in the communication, they set up the values for the employees as another model of behavior consistent with the competencies to model in daily work and dealings in support of the brand." McCreadie had her misgivings about bringing the values in this way. "I will admit to you, it felt a little disjointed to me for a while," she says. But in the end, the idea that Union Gas needed values not only as a set of behavioral work descriptions but also as a brand was a strong one that made sense to all.

To help with the discussion of values between supervisors and reports throughout the company, the public affairs group put together a very powerful video showing the president of the company sitting in the boardroom talking about "how we live the values" with a number of employees from all different areas of the company. Particularly powerful was seeing the president admit that he hadn't always operated according to the values himself in the past, but now that they were articulated, and everyone knew how important they were for succeeding in the new marketplace, he would endeavor to do so, and he gave everyone permission to help hold him to those values in how he acted. All managers throughout the company were asked to use this video in their staff meetings, to talk about it with their reports, and take the understanding of it to a deeper level by relating the values to how people do their jobs and live the values. They asked such questions as, "What are the things you do or could do to demonstrate the values better?" From the top of the organization down to the lower levels where workers walk the line and clear the snow, pocket conversations about the values were under way to help employees internalize them.

Given the profound change that Union Gas was undergoing, it made sense to take the approach they adopted in using values as aspirations to be strived for in order to adapt to new circumstances. Significantly, they backed that rhetoric up by incorporating the values into all human resources programs such as hiring and performance management. And finally, they had the support of the president from the very launching of the initiative, through the communication of the final product to the employees, to his stated commitment to live the values himself in the days to come. He even asked everyone to give him ongoing feedback about whether he was or was not acting according to the values.

LOOK INSIDE THE BOX

Is it acceptable to have only a little of the values some of the time? While the obvious answer is no, why do performance management programs have anything beyond "meets expectations," which is defined clearly as "every opportunity to live the values with all people at all levels the individual demonstrated the correct values behavior."

If the values are black and white, you can't exceed expectation on values or behavioral competencies because they are in fact the definition of what you are to do all the time.

The real question is if you don't act in alignment with the values consistently, perhaps not every time but the clear majority of time, why are you still employed by that firm?

In turn what is the firm saying to their other employees who they know also know that the person is not living the values?

What is being said to the employees if a manager who violates the values is promoted because the employees made their manager look good with the results?

The story, however, did not end there. In the world of energy supply, deregulation had created a wave of mergers. In 2002, Union Gas was purchased by Duke Energy. Union Gas's values had only been in place for six months. It was apparent to Grace Palombo that "the Duke culture was completely different. They had a very different set of values, very different approach to business and a different set of priorities. The resistance of our employees to these values provided a kind of checkpoint showing how strong our values had actually become. People said, 'That's not how we do things.'"

Duke was actually in the process of defining its own values while the merger was proceeding. This heightened awareness of the importance of values on both sides of the merger seemed to facilitate the integration of the two cultures. According to Jane McCreadie, Duke talked early on about the fact that the two sets of values, while not identical, were at least congruent. In terms of business opportunities and the business itself, there was a lot of common ground on which to build a shared sense of purpose and approach. The Duke team offered McCreadie a look at the Duke values when they were in their final stages of development and asked her to run some focus groups in Canada to get input and understanding. "We offered some final feedback, and the values were quickly finalized and communicated after that," McCreadie says.

McCreadie had no illusion that Duke's values would take precedence. "This was not a merger; it was an acquisition, so I began to retract work that we had done at a palatable place, and replace communication about our values with Duke Energy materials." She launched new communication efforts and manager staff meetings to facilitate understanding. "We did a comparison of Duke Energy values, showed the similarities with our own and drew the alignments. That helped our employees get onto the Duke Energy page very quickly."

It also helped that Union Gas had become so practiced at smoothly integrating values and behaviors into people management systems. "Duke Energy had a different performance management system," says Jane, "so we migrated over to that. They had a different set of competencies, so we migrated to those. There were a lot of things to retract and replace. We agreed on the right pace and the right time for those changes. We didn't try to change the performance management system in March, for instance, when the merger went through. We waited to finish the year with the program everyone knew and introduced the change in January for the new cycle."

The most important thing for McCreadie was that this work on the intangibles of the business was considered as essential as the integration of the financial and operating systems. "This wasn't HR trying to sell the need for a strategy. This was the business saying we need to change and we want to do it with guided HR expertise. In a lot of other situations, HR professionals find themselves working with senior management who need to change their business processes, and plan to deal with the people stuff later. This [values work] was top of mind for them and they were tremendously supportive of the people needs that were changing."

Ensuring Your Return on Intangibles

The essential tool in all significant organizational change is clarity of values. When values are well understood and articulated, and are integrated into the people management systems of an organization, then leaders and employees are hyper aware of their importance in daily operations. The question becomes: how do you know that a big change will create a change in values, and do you want to go down that road?

Change is a constant, as we're all tired of hearing. But not all change, no matter how sweeping, touches the ultra-sensitive nerves of values. Strategic change, market change, operational change and even a change of vision or mission do not necessarily require a change in values. Organizations facing such change can assess whether the values are being affected by testing how close to the bone the change feels. Does the change affect who you are, what you're about and what you stand for? Like an exposed nerve, the questions will prompt painful, anxious or even panicked responses if values are involved. If your values do not have to be changed, then the rightness of a major change in direction, strategy or organizational structure needs to be tested for correctness by confirming that such a change is in line with the existing values. If, for whatever reason, a change in values is necessary, then clearly understanding your own values will help you be precise and surgical about the changes to be made, ultimately reducing organizational stress and increasing the likelihood of success.

When values must change, engaging your people and communicating with them is critical. Let them understand the change in values through stories, not just PR-driven words. If your company is about to be acquired, assess the culture and values of your new owner by finding out their stories and legends. Compare them with your own. The understanding that ensues will go deeper than if you simply take down one set of posters and put up another. In a similar way, if your company is going through a change in mission akin to the kind Union Gas experienced during deregulation, allow your people to understand in tangible, concrete ways how that change in values will look, sound and feel. If they can put the change into language and stories that really mean something to them, they will engage with the shift at a gut level.

In the end, all change is personal. If organizations are collections of people who share similar beliefs, language, a sense of purpose and ways of doing things, then dealing with those intangibles is your key to leading them into a new world. If you seek out a solid return on intangibles, then your return on investment will be much more secure.

CHAPTER SEVEN

Measuring Inside-the-Box Success: The Meaning of Integrity, Business Results and Employee Brand

- ❑ Why integrity is not a value.

- ❑ The importance of values to ensure doing what is right, not what is easy or expedient.

- ❑ Values define what employees expect from one another.

- ❑ Using the values as a business tool for decision-making.

- ❑ Integration of values into all aspects of human resources.

- ❑ Living the values makes working in a company predictable.

In the end, do values really make a difference? Does an organization do better when it embraces values and integrates them into the way it does business? How do you measure that impact? In a bottom-line world, it's still an argument that needs proof. In this final chapter, we'll talk about what values will give back to your company.

To some people, values are just words. To cynics and critics, this means that values are empty promises, which a corporation can use as a public relations or recruiting tool when expedient, and cover up or completely ignore when it is more profitable to do so. Those same cynics and critics would accuse the modern corporation of having no integrity. Isn't it ironic, then, that according to Patrick Lencioni's article "Make Your Values Mean Something" in the *Harvard Business Review*, 55 percent of all Fortune 100 companies define integrity as one of their values? People respond to integrity and a sense of authenticity in their leaders. But is integrity important to modern corporations? Let's start to examine that question by looking at one of the corporations that listed integrity as a value — Enron.

Before its fall, Enron was the dream company of consultants, shareholders and a good number of current and prospective employees. It was high on every list of most admired companies, and was considered an employer of choice. For five years running, it was selected as among one of *Fortune* magazine's most innovative organizations. Enron's vision was "to become the world's leading energy company — creating innovative and efficient energy solutions for growing economies and a better environment worldwide." Its values in support of that vision were:

LOOK INSIDE THE BOX

Enron's Values

Respect

We treat others as we would like to be treated ourselves. We don't tolerate abusive or disrespectful treatment. Ruthlessness, callousness and arrogance don't belong here.

Integrity

We work with customers and prospects openly, honestly and sincerely. When we say we will do something, we will do it: when we say we cannot or will not do something, then we won't do it.

Communication

We have an obligation to communicate. Here, we take the time to talk with one another … and to listen. We believe that information is meant to move and that information moves people.

Excellence

We are satisfied with nothing less than the very best in everything we do. We will continue to raise the bar for everyone. The great fun here will be for all of us to discover just how good we can really be.

In its principles, Enron went on to state:

Enron stands on the foundations of its Vision and Values. Every employee is educated about the Company's Vision

Continued

and Values and is expected to conduct business with other employees, partners, contractors, suppliers, vendors and customers keeping in mind respect, integrity, communication and excellence. Everything we do evolves from Enron's Vision and Values statements.

And a little further down the list:
We are dedicated to conducting business according to all applicable local and international laws and regulations, including, but not limited to, the U.S. Foreign Corruptions Practices Act, and with the highest professional and ethical standards.

We still don't know exactly where it all went wrong. On paper, Enron said all the right things. As a company, every employee would be developed and managed according to the vision and values. Those values clearly prohibited activities like falsification of numbers, the trading of bogus contracts and the bilking of shareholders. I could parse the way Enron worded its values, pointing out that they were vague and left a lot of leeway in interpretation. But at the same time, it's difficult to fathom anyone who was actually trained and promoted according to those values putting up with the illegal activities Enron eventually got caught doing.

Given all the other scandals that arose around the time of Enron, cynics and critics must pause to wonder how the modern corporation can lay claim to having any integrity at all. I'm not in that camp, but I do believe they are right when they say that integrity is not a corporate value. Let me explain why and show how that understanding can be the foundation for using values in a way that really counts.

Integrity is Not a Value

Organizations love listing integrity as one of their values, but I always have trouble helping them articulate what integrity means. How can we define it in concrete terms? Other overused abstract words like *respect* and *honesty* create the same kinds of concerns. You can define teamwork, or even excellence, but it's always been difficult, in my experience, to distill the essence of integrity. This confusion came to a head, a few years ago, when a client I was working with to define their values encountered a serious values challenge in the middle of the process.

The organization, an insurance provider, was being sued by a family for coverage that hadn't been provided after an accident because of an issue with a premium. As we worked through the task of articulating the organization's values, newspapers blared headlines about the progress of the court case, putting all of our efforts in an uncomfortable context. Perhaps, because of that contentious atmosphere, our debate was particularly rigorous and thoughtful. When we finally came to an agreement, everyone in the room was happy. Then one executive threw cold water in our faces: "If all of these values are really true, and I think they are, then we're doing the wrong thing fighting this family in court."

It was a sobering thought that galvanized a powerful reaction. Immediately, the top leaders decided that the company would reverse its stand and pay up. The lawyers couldn't believe it, but the executive team had its first good sleep in a while, comforted by the certainty that it had done right by the family — and the organization.

The reaction to this switch was overwhelmingly positive. The press loved the decision. Politicians applauded it. The community genuinely appreciated the gesture. Other companies, at a conference that took place soon after, admired it, knowing

that it took a lot of courage to set such a precedent when profit
was at stake. Most important, the people within the organization
felt good about the decision. In fact, the event clearly had the
makings of a genuine corporate legend, one of those stories I
always listen for, because they often capture the essence of what is
unique and meaningful about a company. One of the executives
seemed to sum up everyone's feeling of pride when he said, "We
acted with integrity."

When I heard him say that, I felt a sense of anxiety. We'd
just finished articulating the company's values and integrity
wasn't one of them. But clearly, integrity had been an emotional
hot button for everyone in the company, something that really
mattered. Did this mean we needed to put our heads down again
and rethink the values we had come up with, replacing one or
more for a value like integrity? The list of values we had drawn
up all pointed to behaving in the same way, and yet it was the
word *integrity* that seemed to capture the actions that had been
taken and deemed so successful and central to the corporation's
culture. There it was again, integrity, my bugaboo, throwing a
wrench into an otherwise agreeable process.

As I thought more about what integrity really means, an
answer occurred to me. *Integrity isn't a value.* Instead, integrity
is the byproduct of living your values. To violate a value, or the
entire set of values, is to diminish your integrity. Integrity is not a
value in itself, but a summing up of the other values together. To
include integrity in a list of values is a redundancy. Organizations
act with integrity only when they live up to all their values with
equal fervor all the time.

A company like Enron did not act with integrity; therefore, it
did not have integrity. With arrogance and disrespect, it rigged
an elaborate accounting shell game, which benefitted some

individuals in the short term while ultimately decimating the share value of the firm and putting its employees out of work. The fact that it failed to adhere to its own values made those acts possible. Given the level of complicity within the organization, it seems likely that a shadow, underground culture with a different set of values thrived while the explicit articulated aboveground values of the firm were all for show. In an amazingly and tragically amplified way, Enron shows the dangers of not walking the talk.

Managers who make even minor decisions contrary to their organization's values act without integrity, too. Under great pressure to make the business run profitably or deal effectively with the political concern of the moment, executives often find it more expedient to succumb to easy priorities rather than struggle for the right decision according to the values. Immediate gratification — the crisis put under wraps, the contrary employee fired, the numbers met — overcome the priorities for longer-term impact. This creates a gap between word and deed, and fosters cynicism. When a manager's actions and decisions are not consistent with what the leadership has articulated as the company's values, employees learn to suspect the truth and expect the worst. They come to see leadership as betraying whatever convictions they pretend to hold, lacking any courage to do the right thing. This default is especially glaring when times are tough.

On the other hand, every decision made in line with the organization's values reinforces those values and makes the tough decisions easier. Values are expressed by all organizations in the way employees, suppliers, customers and shareholders are treated. Organizations with integrity are those whose leaders and employees live those values day to day, in good times and bad.

LOOK INSIDE THE BOX

Seven Steps for Ethical Decision-Making

Step 1: Determine the Facts

Too often people want to make fact-based decisions. This is not in itself a bad thing, but the discussion usually ends up being about emotions not facts. When you act too fast, you spend an equal if not greater amount of time reworking or rediscovering information to make a second decision.

Step 2: Determine the Impact on People

By knowing all the people internal and external to the company who will be impacted in the short and long run, you have the capability to consult with them and make them part of the process. This leads to step three.

Step 3: Consult Your Values

Your values demand an action or response to every situation. Knowing your values allows you to know the ethical correctness of the action sooner rather than later. I have seen heated debate at the executive level come to a sudden halt when one of the parties points out the context of the actions to be taken and how they hold up in light of the values.

Step 4: Realize There is More Than One Right Answer

When you think you have the answer, seek out the second right answer. Just as there are many sides to a story, there are often many right answers. The process of discovering alternative answers opens you up to additional modifications to your actions. Sometimes through an action based on the least harm, you find a way to the greater good.

Step 5: Think Long Term, Not Short Term

One of the biggest flaws in much corporate decision-making is that senior management is too focused on short-term gains. A value-based decision might not provide an instant impact on your people. But if you act for immediate gratification, things might seem good for the short term, but they always turn out wrong in the long term. Cynicism is a delayed reaction. Employees, rightfully, often assert that leadership is lacking perspective or is deficient in long-term thinking. No one value is more important than another.

Step 6: Select the Action

After consideration of all of the above, it is time to act. While working through steps one to five seems a long and drawn-out process, in reality it could take a very short period of time. Many of the aspects of the steps above are intuitive and the answer is obvious. Once you have eliminated the politically expedient action and the other actions that would have violated the company value set or code of conduct, you can make your decision based on the greater good instead of the least harm. This is not to say the action you take will not harm certain people. But in the long term, you will have caused the least amount of harm.

Step 7: Take Action

At this time you begin the execution of the plan knowing that as things evolve and more information comes to the forefront you might have to alter the course of action. Being stuck on a particular decision without being open to the impact of new information on people, progress or long-term business,

Continued

will have a negative impact on what would have been an opportunity for continually improving the decisions you make.

If you follow the values as they actually are lived within the
culture of the organization, you might decide that what initially
appeared to be a financially unsound business decision has
turned out to be the greatest decision you've ever made. You
can also sleep well at night because you will know it was the
right way to go.

Bringing it All Together

The Calgary Police Service (CPS) is a good example of an
organization living its values. The CPS clearly states that a member
of the service will have integrity only when he or she lives the
behaviors that define those values as an absolute priority inside
and outside the organization. Few friends from my "radical" youth
could have anticipated that I would work with a police service
one day. But I have seen no better example of a leadership group
that has used cultural continuity to its advantage in developing
its people and serving its client base — the taxpayers of the city of
Calgary, Alberta. Let me tell you how this organization managed
to do that.

Let me begin with two very powerful stories that exemplify
how living one's values — especially in difficult times when you
could "justify" doing what others have done — is not the right
way of acting. Through its history the CPS has marched to its
values and not the status quo of acceptable policing.

The G8 Meeting
When you imagine a G8 meeting, you visualize what began in
Seattle, Washington, as a violent confrontation between the law

and order of the police service and city officials and the masses of protestors. All G8 and other international world forums have been violent to one degree or another from Quebec City to Évian-les-Bains, France, to Genoa, Italy, to Okinawa, Japan, and Hong Kong, China and many more. What happened in Calgary when the CPS was the focal point of the Kananaskis, Alberta, G8 meeting in 2002 is a sign that even in the face of significant pressure your values will lead you to success.

To me the most telling story of the use of values as the heart and soul of the organization was when the CPS prepared for the G8 meeting. The Service was given the responsibility for security of the members of the G8 nations and other dignitaries. The meeting was to be held in Kananaskis, thirty miles into the Rocky Mountains. Since the first WTO riots in Seattle, these international meetings meant confrontation and conflict, often resulting in damage to commercial stores and injuries to both officers and demonstrators. This would not be acceptable to the Service given the behaviors they had used to define the value of compassion (compassion is coupled with respect and fairness).

As the training of the officers began, the participants were told that if they perceived any of the actions they were being taught regarding crowd control or other activities associated with the G8 meeting as violating the Service's values, they were to speak up. Deputy Chief Hanson was the lead on the G8 preparation. Two weeks prior to the meeting, he was called into the mayor's office. The mayor told Hanson that he had received feedback that the CPS was not preparing for the G8's onslaught of demonstrators in the same way as other services.

Hanson assured the mayor that they would be acting in accordance with the values of the Service and the expectations of the community of Calgary. The mayor continued to express his concern about the Service not following standard operating procedures for crowd control and other activities associated with such a gathering. Hanson clearly and forcefully stated that his officers

would not act in a way that violated the values and corresponding behaviors of the Service, even if it went against the best practices of policing up to that point. The CPS was going to stand
its ground on that point and not compromise the values. The
mayor then backed off and Hanson and his team implemented
their strategy. One reporter described the ensuing G8 protests as
more of a love-in from the 1960s than a demonstration.

By following their values, the CPS developed a plan of action
that respected the rights of the demonstrators to get their message
heard within the boundaries of the law. The CPS actually met
with the local representatives of each of the groups planning
to demonstrate and contacted others who were beyond the city
limits, working with them to develop a means of arbitrating if
one side or the other was getting out of line. The result was
the establishment of a mutually agreed upon go-between, or
arbitrator, to ensure that neither side would go beyond what it
agreed to prior to the start of the meeting of nations.

While other multi-national economic forums have been held
since 2002, Calgary remains the only one in a fully democratic
nation that resulted in no property damage or personal injury.
There were four arrests during the demonstrations, two of which
were for issues not related to the demonstrations. Jurisdictions in
other cities rejected the CPS's approach, however, which led to a
return to violence in subsequent G8 meetings.

Writing this I realized that this was not the first time the
CPS acted counter to standard police practices. In the 1960s,
my college roommate, Van McCleod, came to the Toronto Film
Festival to see the release of the movie *Festival Express*. This film
chronicles the cross-Canada journey of a train full of popular
rock musicians in 1970. The train's journey started in Montreal
and ended in Calgary, making stops for the musicians to give
concerts. Van was on the train, working as the lighting director.

He was part of the jam sessions and wanted to be there with other members of the train who would be in attendance to capture moments of the past.

I recall the images of the crowds of young people in other cities along the route who were held back, often forcefully and without mercy, by the local police. Yet, in Calgary the arrival of the members of the train were greeted by an entirely different experience with the police. In fact, there are scenes in the film of members of the CPS in the crowd just enjoying the music and allowing the events to unfold peacefully. It seems to me that the approach was consistent with the values of the CPS then, as it is now, even in very different times with very different sets of veteran officers. The value of compassion held true.

The Beginning of the CPS Values Journey

It has taken a great deal of work to make the Calgary Police Service such a strong organization. When Christine Silverberg took over as Chief of the CPS in 1995, she came to a Service that had a proud and long history with a strong commitment to the community. But the CPS was also a hierarchy deeply rooted in tradition and seniority. In fact, the CPS possessed strong pride of service, but its culture passively expressed that pride. The Service needed a way to develop its members to a higher level of capability while celebrating their pride and culture.

Prior to Chief Silverberg, Chief Gerry Borbridge had laid the groundwork for the behaviors of community policing. While those behaviors were never defined concretely, their success was linked to the deep roots of the CPS values of community service. The CPS was ready to embark on a more behavior-focused expression of how it conducted business.

When the project began, Calgary was (and still is) growing at an amazing rate. Fast-paced population growth directly affects the amount of public disorder and growing crime in a community. Rapid growth brings increased diversity, a change that needs to be reflected in the Service. Indeed, workforce demographics suggest that a large number of officers will reach retirement age by 2010, and recruiting efforts need to be stepped up. As senior officers retire, those left in senior positions will have less experience collectively. This highlights the need to make learning and training opportunities available to the workforce. For both external and internal reasons, then, the time has come to build a model for sustained change while also celebrating the past.

Silverberg had an abiding belief that organizational development and culture (values) could be the enabling force that would make policy and organizational shifts successful. In her first few months on the job, Silverberg conducted an informal appraisal of what members of the Service wanted, both from her as Chief and from the Service as a whole. This process raised many problematic internal organizational issues, including human resource policies such as hiring, promotion and recognition systems. The Chief determined that her job was "to put in place structures, systems and processes within which the CPS could solve its own problems." From the start, the Chief was interested in getting officers at all levels involved in the process and with the creation of a Service they would be proud to work for. She delegated to the human resources team (then headed by Deputy Chief Rick Hanson and Inspector Dale Burn) the task of creating a holistic approach to engaging the organization, one that would break down systemic biases (that relationships were the key to promotions) and get everyone involved. This process successfully levelled the playing field, as in the first year many people were promoted who previously may not have been.

The work started with the premise that the Service needed to create an integrated, holistic approach to its human capital.

Knowing that a new business plan would have to be drafted for 1999–2001, everyone hoped that the introduction of a behavioral competency process would set about helping the CPS create a uniform and consistent way of operating.

The team of Hanson and Burn instituted a systems approach to capture the advances made by the previous Chief in his move to community policing. This model retained the vertical chain of command but overlaid it with a cross-functional structure, while moving the Service further along its goal of community-based policing. The model is captured in the following table.

LOOK INSIDE THE BOX

Traditional versus Community Methods of Policing:

Traditional	Community
• Reactive	• Proactive
• Conformity	• Creativity
• Enforcement	• Prevention
• Bureaucratized; Manager as controller	• Cross-functional; Manager as learning facilitator / coach
• Command of control	• Empowerment of lower ranks
• Focus on individual performance; technical job skills	• Focus on team and organizational performance; skills of whole person
• Sporadic, isolated and contained training	• Life-long, holistic learning
• Centralized decision-making	• Inclusive, community-based decision-making

The project began with the development of the behavioral profile for the role of constable. During the focus group discussions, we first asked the sworn officers who participated to address their perceptions of the values of the Service. During that discussion, they were asked to identify the aboveground and underground values and provide evidence of incidents to support their claims. The discussions were always lively and enlightening. While we found that the two sets of values were closer than people thought, it was apparent that many were concerned that the stated and real values were drifting apart.

The team of Silverberg, Hanson and Burn realized early on that organizational values were central to aligning the efforts of moving the organization forward based on the strength of its past. They also knew that the leaders of the Service had to initiate, from the top down, the behaviors that defined the values. Further, senior management would have to demonstrate with consistency and vigilance its commitment to the values, in particular, and the human resources project in general. The Chief realized that one way to center everyone's efforts was to work together to achieve a consensus. In November of 1997, the human resources team led a service-wide process of competency profiling. After the focus groups for the first role were concluded, we realized that value identification must be the foundation for all of the work on behaviors.

But as the work on competencies began, it became clear to the team that the credibility of the effort rested with the ability of the system to promote the right individuals. That would mean avoiding choices based rigorously on seniority as in the traditional service, or even on the person with the most capability; instead choices would be based on selecting the person who had the most competence to do the job. In order to do this, the promotional process needed to be fair, and it needed a foundation in the values of the Service. The team realized that promoting an officer with the most number of years of service and the technical knowledge to do the job without the values of the CPS would instantly kill the credibility of the work the team members had started to develop.

Values are strongly held beliefs that are emotionally charged and highly resistant to change. In order for the CPS to use them as a basis for major change, all members needed to believe, share and act on them with consistency. The early work on the first role profile provided an in-depth understanding of the corporate legends of the Service that made the values real, and showed that the aboveground and underground values were truly aligned.

But it would still take the leadership of the Chief and her deputies to articulate the values. After all of the deputy chiefs were interviewed one on one to determine their personal takes on the corporate vision and values, the group went off site to have a conversation to reach a consensus on the values and to uncover stories of clear actions that represented incidents of members of the Service living the values. This group represented over 100 years of collective service, but there was a problem. At such sessions, the CEO is usually present and participates to varying degrees. However, since the Service was a paramilitary organization with a strict hierarchy, the presence of the Chief would undoubtedly shut down the conversation, as her direct reports would have looked to her for the answers. So we informed Chief Silverberg that it would be best that she not come for the one-and-a-half-day conversation.

Initially, the deputy chiefs were reluctant to engage in any kind of conversation without the Chief present. We explained our reasons, and they gradually accepted the idea. The day-and-a-half discussion culminated in a list of values consistent with the culture and history of the service. In the end, the Chief's and her deputies' views were closely aligned with the officers'. As a result, it took little time to articulate the values and behaviors. They are listed below:

The CPS Values

Members of the CPS will be known for our honesty, integrity and ethics as we demonstrate in every situation with all people we interact with when we live our values as defined as follows:

◆ **Respect, Fairness and Compassion** as demonstrated by:

- Actively supports the values of individual difference and that a variety of perspectives can build a better understanding than a single opinion leading to a strong Service.
- Holds individual members who are intolerant of people because of prejudicial words or actions accountable.
- Says "no" when overloaded with work while working to provide alternative suggestions to the person to get the request executed in a feasible yet different manner.
- Finds an appropriate balance between work and personal life, not sacrificing one at the expense of the other.

◆ **Commitment** to our community, people, learning and continuous improvement as demonstrated by:

- Once a decision is taken, supports the ideas of others both in public and in private.
- Provides recognition of individual contribution to the success of the team in particular and the CPS in general.
- Continuously learning and growing professionally by seeking out information from other police jurisdictions, academic research and others to solve our problems and improve the way we deliver services.
- Takes intelligent risk based on research and learning for the experience of self and others.
- Finds creative new ways of doing things that move the results forward to meeting the strategic business plan.

◆ **Courage** as demonstrated by:

- Doing the right thing, even when others hesitate.
- Takes a decisive stand on issues based on past experience, fact and intuition.
- Takes a bullet (literal and figurative) when required.
- States the truth under all circumstances.
- Acts in accordance with the CPS values in all activities, even if it means putting one's self at risk.
- Gives feedback to people at all levels if their behavior is inappropriate, not aligned with the values of the CPS.
- Puts the good of the CPS and the community before personal interests, gain or recognition.
- Admits to mistakes, taking responsibility for one's actions and decisions.
- Applies the learning from mistakes in subsequent situations.

Validating the Values and Developing the Behavioral Role Profiles

Defining the values enabled the Competency Development Team to raise awareness of what behaviors were necessary to achieve success on the job. Moreover, the values provided the guidelines within which a person would be defined as successful within the service overall. We then set out to get feedback on those values and behaviors from a variety of sources.

Through focus groups and individual interviews with both sworn and civilian members of the CPS, the competency team continued the development and validation of competency profiles for the balance of all the ranks within the organization. In layman's terms, the values of the CPS were translated into clearly stated behaviors with measurable outcomes. These profiles were to form the basis, not only of a new approach to promotion and succession planning, but also of revamped hiring, performance development (management) and career development procedures.

From the start, the human resources team and the consultant recognized that it was very important for staff to be involved in the process; they wanted every constable on the force to have a chance to be involved in validating the constable profile. This allowed members to give feedback on the draft profile for their respective rank (or the rank of those they supervised) and ensure that those who do the job agree on the behaviors the job entails.

Promotion and Succession Planning

One of the first issues identified for improvement was the promotional process. As in many organizations, the traditional process for promotions was perceived as unfair and based on political connections internal to the organization. In order to level the playing field and give all prospective candidates for promotion an equal chance, values were made a cornerstone of the promotional process. To do this, the values could not just be stated as words on a page but needed consistency in interpretation so all members of the Service would have a common understanding of the meaning of the values as they lived in real life.

The values had to be written clearly to ensure that the members of the Service would not only be demonstrating them but they would be understood by the members of the Service as a foundation for doing what is right for the community. The addition of the values to the promotion interview was fundamental to ensuring the values would be taken with the seriousness they deserved.

Typical Promotion Ladder

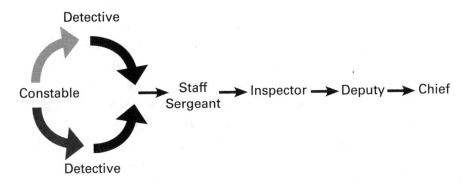

In the pre-behavioral profile system, the CPS used a promotion system called *forced ratings*. It worked like this: candidates' district or section commanders, who, along with staff sergeants and sergeants, ranked the individuals who had applied for promotion in their area, prior to bringing the person forward for consideration for promotion. The district/section would support the individuals with the highest rankings, bringing them forward to citywide ratings. Again, all highly ranked individuals were compared across the city and only certain numbers of the highest ranked individuals continued on to an interview stage. Three one-on-one interviews were conducted and interviewers got together at the end of the process to rate the candidates and prepare a list of promotable individuals. There were three main problems with this system. First, promotion was based on a certain series of activities that had to be completed prior to promotion, but only had to be checked off on a list. This meant important behaviors could have been demonstrated only once, rather than on a consistent and reparative basis. Second, favoritism was inherent in the process. The third and final issue was that seniority was the factor often taken into consideration as the primary consideration.

The Revised Promotional Process

The new promotional system begins with a review of the behavioral profile for the desired job that each person desires to be promoted to. In the past success in your current rank was the foundation upon which you could move forward. Candidates interested in promotion (for example, constables wishing to become sergeants) will meet with their commander for an informal behavioral interview and complete a Competency Assessment form for the rank to which they desire to be promoted. Measurement against the competencies requires the officer to provide to their direct supervisor examples of times, preferably in the last twelve to eighteen months, when they have repeatedly demonstrated some of the desired behaviors for the rank to which they will be applying for promotion. If, in the opinion of the supervisor, the candidate can be supported for a recommendation for promotion, the individual's name is brought forward to a group of their supervisor's peers.

At the peer review meeting, the other sergeants in the unit or district review the individual recommendations. The group cannot deny the recommendation of the individual's direct supervisor unless they have specific anecdotal evidence as to why the incidents that the candidate used to support his or her belief that the candidate demonstrated the behaviors for promotion were not factual based on the first hand observations of another peer of the candidate's supervisor. The credibility of the process is based on several premises. All candidates must have demonstrated situations that required them to live the values. All supervisors recommending a person must come prepared with real and meaningful stories to support the recommendation. No other peer during the peer review session can speak negatively about a person who is being brought forward for recommendation without providing contradictory evidence of the person's inappropriate behavior. If the peers do not recommend the person be brought forward to their commander for recommendation, then the recommending supervisor has to go back to the officer, explain why his or her promotion was not granted permission to move forward along the promotional interview path at this time. The supervisor of this officer and the officer have to immediately build a development plan that, if successful, would lead to a successful recommendation to the commander's peers the following year. That action plan has to be shared with the commander of the unit responsible for officer development, and the supervisor has to report to his or her own commander on the person's progress, or lack thereof during the year.

No officer recommended at this point is ensured of promotion; they are passed along for a promotional interview. If the supervisor does not agree that the candidate is promotable, the candidate can initiate an appeal process to a higher level. Decisions of non-support must be documented and provided to the candidate. If the individual is supported for promotion, he or she is presented to the Candidate Eligibility Board where all candidates are rated based on the competencies and other information (such as exam results) by all members of the next higher rank. Candidates who do not pass the Eligibility Board are provided with information on why they were not supported. They can use this to build their career/development plans. Feedback for the officers is a major benefit as it allows them to understand clearly what they need to do to get a promotion. The successful candidate goes on to a Formal Behavioral Interview stage with a panel of senior members who make recommendations to the Board of Senior Officers. This board makes the final promotion decisions based on all evidence.

Recently, in an effort to ensure that the total background of the officer is reviewed, the service has added to the process senior ranking members of the service to be part of the promotional review process. They are responsible for a background check on the person's capability and competence to perform the role of the next level successfully. That background information is combined with the results of the promotional board panel interview, and recommendations are made accordingly. Third-party observers are always present to maintain the objectivity of the promotional process. The third party is usually a retired officer.

This new process has addressed both problems identified in the old promotion system. Officers can no longer simply check items off a list, or do something only once in the last three months prior to promotion to demonstrate that they're eligible for promotion. They are now measured on how frequently they exhibit a desired behavior over the previous twelve to eighteen months. They must frequently demonstrate the desired behaviors with consistency while always acting according to the values of the CPS. Since all officers are promoted based on the same objective criteria, favoritism has been made effectively obsolete. While the number of people up for promotion has decreased because of the well-published criteria for promotion, the majority of the officers has recognized the fairness of the process. For the first five years of the process, there were no grievances after promotion decisions were made. In the sixth year, there was a challenge to the process and the challenge was not successful. After a consideration of the evidence the decision to dismiss the grievance was based on the solid evidence that the interview process is in fact equal and fair for all candidates. This conclusion was made because the competencies that defined the position and the questions were valid as there is a clear link between the questions and the behaviors of the profile. The outcome was that the interview was done in a fair manner and the decision of the promotional board of the CPS stood.

Hiring New Officers

Since the CPS operates an internal labor market with only one port of entry at the constable level, the constable behavioral competency profile is now used for hiring new constables. Previous to the use of competency profiles, the CPS had another set of criteria they used to hire constables. Individuals were hired based on KASPs, or knowledge, ability, skills and personality traits. Previously, new recruit interviews were behavioral in nature, but were not based on competencies that employees themselves had helped to create. Current recruit course content has been successfully rewritten to reflect a values-based and behavioral competency-based learning approach. This teaches new recruits critical thinking skills and decision-making abilities based on the values of the CPS and the community they serve.

New officers are now trained using the behavioral profiles. All officers in the service have access to all profiles, allowing people at each rank to be aware of the behaviors of the rank above them when they are aiming for promotion. Certain "knockout factors" (those skills, knowledge and/or behaviors necessary to begin the role successfully) of the profile above them need to be demonstrated before they will be considered for promotion. Clearly, new performance management tools need to be developed to support the new competency-driven system.

Given the workforce demographics mentioned earlier, it is expected that hiring will increasingly need to be a consistent process. For example, 1998 statistics showed that 34 percent of Calgary police officers had between sixteen and twenty years of experience. Over half the sworn personnel at the time had sixteen or more years of service. Assuming retirements coincide with twenty-five years of service, and all eligible individuals retire at twenty-five years, the CPS will need to replace almost 650 officers before 2008 just to maintain existing staffing levels. It was expected that 313 members would retire by 2003 and there continues to be a significant number of senior tenured officers retiring each year. Recall, however, that the city is growing, and staffing requirements will grow too, making this a conservative estimate. The Chief's decision to implement a fair and equitable process for hiring could not have been more timely, and adherence to the system will no doubt continue to improve efficiency of the hiring system as the demand for officers and civilian members increases.

The first proactive application of the values was the hiring of new recruits. New possible cadets are put through a rigorous process. They have to pass the following tests: psychologist interviews, physical capability, background check, lie detectors, mental health, as well as have a B.A. or B.Sc. (Some members of the Service have already attained Master's Degrees and some even have MBAs, and one is even a lawyer.) But the final interview prior to the final offer to join the cadet class is now a behavioral interview that is focused on the values of the CPS.

Performance Management

Performance management was the least well developed of the competencies used by the Service. Over the last six years, the organization continued to have difficulty getting the message across to members of the importance of giving feedback for the purpose of improvement. Not unlike other organizations, the performance feedback process was less honest and forthcoming than it should be. Members were reluctant to give one another negative feedback in a formal setting.

Recently, CPS replaced the Performance Management Program with a Development Assessment Review process. In this process, officers are given the opportunity of sharing with their supervisor how the officer perceives he or she is doing on the job. Based on first-hand observations, the supervisor can then provide immediate feedback and reinforce the improved behavior or help the officer. A self-assessment is currently developed for each profile as part of the developmental discussion process. When completed correctly, these assessments allow the officer, his or her commander and the Service in general to see the importance of feedback and continual learning and development as a requirement of the job and a value of the Service. The process is no longer simply about getting results. The focus is now on both the results and how the results are achieved — what behaviors are demonstrated — and how those behaviors reflect the competency profiles driving the system.

In a community policing organization, emphasis is on the whole set of skills each individual brings to the organization, and on life-long, holistic learning. Developmental assessment reviews allow members of the CPS to play active roles in their own careers, providing myriad opportunities to grow as team players and as individuals. This growth is achieved in many ways — through partnerships with community groups, for example. It may also be achieved through internal initiatives such as involvement in the process by which issues identified within the system are assigned a team for resolution or being fully responsible and accountable when acting in the more senior role for a senior officer off on vacation or a special project. Learning on the job is also essential for the transfer of knowledge from the veteran officers to the younger members of the service. In order to do that, officers with more years of service are being rotated out of specialty units and placed in frontline constable roles and paired with newer members of the Service. This tenure project allows officers with the greatest capability and competencies to apply for specialty roles as no one can now serve in a specialty unit for more than five to seven years, depending on the complexity of the unit.

The CPS has also built into the review discussion a means of goal setting for the individual in order to measure his or her contribution in meeting the Service's strategic plan. In order to do this, each supervisor meets with his or her direct reports and ensures they receive the following: a full understanding of the strategic goals of the organization; how to translate those goals into action plans for groups; a clear communication of what measures will be used to assess behaviors (namely, the behavioral profiles); and, finally, clear communication of the drivers and measures used to establish individual objectives as well as how the individual's and team's results add up to the district or unit results, which, in turn, help the Service meet the strategic business plan.

Senior officers increasingly need to be able to guide and advise their staff. As part of the continual improvement in performance initiative, these officers have participated in a workshop on how to conduct effective constructive coaching conversations with their staff. In addition, senior officers have to understand the business plan and the contribution expected from their departments to help achieve organizational goals. Each rank goes to the one below it and says, "If I commit to this part of the plan, how are you going to help me achieve it?" This system even allows constables to help achieve organizational goals and/or point out mistakes. Initiatives in the area of managing performance can be seen to be effective by examining, for example, education embarked upon by CPS members. Both internally and externally, CPS employees seem to be embracing the values. Introducing competencies into the CPS has resulted in measurable outcomes that illustrate its effectiveness and will continue to drive the CPS toward its very ambitious goals for the future.

Leadership and coaching based on the values, actually celebrating the long history of the values of the CPS, served as a catalyst to moving the organization strategy forward without compromising the values. It went from being a traditional policing organization to an open, organic community-based policing service that can adapt to the changes it knows will bring about more effective and efficient means of policing. Years after the Service introduced the behavior-based human resources process, the CPS continues to use the programs and the business results of the Service have been world-class.

Values Trump Strategy Every Time

I believe deeply in the importance of values, not for any personal or moral reasons but because the values are the foundation upon which one knows right from wrong — ethical from non-ethical behaviors. And because values also demonstrably enhance an organization's success by guiding the decision-making process, creating leadership that fits, providing focus and energy to collective efforts and motivating employees like no other tool. In fact when the aboveground and the underground values collide employees are not engaged no matter how much effort you put into "engagement" activities. The employees see through the rhetoric, the leadership and human resources teams believe they are living the aboveground values or aspire to live them although in reality they are not perceived as living them. The consequence to the organization is a negative impact beyond the box in that when prospective employees talk to current employees they learn of what is happening inside the box and don't apply for roles in the company. Employees need stability and consistency, but they also need energy and emotional commitment. Leaders need grounding and purpose. Managers making decisions need a touchstone or compass to guide their way.

When organizations embrace a clear and consistent set of values at all levels, they generate tremendous energy. It doesn't matter how arduous circumstances may make the pursuit of a compelling vision. As long as values are aligned throughout the organization and consistently followed, employees will feel safe and supported in their work, the motivated to act with a sense of ownership and responsibility, and the free to innovate and improve processes and productivity. Organizations that live their values have integrity. Organizations with integrity live the formula mentioned at the beginning of this book.

Values ×	**Vision** ×	**Leadership** ×	**Execution** =	**Greatness**
(What an organization holds to be true)	(What an organization strives to become)	(How managers hold themselves and their direct reports accountable)	(How employees do their jobs within that discipline)	(Measured by integrity, business results and employee engage-ment)

When this formula comes together, the resulting positive energy creates an organization that employees want to belong to and are motivated to help make the organization a sustained success.

Every Company Has its Own Values

In the introduction to this book, I told the story of my father and the box company he ran based on his strongly held beliefs. I did not mention that my father was not the first person in my family to run a box company. In fact, my mother's father, my grandfather, owned a paper box company called Roth Paper Box.

My grandfather was a first-generation American, raised in Newark, New Jersey, from the age of three. He dropped out of school in the primary grades and went on to a long and successful career as a box maker. Roth Paper Box started in the mid-1920s. Establishing a business at this time turned out to be a calculated risk but, nevertheless, one that a first-generation immigrant with entrepreneurial instincts eagerly took on. The risk paid off in many ways and the firm expanded and flourished.

When World War II arrived, grandfather Ed Roth found himself with a dwindling male workforce. Eventually the demand for boxes outgrew the manpower capacity. Seeking out new employees, Ed turned to the only source he knew was available, females. His daughter, my mother, having been steeped in his values, thought of the family's roots and went back to the women of Newark. What they did not anticipate was the established female employees' unwillingness to work with African-American women in the early 1940s.

When my mother arrived with a busload of new employees, she was eager to bring them on-board and knew the actual work would be easy to learn. After all, it was not difficult for new employees to be successful in running the machines, as long as they were willing to work in the summer in a very hot environment. Unfortunately, my mother was a bit naive! The established workforce of white women refused to work with the new employees. They wanted a separate locker room, and they wanted to work on separate machines.

My mother brought the white women together and let them know that people are people; no matter their color. She explained that everyone has the right to work, and they all needed the income. She shocked those at the meeting when she said, "you can either work together or not work at all." The women responded with shocked silence. To break the awkwardness, my mother echoed one of her father's favorite lines: "If you don't like it, don't let the door hit you in the rear on your way out."

My mother expected more resistance, but this was not to be the case. The employees began to work together. Over time, they started sharing pictures and stories of their loved ones overseas. They began to exchange tales about their children and even began eating lunch together. Not everyone was successful in making the transition, but the majority of women came to understand that the values inside that box company were the foundation for all decisions and actions; the basis for right and wrong. It didn't matter if the people were inside or outside the box, the values stayed the same. The business remained successful and women would become the lifeline of the company

My father, in turn, ran his box company according to the same values. Values are passed along within the family from generation to generation. Values are also passed along within the organization from your established employees to your newly arrived employees. The new employees learn from those that came before them about the actions that will define right and wrong and lead to success within the firm. When leaders are consistent and relentless in their application of the values, in making decisions, large and small, they become predictable. It is their predictability that makes the organization a safe place to work. When leaders forget to communicate and celebrate the meaning of the values, employees go astray. In turn, the company goes off course. When the firm tries to right itself, it inevitably goes through an assortment of trendy new ideas or strategic directions to accommodate this ruptured culture. In fact, what it needs more than anything is to go back to what made it special and authentic in the first place.

Despite being invisible and intangible, values are one of the few things in every organization that are lasting and real. Above or below ground, they create the environment in which employees work and play. Every long-term successful company goes through trials and celebrations, faces setbacks and generates achievements. But the existence and continuity of the organization is nothing more than a reaffirmation of the values its people share over generations, and what they have accomplished by staying true to them.

Bibliography

Albrecht, Karl. *The Northbound Train: Finding the Purpose, Setting the Direction, Shaping the Destiny of Your Organization.* New York: Amacom, 1994.

Argyris, Chris. *Flawed Advice and the Management Trap: How Managers Can Know When They're Getting Good Advice and When They're Not.* New York: Oxford University Press, 2000.

Barnard, Chester I. *The Functions of the Executive: 30th Anniversary Edition.* Cambridge, MA: Harvard University Press, 1938; Cambridge, MA: Harvard Business Press, 2005.

Barth, Roland S. *Run School Run.* Cambridge, MA: Harvard University Press, 1980.

Bennis, Warren. *On Becoming a Leader.* Cambridge, MA: Addison-Wesley Publishing Company Inc., 1989.

Campbell, Sarah F. *Piaget Sampler.* Lanham, MD: Rowman & Littlefield Publishers, 1987.

Cannon, Jimmy. "Why the Yankees Are So Great," *The New York Daily News* (June 2, 2002).

Chernow, Ron. *Titan: The Life of John D. Rockefeller Sr.* New York: Random House, 1998; New York: Vintage, 2004.

Cohen, David. *The Talent Edge: A Behavioral Approach to Hiring, Developing, and Keeping Top Performers.* Toronto: John Wiley and Sons Canada, Ltd., 2001.

Collins, J. and J. Porras. *Built to Last: Successful Habits of Visionary Companies.* New York: Harper Business, 1994.

Collins, James C. and Jerry I. Poras. "Building Your Company's Vision," *Harvard Business Review* (September – October 1996).

Collins, Jim. *Good to Great: Why Some Companies Make the Leap ... and Others Don't.* New York: HarperBusiness, 2001.

Costa, John Dalla. *The Ethical Imperative: Why Moral Leadership is Good Business.* Cambridge, MA: Perseus Books, 1998.

Deal, T. E. and A.A. Kennedy. *Corporate Cultures: The Rites and Rituals of Corporate Life.* 1984. Reprint. Cambridge, MA: Perseus Books, 2000.

Downs, Alan. *Beyond the Looking Glass: Overcoming the Seductive Culture of Corporate Narcissism.* New York: Amacom, 1997.

Drucker, Peter F. "Managing for Business Effectiveness," *Harvard Business Review* (May 1, 1963).

Foust, Dean. "The GE Way Isn't Working at Home Depot," *Business Week* (January 17, 2003).

Gerstner, Lou. *Who Says Elephants Can't Dance?: Inside IBM's Historic Turnaround.* New York: HarperBusiness, 2002.

Gladwell, Malcolm. *Blink: The Power of Thinking Without Thinking.* New York: Little, Brown, and Company, Time Warner Book Group, 2005.

Hall, Robert T. and John U. Davis. *Moral Education in Theory and Practice.* Buffalo: Prometheus Books, 1975.

Herzl, Theodor. *Altneuland.* 3d ed. Haifa, Israel: Haifa Publishing Co., 1964.

Howard, Robert. "Values Make the Company an Interview with Robert Haas." *Harvard Business Review* (September – October 1990).

Kohlberg, Lawrence. "The Philosophy of Moral Development: Moral Stages and the Idea of Justice." *Essays on Moral Development,* vol. 1, San Francisco: Harper & Row, 1981.

Kotter, John P. *Leading Change.* Boston, MA: Harvard Business School Press, 1996.

Kouzes, James M. and Barry Z. Posner. *The Leadership Challenge: How to Get Extraordinary Things Done in Organizations.* San Francisco, CA: Jossey-Bass, 1988.

Kunde, Jesper. *Corporate Religion*. London, England: Pearson Professional Education, 2002.

Lager, Fred. *Ben & Jerry's: The Inside Scoop*. New York: Crown Publishers, 1994.

Langeler, Gerard H. "The Vision Trap." *Harvard Business Review* (March – April 1992).

Lederer, William J. and Eugene Burdick. *The Ugly American*. New York: W. W. Norton & Company, 1958.

Lencioni, Patrick M. "Make Your Values Mean Something." *Harvard Business Review* (July 2002).

Mintzberg, Henry. *Managers Not MBAs: A Hard Look at the Soft Practice of Managing and Management Development*. San Francisco, CA: Berrett-Koehler Publishers, May 2004.

Mintzberg, Henry. *Strategy Bites Back: It Is Far More, and Less, than You Ever Imagined*. New Jersey: Financial Times Prentice Hall, 2005.

Moral Education: It Comes With The Territory. Edited by David Purpel and Kevin Ryan. Berkeley, CA: McCutchan Publishing Corporation, 1976.

Neuhauser, Peg, Ray Bender, and Kirk Stromberg. *Culture.com: Building Corporate Culture in the Connected Workplace*. Toronto: John Wiley & Sons Canada, Ltd., 2000.

Norman, Al. "A Citizen's View of Home Depot: Not In Our Hometown." From http://www.sprawl-busters.com/hometown.html.

Piaget, Jean. *The Psychology of the Child*. New York: Basic Books, 1969, 2000.

Oliphant, Thomas. *Praying for Gil Hodges*. (New York: St. Martin Press, 2005), 48-49.

Reimer, Joseph, Diana Pritchard Paolitto, and Richard H. Hersh. *Promoting Moral Growth: From Piaget to Kohlberg*. New York: Addison Wesley Longman, 1979.

Roush, Chris. *Inside Home Depot*. New York: McGraw Hill, 1999.

Schein, E.H. *Organizational Culture and Leadership*. 3d ed. San Francisco, CA: Jossey-Bass, 2004.

Sellers, Patricia. "Home Depot Something to Prove," *Fortune Magazine* (June 27, 2002).

Selznick, Philip. *Leadership in Administration: A Sociological Interpretation.* California: University of California, 1984.

Snyder, N.H., J.B. Dowd, Jr., and D.M., Houghton. *Vision, Values, and Courage: Leadership for Quality Management.* New York: Free Press, 1994.

Stewart, James B. *Disney War.* New York: Simon & Schuster, 2005.

Tabak, Lawrence "If Your Goal Is Success, Don't Consult These Gurus," *Fast Company Magazine* 06 (December 1996): 38.

"The Best CEOs," *Worth* (May 1999): 102–148.

"The Entrepreneurial Leadership of Thomas Edison: America's Inventive Colossus." In *Babson Insight e-magazine.* Babson College, 2005. www. babsoninsight.com.

Tichy, Noel M. *The Cycle of Leadership: How Great Leaders Teach Their Companies to Win.* 2002. Reprint. New York: HarperCollins, 2004.

Tichy, Noel M. *The Leadership Engine.* 1997. Reprint. New York: Harper Business, 2002.

Wall, Bob, Robert S. Solum, and Mark R. Sobol. *The Visionary Leader.* Rocklin, CA: Prima Lifestyles, 1992.

Warner, Melanie. "New McDonald's Chief Vows To Keep Strategy Unchanged." *New York Times* (Saturday, December 4, 2004): C1, C12.

Index